THE INK IN THE GROOVES

The Ink in the Grooves

Conversations on Literature and Rock 'n' Roll

Edited by Florence Dore

Cornell University Press
Ithaca and London

First published 2022 by Cornell University Press

Printed in the United States of America

Page 302 constitutes an extension of this copyright page.

Library of Congress Cataloging-in-Publication Data

Names: Dore, Florence, editor.
Title: The ink in the grooves : conversations on literature and rock 'n' roll / edited by Florence Dore.
Description: Ithaca [New York] : Cornell University Press, 2022. | Includes bibliographical references.
Identifiers: LCCN 2022005319 (print) | LCCN 2022005320 (ebook) | ISBN 9781501766206 (paperback) | ISBN 9781501766251 (epub)
Subjects: LCSH: Music and literature—History—20th century. | Music and literature—History—21st century. | Rock music—History and criticism. | Rock musicians' writings.
Classification: LCC ML3849 .I47 2022 (print) | LCC ML3849 (ebook) | DDC 781.6609—dc23/eng/20220225
LC record available at https://lccn.loc.gov/2022005319
LC ebook record available at https://lccn.loc.gov/2022005320

Contents

PART II. ROCK 'N' ROLL SAVED MY LIFE: WRITERS ON MUSIC

PART III. ROCK'S LITERARY IDENTITY: MUSICIANS ON LITERATURE

PART IV. DON'T LET ANYONE WRITE YOUR STORY: MUSINGS ON ROCK AS LITERATURE

Acknowledgments

The Ink in the Grooves originated before the COVID-19 pandemic struck and just as I was getting the wheels turning again on my recording career. A world-shattering break, it turns out, will bring some changes. *The Ink in the Grooves* now includes an essay by John Jeremiah Sullivan, for example, on a song made famous by Canned Heat, and an essay by Dave Grohl about what it was like for him not to be playing live concerts. John Prine was on the list of artists I was hoping to include in the collection. Instead, readers of *The Ink in the Grooves* will find an interview with members of his band reminiscing about a legend lost.

When the first lockdown edicts were issued in March 2020, I had just finished my first tour in many years and was set to record my new album, *Highways and Rocketships*. As my band and I were preparing for both tour and studio, the five of us in all of our maskless oblivion crammed into a tiny practice space in Carrboro, Peter Holsapple suggested that we play Marshall Crenshaw's "Somewhere Down the Line" as the cover for our live set. Eager to make my return with louder drums and a telecaster, I opted for Patty

Griffin's "Silver Bells" instead. When everything closed down, though, and the world began to feel like a void, I kept hearing Crenshaw's gentle lyrics in my head: "Somewhere down the line / It's gonna be more than fine / These days will never cross our minds / Somewhere down the line."

So we set up Will's drums in front of the television, a friend left a good vocal mike out on his screened in porch for us to grab, and Peter dropped off a mixer and some mike stands in our driveway. A few bleach-soaked paper towels and some Facetime calls later, there I was, recording Will's drums in front of the television. With Don Dixon's production wizardry, as well as Jefferson Holt's abiding support and vision—we managed a social-distanced version of recording and kept the musical wheels turning, each band member recording separate parts in his own home, sending tracks to Don via WeTransfer. We were off the road, but we were still moving.

What to do with this track now that violins had been added, vocal tracks had been layered, and all had been mixed? When everything shut down, I had begun scheduling a gig at the legendary Cat's Cradle. As the panic and fear of those early days set in, I started worrying that there would not be a Cradle to come back to when all this was behind us. What will happen to the rock venue that make this town what it is, I wondered, and clubs like it all over the country, which fix distant locales in a sprawling rock network—that web of inconsistent PAs and graffitied rooms into which musicians pour their hearts and souls every night? I ended up joining forces with Steve Balcom, Lane Wurster, and Shawn Nolan, all of whom have deep roots in the Chapel Hill music world, and together we created *Cover Charge*, a record to benefit Cat's Cradle.[1] My band's version of "Somewhere Down the Line" would be transmitted that way. The dB's immediately offered up an unreleased cover of "I'm on an Island" by the Kinks; I called my former student Libby Rodenbough, and her band Mipso gave us "Long-Distance Love" by Little Feat. Steve, Lane, and Shawn brought in more and more acts. I wiped down my little red audio interface with a Clorox wipe and placed it in the mailbox for John Wurster, who used it to record drums for Superchunk's version of the Go-Go's' "Can't Stop the World." *Cover Charge* gained momentum, revered NC bands jumping on right and left to record their covers for the Cradle. Southern Culture on the Skids covered Wilbert Harrison's

1. Various, *Cover Charge: NC Artists Go Under Cover to Benefit the Cat's Cradle*, Bandcamp (Chapel Hill, NC: Cover Charge Music, 2020), https://coverchargemusic.com/.

"Let's Work Together" for the record, and I asked Sullivan to write something up to help publicize *Cover Charge* in our local free weekly, the *INDYweek*. Sullivan's piece, as noted, is now gathered in *The Ink in the Grooves*.

This endeavor, as well as finally finishing *Highways and Rocketships* once recording in person became safe, made *The Ink in the Grooves* a different book. I came up with the idea for *Ink* for old personal reasons, which I discuss in the introduction—and because I kept finding myself in conversation both with musicians who considered their craft as related to literature and with novelists indebted to rock. It made sense to bring these musings together. But since the pandemic, *The Ink in the Grooves* has become more than a conversation. *The Ink in the Grooves* was amplified by essays, like Sullivan's, that came into existence because of the pandemic. But its essence was also touched by the irrepressible musical life force that erupted as the book evolved.

The contributors to *The Ink in the Grooves*, supreme purveyors of this force, deserve all my gratitude, both for allowing me to bring their moving reflections on the reciprocal links between rock and literature into one place. I owe a debt to them as well for waiting through the months while work on *The Ink in the Grooves* ground to a halt when musical projects consumed my life. I thank my literary agent David Dunton as well, for jumping on board before this project was fully formed, and Mahinder Kingra, my editor at Cornell University Press, for his superb editorial suggestions. I may have been driving *The Ink in the Grooves*, but it was Mahinder who kept the motor running. I am grateful for his monumental patience in letting the project sit while first *Cover Charge* and then recording *Highways* took priority. And speaking of time, Will and Georgie Rigby—both so sweet to me—fill mine up with love, music, and the kind of support without which nobody could accomplish anything. Will, master of pith *and* groove, deserves credit for coming up with the title.

Funding for this book came from two generous sources at the University of North Carolina, Chapel Hill: the Department of English and Comparative Literature and the Institute for the Arts and Humanities. I am deeply grateful to both, as well as to Robert Newman at the National Humanities Center, who hosted the Novel Sounds conferences in 2016 and 2017 that provided a platform for the initial conversations that sparked *The Ink in the Grooves.*

The Ink in the Grooves

Introduction

Needles and Pens

By Florence Dore

Drop the record needle. Drop it on any piece of vinyl in your collection, then go crack open that novel you've been meaning to read. Can you feel the reverberations? Do the lines in the song merge with the sentences on the page? For me, when things settle just right, the world goes away, and I am suspended in a cloud of something bigger than the music or the prose alone. Guitars, sometimes strumming, sometimes screaming; snare snaps; buzzes; the muted pops of *p*'s and *t*'s in the vocals. Sounds blend with other sensations harder to identify: the satisfactions of recurring imagery dawning on the brain, pleasing plot turns, suspense, anticipation of what Vladimir Nabokov described as that "golden peace" of the story reaching resolution. I was recently visited by a version of this lovely brain fog while staring through the window of my study onto the moss covering the yard, having just immersed in *A Gate at the Stairs* by Lorrie Moore, the image of a broken gate in my mind, the sound of the knell in Amy Helm's voice ringing behind the beat of descending pitch from snare to tom and into the final words of the first verse: "Drop the record needle anywhere you please."[1] What I am describing here is a quintessentially contemporary experience—a trance induced by the needles and pins (-ah) produced by the needles and pens of the now. This is a feeling that, in the wake of stay-at-home orders and the shuttering of revered rock venues, has the potential to deliver partial inoculation against what Peter Holsapple of the dB's once called "the death of rock."[2]

Ask dB's drummer Will Rigby what first got him into playing the drums, and he will tell you: "It's a cliché. I wanted to play drums after I saw the Beatles play on Ed Sullivan. Most people wanted to be John or Paul; I wanted to be Ringo." When I was in college during the late 1980s, I was a dB's fan and an English major, writing papers on "Ode to a Nightingale" and rehearsing with my own band in a windowless underground tunnel that smelled like socks. After classes were over, in the glare of lamps stolen from dorm rooms above, I immersed myself in the study of singing in a rock band, careful not to put my mouth too close to the microphone, avoiding that tiny but potent shock. I'd go home and stare at the lines of poetry and type, never quite catching up on sleep.

I imagine someone telling me in those days that I would end up marrying the dB's drummer or that I would become a literature scholar. By now, I have heard Will give the Ringo answer more than once. And he's not the only one. How many great American rock musicians born in Will's generation started their bands after seeing the Beatles on Ed Sullivan? That particular episode of *The Ed Sullivan Show* was the glue binding a slice of one generation—white guys, for the most part, who in the midst of the nation's push to integrate (Will's class was the first in his Winston-Salem high school to get bused), came to learn and love the music of the Beatles and of the African American artists who inspired them.

And what about those of us born ten years later? The younger members of future rock bands, still finding our fingers when the Beatles' guitars beamed into American living rooms? What would be our way in? I ponder what it was like for Will, not (like me) born into a rock evolution already in

1. The song is "Record Needle," by Amy Helm's band Ollabelle. Ollabelle, *Neon Blue Bird*, compact disc, Ollabelle Music, 2011.

2. Peter Holsapple's "The Death of Rock" was written in 1977 and 1978. The lyrics were rewritten and the song was recorded by the Troggs as "I'm in Control" in 1992 on their album *Athens Andover*. The Troggs, *Athens Andover*, Rhino, 1992. Peter's 1978 version was finally released in 2019. Peter Holsapple, *The Death of Rock: Peter Holsapple vs. Alex Chilton*, Omnivore, 2019.

progress. He and his peers were surprised by it—discovered and shaped it as it was happening. Those who were startled by the Beatles were also old enough to be aware of the March on Washington, of Bob Dylan singing "Only a Pawn in Their Game," cementing the link between popular music and the civil rights movement. What was it like in those years?

I sang along to The Who's "My Generation" with my friends in college, but I knew we were late. My generation was in fact the first with no moment before, the first for whom there was no time when rock had not already arrived and infused everything. In 2003, Jonathan Lethem, whose interview with the actual Bob Dylan appears in the pages that follow, wrote into being the fictional character Dylan, named by his rock-awakened parents after the real guy. For that novelistic Dylan, as for Lethem and for me, vinyl was something mothers had (I lost my copy of *Rubber Soul*, Scotch-taped and pilfered from my mother, in an unfortunate purge of "my stuff" that I will forever regret), and rock was transmitted through the umbilical cord before we ever arrived.[3] For us—that is, for people born around the mid-1960s—rock was not revolutionary, not a shock, and the Black vernacular from which it clearly grew was obviously part of the cultural fabric that swaddled us. Our moms listened to it; they marched for civil rights. And so there was nothing scandalous about rock's lure. The idea that rock is as important culturally as literature? That they live in the same domain? Of course. No problem. The collection that follows, which includes an interview with Lethem and Dana Spiotta discussing this very issue, examines the historical evolution of this *Weltanschauung*, following its rise to dominance. Born as startling, the idea that rock should enjoy literary status—and, conversely, that literature is indebted to rock—came of age as I did.

I am pretty sure I knew how to "drop the record needle" before I knew how to write. I remember when, in 1970, as I was walking past the living room in my yellow house on Sunset Place in Nashville, something stopped me. My hand halted, resting on the swirl of wood at the top of the newel post in the front hall—the post behind which my brother had recently anchored himself to launch a fork at my older sister, and that had steadied my inebriated father

3. See Lethem's *Fortress of Solitude*, as well as my reading of mothers in that novel. Jonathan Lethem, *The Fortress of Solitude* (New York: Vintage, 2003); Florence Dore, "The Rock Novel and Jonathan Lethem's *The Fortress of Solitude*," Nonsite.Org, no. 8 (January 20, 2013).

several weeks prior on his tilted, careening path to the front door through which he had been asked by my mother to exit. In that moment, the post was there for my hand, not someone else's. And it just rested there. A nasal "na na, na na, na na, na na, nanaaaah" with honey-high harmonies, chunky guitar, and rolling snare was floating on the air from behind me into my ears. Arresting, other—sweet, this sound. "The niiiight they drove old Dixie down": me listening, frozen in place. And then again those nas. After some duration of time I went over to the turntable and stared, mesmerized, plunged into the melody. I remember feeling my heart rising and falling with Levon Helm's voice, watching the logo in the center of the record going around and around, wondering at the sound emerging from that hard, black disc. It was not long after that that I figured out how to thread the LP onto the metal stem by lining up the hole in the center. The pleasing click as the record descended, the thwack of the vinyl landing, the hum of the needle making contact. Then the song.

The Ink in the Grooves began not as a book, but as an exercise in middle-aged introspection after my father died. Clem's death was a moment of personal inventory—an attempt to bring all the parts of my own story together. When I arrived in Berkeley for graduate school, I was in my twenties, having just broken up with Joe Harvard, the cofounder of Fort Apache Studios in Boston. Joe's real last name was Incagnoli; he was, like my dad had been, an unlikely Harvard student—a townie, a genius, someone who got in on brains alone and did not otherwise fit the bill. The kids in south Boston where Joe grew up gave him the moniker Joe Harvard, and it stuck. I felt like I was leaving music when I left Joe to go and get a PhD (he was, like my dad, a drug addict), and when I showed up at Berkeley I was still grieving a musical life lived in Boston—playing at the Rathskeller and Bunratty's, catching the Titanics at Chet's. Clem graduated magna cum laude in English at Harvard in 1953, going on to earn his MA in 1954 and a PhD in philosophy in 1961. He had instructed me, upon arrival in California, to go and say hi to his former roommate from Harvard, a guy named Paul Alpers, who was on the faculty at Berkeley. The first thing Alpers said: "Clem Dore! I owe my love of jazz to your dad. He was my ambassador to the Boston music scene." I learned from this man that as a Boston local, Clem had introduced many a Harvard student to music, taking them to see live performances by Billie Holiday and Miles Davis in a club where his friend ran the spotlight. I listened to this in Alpers's office, stunned, experiencing déjà vu. But it wasn't mine. This repeat felt like a snag on some giant cosmic record, making me feel the second version of something I thought I originated—and of something bigger and more important than me.

Did I learn how to pull the plastic lever down to "on" and get the thing spinning before I was able to write my name? Levon has a daughter about my age, Amy Helm. As noted, she's a singer. (My interview with her can be found at the close of *The Ink and the Grooves.*) She and I have a few things in common. Even without the addicted father, the lifelong pull to sing, what we share, we share with everyone in our generation: needles and pens came into our hands at the same time. The idea, which I gleaned much later, that rock is "low" culture to literature's "high" seemed patently absurd. I can't remember where I first encountered that claim, but I never paid it any mind. Nor, apparently, did Amy, or Spiotta, Lethem, Colson Whitehead, or Rick Moody. I have gathered writing from some of the best novelists of our generation in the pages that follow. All will show a tendency to move seamlessly between books and records, between what Amy describes as a canon of rock classics created by radio and the written word.

The Ink in the Grooves brings two parts of me together—the me studying rock in underground spaces over the years and the me who is a close reader of difficult literature. This collection also seeks to encapsulate a bigger sea change, however, one whose steering duties seem to have landed on people in my generation. There has always been bleed between perceptions of high and low culture, but at present we are witness to its utter erasure. We have arrived, it seems, at the absolute end of the line for the cultural elitism that fueled that division, and the collection that follows clarifies and celebrates this end, freshly unpacking rock and literature's basic kinship. *The Ink in the Grooves* collects greatest hits, you could say, key statements of the collapse that has been developing since at least since the publication of Greil Marcus's *Mystery Train* in 1975. And it only makes sense that the examination of the cultural phenomena *The Ink in the Grooves* examines has landed on middle-aged persons. Our parents already loved popular music, and when we arrived on the planet, it had already morphed into rock and roll. We, who are at the time of this writing, fiftysomethings were the first to be born into rock; the last rock fans whose only access to the music we loved was buying vinyl. Collectors persist, but we bought LPs because it was the only way to listen to music.

The most celebrated—and for people like me, the most boring—event of rock's ascendance to the "heights" of literature was that which the *New*

Yorker editor David Remnick called an "astonishing and unambiguously wonderful thing": the conferral of the Nobel Prize for Literature on Bob Dylan. For all the hubbub surrounding that single prize, the essays, stories, reviews, and interviews in *The Ink in the Grooves* clarify that Dylan's win was anything but anomalous. On the contrary, it was just one of many instances of a convergence between literature and rock in the early twenty-first century. In hindsight, it seems inevitable. Dylan's Nobel was announced by a middle-aged woman, one Professor Sara Danius, a member of the selection committee born around the time I was. Did she steal records from her mom? I don't know. As those of us for whom rock always existed become old enough to take seats on committees, in any case, culture is becoming redefined according to our vinyl-inflected worldviews.

Like Lethem, the best authors in this same generation of American novelists put pen to paper ready to draw on rock and roll to craft plots and characters. The lyrics to "Chimes of Freedom" float through the protagonist Dylan's mind in Lethem's *The Fortress of Solitude*; the Beach Boys' "Caroline, No" occasions a name change in Spiotta's 2006 Dylan-inspired *Eat the Document*; "Oh Babe, What Would You Say" by Hurricane Smith encapsulates teen angst in Whitehead's 2009 *Sag Harbor*; and so on.[4] These novelistic nods to rock and roll by middle-aged writers, potent examples and discussions of which—by Spiotta, Randall Kenan, and Whitehead—are excerpted here, started to appear around the year 2000, heralding in that moment the collapse Dylan's Nobel win made explicit. Richard Linklater is a

4. Elsewhere, I have shown that finds an explosion of fictional references to historical rock bands and their songs, and the authors portray these in strikingly literal terms. So, in *Fortress of Solitude* (2003), we find Lethem glossing his fictional Dylan's consciousness with the lyrics of one-hit-wonder Wild Cherry's "Play that Funky Music" (1976) when he is a teen. The somber "Another Green World" (1975) does the job later in his life, Brian Eno's intellectualized rock the better to match a more mature Dylan's complex existential emotions. In his 2016 *A Gambler's Anatomy*, Lethem again turns to rock, bringing us an eccentric rock-fan-turned-neurosurgeon trying to bring Jimi Hendrix back from the dead with every surgery he performs. Also apposite here are Dana Spiotta's *Eat the Document* (2006), a novel whose title she took from Bob Dylan's unreleased 1972 documentary with the same name; and Lorrie Moore's story "People Like That are the Only People Here: Canonical Babbling in the *Peed Onk*," in which a bereft mother sings the Animals' 1965 "We Gotta Get Out of This Place" to comfort her infant, who is strapped down to a hospital bed after a cancerous tumor has been removed from his tiny body. The list goes on: Jennifer Egan, Hari Kunzru, and Hanif Kureishi all make use of rock in their novels. See Dore, "The Rock Novel and Jonathan Lethem's *The Fortress of Solitude*"; Florence Dore, *Novel Sounds: Southern Fiction in the Age of Rock and Roll* (New York: Columbia University Press, 2018).

fellow Gen Xer, and although no novel appears in his 2003 *School of Rock*, we might think here of the scene in which Dewey Finn (played by Jack Black) wields his pointer in front of a blackboard on which the chalked genealogy of iconic American rock bands is mapped. This scene marks the historical moment *The Ink in the Grooves* examines, in high comic form, tipping us off to the emerging sense that rock has scholastic value even given its scruffy guardians. Dewey teaching future Princeton students is the embrace of rock as legitimate that informs contemporary culture at large.

After all, at the same time their songs are literally turning up as background music in the plots of some of the most celebrated fiction of the twenty-first century, the same pioneers of rock whose bands appear on Dewey's blackboard have begun to exit the stage and head for the page, setting down their guitars to write memoirs. The era I am describing is also defined by a veritable deluge of aesthetically elevated rock memoirs: *Life* by Keith Richards and *Just Kids* by Patti Smith—both out in 2010; Viv Albertine's 2014 *Clothes, Clothes, Clothes. Music, Music, Music. Boys, Boys, Boys*; Kim Gordon's 2015 *Girl in a Band*; Bruce Springsteen's 2016 *Born to Run*; Patti Smith's *M Train* (also 2016); John Prine's 2017 *Beyond Words*; Richard Thompson's *Beeswing: Losing My Way and Finding My Voice* (2021). Richard Hell, Robbie Robertson, my initiator into the thrills of rock Levon Helm, and many more: all saw fit to write memoirs around the turn of the twenty-first century. This spate of rocker narratives clarifies the current push to embrace both record needle and pen—the easy move from songwriting to prose. What was once conveyed by needle alone now finds expression in the rock icon's written word as well. These phenomena—Dylan's win, the new fictional focus on rock, the foray into rock memoir—provide a backdrop against which to understand the writings collected in *The Ink in the Grooves.* All show rock and literature to be woven into the same cultural cloth.

What does it mean to describe the melding of literature and rock as a "contemporary" phenomenon? I have already mentioned that I ended up a literary scholar as well as a musician, and those of us who specialize in the period of literature now called Post45 (literature written after 1945) have thought a lot about the problem of describing aesthetic objects as "contemporary." It is a weird thing to do. Unlike describing a piece of literature as Victorian, say, because Queen Victoria always defines that epoch, a novel can only be contemporary until its moment passes. Thus, the aesthetic inventory of the contemporary era must by definition always change. In 2008, Amy Hungerford, a Yale English professor, wrote "On the Period Formerly Known as Contemporary," an academic article about this very problem, in which she announced that the then-new field should be called Post45.[5] I was thinking about the reference to Prince in her title and wondering why a literature scholar would reach for a rock legend to define the period of literature written after World War II. I think it's more than a cute quip. Although she doesn't delve into the topic in her article, I am going to venture that Prince came into her musings because all culture produced between 1945 and the present—whether mapped as high, low, or anything in between—swiftly became enmeshed with the popular art form that began to develop at the end of World War II. In other words, I think it is very difficult to separate any cultural expression since the birth of rock and roll music from the form. Whatever divisions appeared to exist between literature, which, as I have written elsewhere, was at that time defined by dwellers in the ivory tower as white, and rock—understood, in its early days, as interracial—were superimposed upon what was in fact their root interconnection in that original moment.[6] That doesn't mean the divisions didn't have impact. They did. What we are witnessing in the current moment is, precisely, the melting away of the final traces of that impact—the total evaporation of an illusory distinction.

Although rock 'n' roll was born as an adolescent form—anti-institutional, irreverent—it survives even in old age. As pioneers of rock grow old, become frail, and pass away, defying rock's early iconic images, we rush in to preserve their artifacts. The Smithsonian Institution has been archiving popular music since John Lomax set out to record Lead Belly's "Goodnight Irene" with his three-hundred-pound "portable" phonograph in the 1930s. But archivists at the Rock and Roll Hall of Fame, the Southern Folklife Collection at the University of North Carolina Chapel Hill, and at the Bob Dylan Archive at the University of Tulsa have more recently begun indexing the posters, albums, early analog demos, and letters of rock icons. As our im-

5. Amy Hungerford, "On the Period Formerly Known as Contemporary," *American Literary History* 20, no.1 (2008): 410–419. J. D. Connor, another member of the Post45 steering committee, coined the term "Post45."

6. For a more detailed account of the longer history of overlap between literature in the academy and rock, see Dore, *Novel Sounds*. See also Maureen Mahon, *Right to Rock: The Black Rock Coalition and the Cultural Politics of Race* (Durham, NC: Duke University Press, 2004); Jack Hamilton, *Just around Midnight: Rock and Roll and the Racial Imagination* (Cambridge, MA: Harvard University Press, 2016).

mortal rude boys and girls appear before us as so many graying grandparents, the form's legitimacy has become easier to accept. From one point of view, the archived collections of rock's things might look like anxiety about the death of rock. Peter's song "The Death of Rock" comes to mind again here: "Better put your records / Under key and lock." The capture of rock in the nation's longstanding preservationist traditions and institutions, however, as importantly validates rock as part of our national cultural heritage. We catalog handwritten posters and cassettes, we install Greil Marcus as one of the gatekeepers of literary studies, and, courtesy of the State Department, we send Mary McBride and her band to Benghazi and Pakistan to engage in acts of cultural diplomacy.[7] And we bestow the Nobel Prize for Literature on the man who wrote "Like a Rolling Stone," once hailed by *Billboard* magazine as the greatest rock and roll song of all time. Rock and roll, once the signature form of adolescence—the "new pornography," as the Canadian musical collective who took that name reminds us—is now dignified.

Rather than an indication that rock and roll is dying, however, through the changes that bring us rock's septuagenarians, rock and roll has remained vibrant. Even through COVID-19. In March 2020, with live music entirely shut down, the death Peter narrated in the 1970s seemed closer at hand. But in his essay here, Dave Grohl extols rock's lasting vibrancy. "The Day the Live Concert Returns" is Grohl's celebration of what had so recently been lost when he first wrote the essay in May 2020. His exuberant recollections in this piece do not resemble an epitaph in any way. The article is rather an embodiment of the phenomenon I am describing here: an expression of that vibrancy that both needle and pen seek to capture in current expressions of rock and roll. The piece by Greil Marcus, as well, keeps our attention on live shows, narrating an incredible moment during one, in essence placing readers in the audience, making of us avid listeners. Also included in *The Ink and the Grooves* is an attestation to rock's life force in memorialization. The heart-searing loss of John Prine to COVID-19 is honored here in an interview with his band members: Dave Jacques, Jason Wilber, Pat McLaughlin, and Fats Kaplin. Their words about Mr. Prine, the "reluctant genius," as his longtime guitarist Wilber calls him, make vivid a fact that all the essays in *The Ink in the Grooves*

7. Kiran Nazish, "'Home Tours' Take Mary McBride Band to Zones of Conflict and Calamity," *The New York Times*, July 3, 2015, https://www.nytimes.com/2015/07/05/nyregion/home-tours-take-mary-mcbride-band-to-zones-of-conflict-and-calamity.html.

touch on: the wrenching losses in music—of John Prine, Charley Pride, Adam Schlesinger, and so many others—underscore the endlessness of the contribution, the lasting vitality of the art form those who have died helped create. I ask Peter what "The Death of Rock" is about, and he says, "Hard to say, really. . . . I think I was trying to write a 'dumb rock and roll song' and I may have succeeded. I don't think it was anything like the Advent of Cassettes or the CD Era that prompted it. I just wanted something I could really holler." Even "The Death of Rock" is about rock's vitality.

"The niiiight they drove old Dixie down." I eventually learned what Dixie was, of course, and that "The Night They Drove Old Dixie Down," written not by Levon Helm but by fellow member of The Band Robbie Robertson, is included in *Rolling Stone*'s "500 Songs That Shaped Rock and Roll." Have a quick look at Wikipedia and you can find that in 2011, *Time* magazine included it among the top 100 all-time best popular songs, and that in a 1969 review, the music critic Ralph J. Gleason describes "The Night They Drove Old Dixie Down" as literature. Gleason describes the "overwhelming human sense of history" conveyed in the song, declaring "the only thing I can relate it to at all is *The Red Badge of Courage*." I thought about this claim in relation to Ta-Nehisi Coates's deeply moving statements about "The Night They Drove Old Dixie Down," published in a 2009 issue of the *Atlantic*: "I was thinking about Richmond yesterday, and The Band's 'The Night They Drove Old Dixie Down.' I started to play the song and stopped myself." He's angry. "'These motherfuckers,' I mumbled to myself. Again, another story about the blues of Pharaoh, and the people are invisible. The people are always invisible." Coates ends with the words of an African American soldier fighting for the Union, a chaplain named Garland H. White, who describes finally being reunited with his mother: "Among the densely crowded concourse," Coates quotes White as reporting, "there were parents looking for children who had been sold south of this state in tribes, and husbands came for the same purpose." White explains that among "the many broken-hearted mothers looking for their children who had been sold to Georgia and elsewhere, was an aged woman, passing through the vast crowd of colored." This was White's own mother.

I think back to the stillness, to that the moment in 1970 when I was transported by Levon's voice. Coates's essay about "invisible" people makes me wonder about a related problem: how the racial makeup of conversations about rock comes into the familiar and fraught American story of how Black vernacular music was resurrected and reused by white rock and rollers. I have written about that before.[8] Now I wonder: How should Coates's sentiments come into my memory of being transported from the chaos on Sunset Place by "The Night They Drove Old Dixie Down" when I was five? In his memoir *This Wheel's on Fire*, Levon talks about being eleven and catching a ride on a farm truck to Helena to watch "local musical hero" Sonny Boy Williamson play on Interstate Grocery Company's King Biscuit Time Show on KFFA, 1220 A.M. radio.[9] Eventually introducing himself to Williamson, Levon ends up playing with him. He recounts a story about a "perfect" day in 1964 that ended with Levon and band and Sonny Boy Williamson being run out of a barbecue restaurant by a racist cop who harassed them for sitting together. Rather than waiting around, "since the next step was getting the shit kicked out of us by a bunch of cops," the band heads to Fayetteville.[10] Helm's admiration for Williamson shines like a beam through the entire memoir. When he explains that he had taught himself to play the drums by playing along with Sonny Boy Williamson records, I think about what Bob Dylan and Eric Lott have referred to as "love and theft." Here is what Levon says about the origins of rock:

> Our early career coincided with the birth of rock and roll. We literally watched it happen in our part of the country. Traditionally, white people played country music, and black [*sic*] people played the blues. But in the thirties white musicians like my dad began to sing the blues with a twang, and it became something else with a different bump to it. That was the seed. In the late forties and early fifties Muddy Waters came out with the first electric R&B band and a string of R&B hits—"She Loves Me," "I'm Your Hoochie Coochie Man," "I Just Wanna Make Love to You," "Got My Mojo Working"—that appealed to black [*sic*] and white people alike where we lived. Over at KFFA, the radio people noticed that telephone requests for Sonny Boy Williamson were as likely to come from the ladies at the white beauty parlor as from the black.[11]

---

8. Florence Dore, "Who Owns the Blues?" *Public Books*, July 5, 2017, https://www.publicbooks.org/who-owns-the-blues/.

9. Levon Helm with Stephen Davis, *This Wheel with Step: Levon Helm and the Story of the Band*, 2nd ed. (Chicago: A Cappella, c. 2000, 1993), 27, https://catalog.lib.unc.edu/catalog/UNCb7592726.

10. Helm with Davis, *This Wheel with Step*, 120.

11. Bob Dylan, *Love and Theft*, Columbia Records, 2001; Eric Lott, *Love and Theft: Blackface Minstrelsy and the American Working Class* (New York: Oxford University Press, 1993), 36.

Helm was directly influenced by African American musicians. Was it love, theft, or both? Hurricane Smith was a white Englishman who engineered several Beatles albums. What should we make of the impact of his "Oh Babe, What Would You Say" on the teenaged African American narrator of Whitehead's *Sag Harbor*? This section of the novel is included *The Ink in the Grooves* for readers' consideration. Founding member of the Carolina Chocolate Drops, and now a solo artist, Dom Flemons found inspiration from three-dollar LPs by Joni Mitchell, Joan Baez, and Van Morrison, purchased when he was an English major at Northern Arizona University. My interview with Flemons, included here, gives me food for thought as I ponder the question of Sonny Boy Williamson's invisible role in making me feel safe in that yellow house in 1970. I have also included the magisterial story "When We All Get to Heaven," written by my friend and colleague, the dear departed Randall Kenan, in which rock's difficult racial history is reimagined as a present-day chance encounter between a Black preacher and Billy Idol in a New York club. That helps me think about these thorny questions too, as does John Jeremiah Sullivan's essay on "Let's Work Together," a hit for the all-white band Canned Heat written by the African American bluesman Wilbert Harrison. *The Ink in the Grooves* does not attempt to repair the erasures Coates decries. But the writings gathered here ask me, and readers of this book, to remain attentive to them.

This volume gathers work that clarifies the establishment of rock's new, more august cultural stature—Lethem's interview with Dylan, for example, and Michael Chabon's "Let It Rock"—with previously unpublished work exploring rock and literature's forceful melding by some of rock's most influential architects. *The Ink in the Grooves* offers a backstage pass into a new cultural arena, one inhabited by key architects of rock and novelists alike. Among the pieces to be found in *The Ink in the Grooves* are a new essay by *The Commitments* author Roddy Doyle on how rock helped him hate Irish music less; Tom Petty biographer Warren Zanes's account of overlaps between Dr. Seuss and Chuck Berry; and interviews with Grammy Award winners Steve Earle and Lucinda Williams on the ways in which their musical lives were shaped by a deep relationship to literature. There is an essay from Columbia graduate and WFMU *Radio Thrift Shop* disc jockey Laura Cantrell, whose first record, 2000's *Not the Tremblin' Kind*, was championed by BBC legend John Peel. Laura writes of how she got her start in rock studying Shakespeare in the hallowed halls of Columbia over which Hungerford eventually came to preside as dean—a point of contact that makes vivid the importance of generational shifts to rock's legitimation among the literati.

While the writers gathered here all locate the ultimate merging of rock and literature in the contemporary moment, their writing also asks us to hearken back to earlier cross-pollinations as well. For example, the iconic Richard Thompson describes for us in "Sir Patrick Rocks!" the magic that drew ancient ballads into the early recordings of his seminal British folk revival band Fairport Convention. The essays here also clarify that, for all the noise generated by Dylan's win—and for all the legitimate genre-busting that went into making rock and roll a key feature of the American novel—the presence of literature in popular music is by no means new. Indeed, the relation between popular music and literature goes back a long, long time, and in addition to revelations about the twenty-first century, the authors included here also make it clear that they are pulling from a longer history of exchange between vernacular music and literature, accepting as given the idea that popular music is a form of literary expression, and that literature would be understood in rock's legacy. In his Nobel Lecture, Dylan tells the story of how Buddy Holly and Lead Belly combined in an alchemical mixture in his person just after Buddy Holly died. Dylan explains that he went to see Buddy Holly the day before his plane crashed, when "out of the blue, the most uncanny thing happened":

> He looked me right straight dead in the eye, and he transmitted something. Something I didn't know what. And it gave me the chills. I think it was a day or two after that that his plane went down. And somebody—somebody I'd never seen before—handed me a Leadbelly [*sic*] record with the song "Cottonfields" on it. And that record changed my life right then and there. Transported me into a world I'd never known.[12]

Elsewhere I have written about Lead Belly's astonishing appearance, in 1934, at the annual meetings of the Modern Language Association—performing on a panel as Exhibit A of living literature for the foremost literary scholars in the country. Lead Belly seems to carve out a space where literature and popular music are one. But was Lead Belly the first to arrive in this space? This moment and others might prompt us to keep rolling back, to search for a point

12. Bob Dylan, "The Nobel Prize in Literature 2016," NobelPrize.org, June 5, 2017, https://www.nobelprize.org/prizes/literature/2016/dylan/lecture/.

before—a before when vernacular music was clearly distinct from literature. But where would the overlap begin? Surely it must be earlier than 1934, at least as early as when Geoffrey Chaucer turned ballads into *The Canterbury Tales*. The persistence of "Sir Patrick Spens," the eleventh-century ballad Richard Thompson writes about here, or the appearance of Billy Idol in a story by one of our most beloved African American fiction writers: the undeniable literary status of rock is only one version of a broader narrative that has, from the beginning, woven vernacular song into literature, literature into vernacular song. We can at last look with clarity at this past.

Skipping the record needle back to where we started: I knew how to put that song on the record player by myself, and I did—over and over and over again. I didn't understand the words, had no idea what "Dixie" meant, and knew nothing about the night they drove it down. I was just grabbed by the sweet sound of Amy Helm's father singing those nas. As I come to the end of this introduction, it dawns on me that for me, staring at the lines of poetry or into space thinking about a novel—these are versions of standing in front of that turntable. My penchant for close-reading literary texts is the embrace of a soothing *in*ability—standing before the complexities of literary logic in William Faulkner or Ralph Ellison or Lorrie Moore and letting it stop everything. Perhaps it is a pleasure taken in the suspension of thought, a return to the lovely stillness that gripped me there in the violence swirling around that yellow house, listening to those nas. I would later learn that the singer of "The Night They Drove Old Dixie Down" was also keeping that gentle but solid beat, that he was in the band that backed Bob Dylan when he "went electric," the same year I was born, and from Levon's memoir, that Sonny Boy Williamson worked on him the way Levon's voice worked on me. But none of what I have since learned or done, including making a new home with a drummer of my own, changes what happens to me when I hear "The Night They Drove Old Dixie Down." When those nas start, everything stops all over again. I am again in my living room in Nashville, watching the record turn, again swallowed up by a feeling that is all guitars and snare snaps and harmonies and sweetness.

I hope you enjoy reading the writings collected here as much as I have enjoyed bringing them together. Read from the start; dive in at the middle; read the last essay first. Or, in the words of Amy Helm, "Drop the record needle anywhere you please."

PART I

The Inescapable Dylan

1

Let It Rock

By Michael Chabon

One day in the late spring of 1983, toward the end of my junior year at the University of Pittsburgh, I stopped by during office hours to see my poetry teacher, Ed Ochester, up on the fifth floor of the Cathedral of Learning. I had just been asked to join a band that some guys I knew were putting together. It's possible, looking back, that I went to see Ed because I was excited and wanted to share the news with a paternal figure who was likely to be more excited than my father about my imminent baptism in the church of rock 'n' roll, but I'm not sure. You didn't really need a reason to stop by and see Ed Ochester. He would always make time for you and your poems, even when your poems, like mine, were nothing special.

In class, Ed always used to start by reading to us, his voice roughened by a Queens accent and the unfiltered Pall Malls he smoked, his straight hair falling from his big square brow down across his big square glasses. With his Auden haircut and his flannel shirts and blue jeans, Ed looked the way that I thought a poet ought to look, at the time; blue-collar but intellectual, like an old-school folk singer, or a man who was sent by the union to organize lumberjacks.

Ed spoke with a mild stammer that disappeared when he read aloud to us. The poetry he favored tended to have a deceptively conversational tone: somebody just talking, yet saying things that no one would ever say, in language that—unlike conversation—was intended to catch you off guard and surprise you. Ed read us plainspoken, sometimes ribald poems by people like Edward Field, David Ignatow, Linda Pastan, and Etheridge Knight, and then with an effortless zigzag he might take up some thorny and austere piece of Eliot or Stevens, and make it sound like Rodney Dangerfield in a pensive mood.

When he had finished reading us a poem, he would open it up like a watch and show us the inner works, all the decisions the poet had made about line breaks and rhyme schemes (if any), vocabulary and diction, rhythm and tone. He emphasized accuracy and precision in language, the sadness of cliché, the need to find newness in the way one wrote about the world, and, unconsciously I think, the supreme importance of exuberance, the kind of mordant exuberance he discovered to us when he read William Carlos Williams's famous number about the mooched plums, so sweet and so cold.

It was Ed who introduced me to the work of the most exuberant poet who ever lived, Frank O'Hara, giving us the one that begins:

> How funny you are today New York
> like Ginger Rogers in Swingtime
> and St. Bridget's steeple leaning a little to the left

The voice of O'Hara was the voice of a friend, a best friend. It was intimate and casual. And yet at the same time it was also refined, literary, erudite, capable of hopping like a sparrow down a sidewalk from densely imagistic to dishy and familiar in the space of a single line. Over that semester Ed read us a bunch of other O'Hara poems, among them "The Day Lady Died," "Lana Turner Has Collapsed!," and my favorite, "Autobiographia Literaria":

> When I was a child
> I played by myself in a
> corner of the schoolyard
> all alone.

I hated dolls and I
hated games, animals were
not friendly and birds
flew away.

If anyone was looking
for me I hid behind a
tree and cried out "I am
an orphan."

And here I am, the
center of all beauty!
writing these poems!
Imagine!

In the thirty years since I left Pittsburgh I've written exactly one indisputable poem. Now, if you plan to write only one poem every thirty years, you should probably make it a love poem; and indeed this one indisputable poem of mine, composed in 2003, is addressed to my beloved. She keeps it folded in the top drawer of her lingerie chest, I believe, with her good jewelry and our children's baby teeth. Over that span of decades, however, I've also written a bunch of what, until now, I've always considered to be my "other poems," poems so disputable that no one apart from me has ever considered them to be poems at all.

They're too long, for one thing, crazy long; some of them go on for hundreds and hundreds of pages. Each of their lines breaks arbitrarily, at the right-hand margin of every page. For stanzas they have paragraphs, and for cantos, chapters, and while they revel freely in the rhythmic antics of anapests, iambs, trochees, and dactyls, they shun rhyme. They have plots and characters, and everyone who looks at them seems to regard them as novels. A number of readers have wondered, at times publicly and not without exasperation, if the things I write really ought to feature quite so many similes, which is not a question that people tend to bother poets with. They point to my fondness for extended metaphors and shake their rueful heads. Nobody ever gives poets a hard time for their extended metaphors! On the contrary. John Donne's been cashing in on them for years now.

But if you build for a campanile you are no less a horologist than if you build for a dainty wrist. I tweeze each whirring word into its little niche in the clockworks, and the stroke of my hammer is a gentle tap, tap. To set the hands of plot into motion and to make the carillons of character chime, I wind the language of my five-hundred-page mainspring ever tighter, striving, the way the poet Ed Ochester taught me to strive, to combine conversation with surprise, dishiness with density of imagery, to bring my consciousness to bear on the world around me with the darting flash of Frank O'Hara, who noticed everything.

I know the books I've written may look, feel, and tip the scales like novels, but to me they have always felt like poems, because when I was writing them—and only when I was writing them—I, too, became the center of all beauty. When I was done for the day I would go back to hiding behind that same old schoolyard tree.

But in trying to consider the impact that the work of Bob Dylan has had on my own writing—as only seems fitting since he has just been inducted into the American Academy of Arts and Letters—I've found myself thinking back on that afternoon in the Cathedral of Learning when I hung out in Ed's office for a while, smoking and talking on and on, with all the tedious vainglory for which Ed, God bless him, had such an apparently high tolerance, about the band I was going to be in, to be called Lunchmeat Island or Hex Wrench or the Bats or Dannon Yogurt Steam-Shovel (in the end we would go with the Bats), writing song lyrics and "singing." As I was leaving his office, Ed handed me a book, an advance copy of an anthology some textbook publisher had sent him for consideration, called *Rock Lyrics as Poetry*, or something like that. The idea that rock lyrics might (or might not) be a new, modern form of poetry was a meme of the seventies that was still hanging around even as late as 1983, and even though nobody used the word "meme" back then; not in Pittsburgh, anyway.

I didn't quite know what to make of Ed's gift, which featured the lyrics to dozens of well-known songs by Bob Dylan, the Beatles, Joni Mitchell, and many other artists whose work was beloved by and important to me. In 1983, I loved rock 'n' roll music no less than I do now—the love of rock 'n' roll is probably the most durable and unvarying passion of my life. Many, many lyrics and bits of lyrics mattered a lot to me, then as now—like, for example:

I remember
How the darkness doubled
I recall
Lightning struck itself

or

Then I woke up, Mom and Dad
Are rolling on the couch
Rollin' numbers rock and rollin'
Got my KISS records out

or

Beat on the brat
with a baseball bat
Oh yeah.

It was interesting to learn, from the book Ed gave me, that the first line of Dylan's "Chimes of Freedom" went "far between sundown's finish an' midnight's broken toll" and not, as I had always heard it, "far between sundown's finish and midnight's broken toe." But the question, the debate as to whether or not rock lyrics were poetry, did not really interest me. I had always assumed that they weren't, even though one day in class Ed had read to us, as if it were just another poem, the lyrics to "Suzanne" by Leonard Cohen, getting us to pay close attention, the way Cohen was paying close attention, to the Chinese provenance of the tea and oranges; and the fact that Suzanne's rags and feathers had been purchased, no doubt on a tight budget, at the Salvation Army; and the beauty of the metaphor comparing Christ's view of the world atop his fatal cross to the lookout from the crow's nest of a ship.

But Leonard Cohen was a special case, a published, acclaimed young poet before he ever wrote his first song, and even Cohen had resorted, as Ed duly pointed out to us, to a cheesy pop cliché like "When she gets you on her wavelength."

Anyway, it turned out not to be elitist snobbery that made me dubious of the thesis of *Rock Lyrics as Poetry*, or some clear sense of the boundary between a poem and a song lyric. As I read through the book Ed had given me I saw that rock lyrics could not really be poetry because when you took away the melody, the instrumentation, and above all the voice of the singer, a song lyric just kind of huddled there on a page looking plucked and forlorn, like Foghorn Leghorn after a brush with the Tasmanian Devil. I remembered how absurd the lyrics to the song "She's Leaving Home" had seemed, mimeographed on a sheet passed out in my eighth-grade English class by an earnest student teacher who was trying to help us find profundity in the song's social commentary. I had always felt a sense of exaltation at the end of that song when I listened to *Sgt. Pepper*, as ascending angelic voices triumphantly asserted "*She* . . . *is having* . . . FUN . . ." But typed out on a ditto, those words had looked banal, trivial, even to a twelve-year-old who hoped to slip out the back door into the world someday and have fun, too, although not necessarily by meeting a man from the motor trade.

Now when I think about Ed Ochester and the book he gave me, back when he was trying to teach me how to be a poet, the question of whether or not Dylan's lyrics are poetry feels irrelevant. Dylan's lyrics are writing, and as writing they have influenced my own writing as much as if not more than the work of any poet apart from O'Hara and maybe Edgar Allan Poe. In fact, song lyrics in general have arguably mattered to and shaped me more, as a writer, than novels or short stories written by any but the most crucial of my literary heroes.

Ask me to name a few of those heroes, and I'm likely to come up with a random sample of literary crushes: Cheever, Welty, Pynchon, Fitzgerald. I might try to mix things up with a genre wild card like Chandler or Ursula K. Le Guin, or even Ian Fleming. Maybe reach across forms to a poet like O'Hara, or an essayist like S. J. Perelman. But I have never once told the deeper truth, and answered Dylan, or Rakim, or Mitchell, or Verlaine (Tom, not Paul).

And yet the words chosen, resorted to, or arrived at by the lyricists of rock, soul, and hip-hop constitute the body of writing that I know best, that I have studied most intensively, puzzled over longest. (I can't begin to calculate or tell you how many hours I had devoted, before Ed Ochester handed me that book, to trying to understand, to really feel, that midnight had toes, and that one of them—the big toe?—could be broken.) Lyrics are the only written works that I have ever reliably committed to memory, apart from a touch of Poe, a smidgen of Kipling's "If," bits and pieces of Shakespeare. I have memorized thousands of song lyrics. Sometimes at night, I lie in bed waiting to fall asleep with a radio in my head playing "Wild West End" by Dire Straits, or Rakim's "I Know You Got Soul," or "Hejira" by Joni Mitchell, or some random piece of pop craftsmanship from my childhood like "Brandy" by Looking Glass, and the remembering of every word of every verse is perfect, and completely involuntary. Song lyrics are part of my literary firmware, programmed permanently into my read-only memory.

Not just words: writing. Tropes and devices, rhetorical strategies, writerly techniques, entire structures of allusion and imagery: entire skeins of the synapses in my cerebral cortex by now are made up entirely of all this unforgettable literature. In the above tunes that I cited as playing on the radio inside midnight's broken brain, we find instances of a well-observed bit of characterization from Dire Straits's Mark Knopfler (an underrated lyricist), *"Now my conductress on the number 19 / She was a honey / Pink toenails and hands all dirty with the money"*; two beautiful images, Mitchell's *"White flags of winter chimneys / Waving truce against the moon"* and Rakim's thrilling simile for the act of writing itself, *"I start to think / and then I sink / into the paper / like I was ink / when I'm writin / I'm trapped in between / the lines / I escape when I finish / the rhyme"*; and even, in the more workmanlike "Brandy," the efficient, patient setting of scene, the port on the western bay that serves a hundred ships a day, the girl in the harbor town who works laying whisky down, the care taken with these lines that open the extended, Dubliners-esque portrait of poor Brandy, that fine girl, with her love going endlessly to waste.

I don't think I could have learned more about the joy and sensuous appeal of alliteration, assonance, and consonance from any poem of Gerard Manley Hopkins than I did from Warren Zevon's wonderful line in "Werewolves of London": *"Little old lady got mutilated late last night"*; more about elliptical storytelling from Raymond Carver than from "Ode to Billy Joe" (Bobbie Gentry is another underrated writer); more about unreliable narrators from Poe or Nabokov than from Steely Dan (passim). And yet while songwriters are given the opportunity, often enough, to cite their literary influences, no one has ever thought to ask me about the songwriters who have shaped my work, any more than I have asked myself, until now. I'm not sure why. Maybe it's the sha-la-la-las and the wo-o-wo-os. Maybe it's the fact that so many lyrics are nothing but clichés strung like costume jewelry beads on a string of backbeat. Maybe it's all the fault of poet manqués like Jim Morrison, the rock 'n' roll equivalent of the pretentious actor in *Annie Hall* who hopes to be torn apart by wild animals and asks Annie to touch his heart with her foot. You write enough lines like *"There's a killer on the road / His brain is squirming like a toad"* or *"If they say I never loved you / You know they are a liar"* and the stock of rock lyricists as influential literary figures is bound to go down.

Of course rock lyrics are not poetry. They don't need to be. What they may lack, on the page, in figurative ambition, in ruthless antipathy toward cliché, and above all in the combination of stance, diction, and point of view that we call a voice, is made up for by guitars, keyboards, drums, and by the living, infinitely expressive voice of a great singer like Bob Dylan, the ache and rasp of that all-too-human voice, now snarling, now weary, now sweet, now brokenhearted.

I wonder if, in handing me that book, Ed Ochester hoped to get me to see that even if the finest lyrics lacked something, on the page, it was not through insufficient craft or "poeticalness" but by their very nature, by design, the way a great play on the page lacks actors, scenery, lights, and costumes and yet remains, powerfully and indispensably, a work of literature. Maybe Ed gave me *Rock Lyrics as Poetry* because he wanted me to think about everything my poetry needed to do to make up for its grievous lack of Gibson guitars, Marshall amps, Slingerland drums, of a voice as full of fire and longing and wit as Bob Dylan's, or as Frank O'Hara's.

When the term ended I moved on from Ed Ochester's tutelage and left the Bats behind, having contributed very little to the ensemble or to the greater glory of rock. For many years after that I was in and out of fiction workshops, writing short stories and first chapters of abortive novels, and never looking back except insofar as I continued to believe that my chapters were cantos, and my paragraphs stanzas, and my sentences lines of free verse that broke where they ran out of space at the right side of the page. Little by little, I began to grope my way toward a style that attempted to mingle the down-to-earth with the high-flown, or rather to fit everyday speech with antigravity discs and build elegant rhetorical flying machines out of common household objects. And I thought of the style that resulted, and that ever since has served, with steady adjustments and modifications, to let me write my books, as a poetic style.

Now it strikes me that all these years I may have had it wrong, that the lesson that I learned in Ed Ochester's class ought not to have been to think of my prose as poetry. Maybe the stories that fiction writers tell, their characters and settings, are only the lyrics to a song the writer is called upon to sing and play. Those characters and stories must be founded in an eye for people and the world as keen as that of the Kinks' Ray Davies, with a grasp of structure as careful as Elvis Costello's, according to a vision of life as dark as Tom Waits's, as luminous as Kate Bush's, as loopily grand as the vision of the Flaming Lips' Wayne Coyne. But the stories and characters won't come alive, won't catch the reader up, won't lift free of the page that imprisons them, until you plug your nouns into the stacks of your adjectives, settle into the pocket behind the drum kit of your verbs, throw back your head, open your mouth, and let it rock.

2

The Genius and Modern Times of Bob Dylan

By Jonathan Lethem

> "Did I ever want to acquire the sixties? No. But I own the sixties—who's going to argue with me?"

"I don't really have a herd of astrologers telling me what's going to happen. I just make one move after the other, this leads to that." Is the voice familiar? I'm sitting in a Santa Monica seaside hotel suite, ignoring a tray of sliced pineapple and sugar-dusty cookies, while Bob Dylan sits across from my tape recorder, giving his best to my questions. The man before me is fitful in his chair, not impatient, but keenly alive to the moment, and ready on a dime to make me laugh and to laugh himself. The expressions on Dylan's face, in person, seem to compress and encompass versions of his persona across time, a sixty-five-year-old with a nineteen-year-old cavorting somewhere inside. Above all, though, it is the tones of his speaking voice that seem to kaleidoscope through time: here the yelp of the folk pup or the sarcastic rimshot timing of the hounded hipster-idol, there the beguilement of the seventies sex symbol, then again—and always—the gravel of the elder statesman, that antediluvian bluesman's voice the young aspirant so legendarily invoked at the very outset of his work and then ever so gradually aged into.

It's that voice, the voice of a rogue ageless in decrepitude, that grounds the paradox of the achievement of *Modern Times*, his thirty-first studio album. Are these our "modern tunes" or some ancient, silent-movie dream, a fugue in black-and-white? *Modern Times*, like *Love and Theft* and *Time Out of Mind* before it, seems to survey a broken world through the prism of a heart that's worn and worldly, yet decidedly unbroken itself. "I been sitting down studying the art of love / I think it will fit me like a glove," he states in "Thunder on the Mountain," the opening song, a rollicking blues you've heard a million times before and yet which magically seems to announce yet another "new" Dylan. "I feel like my soul is beginning to expand," the song declares. "Look into my heart and you will sort of understand."

What we do understand, if we're listening, is that we're three albums into a Dylan renaissance that's sounding more and more like a period to put beside any in his work. If, beginning with *Bringing It All Back Home*, Dylan garbed his amphetamine visions in the gloriously grungy clothes of the electric blues and early rock 'n' roll, the musical glories of these three records are grounded in a knowledge of the blues built from the inside out—a knowledge that includes the fact that the early blues and its players were stranger than any purist would have you know, hardly restricting themselves to twelve-bar laments but featuring narrative recitations, spirituals, X-rated ditties, popular ballads, and more. Dylan offers us nourishment from the root cellar of American cultural life. For an amnesiac society, that's arguably as mind-expanding an offering as anything in his sixties work. And with each succeeding record, Dylan's convergence with his muses grows more effortlessly natural.

How does he summon such an eternal authority? "I'd make this record no matter what was going on in the world," Dylan tells me. "I wrote these songs in not a meditative state at all, but more like in a trancelike, hypnotic state. *This* is how I feel? Why do I *feel* like that? And who's the *me* that feels this way? I couldn't tell you that, either. But I know that those songs are just in my genes and I couldn't stop them comin' out." This isn't to say *Modern Times*, or Dylan, seems oblivious to the present moment. The record is littered—or should I say baited?—with glinting references to world events like 9/11 and Hurricane Katrina, though anyone seeking a moral, to paraphrase Mark Twain, should be shot. And, as if to startle the contemporary listener out of any delusion that Dylan's musical drift into pre-rock forms—blues, ragtime, rockabilly—is the mark of a nostalgist, "Thunder on the Mountain" also name-checks a certain contemporary singer: "I was thinking 'bout Alicia Keys, I couldn't keep from crying / While she was born in Hell's Kitchen, I was livin' down the line." When I ask Dylan what Keys did "to get into your pantheon," he only chuckles at my precious question. "I remember seeing her on the Grammys. I think I was on the show with her, I didn't meet her or anything. But I said to myself, 'There's *nothing* about that girl I don't like.'"

Rather than analyzing lyrics, Dylan prefers to linger over the songs as artifacts of music and describes the process of their making. As in other instances, stretching back to 1974's *Planet Waves*, 1978's *Street Legal*, and 2001's *Love and Theft*, the singer and performer known for his love-hate affair with the recording studio—"I don't like to make records," he tells me simply. "I do it reluctantly"—has cut his new album with his touring band. And Dylan himself is the record's producer, credited under the nom-de-studio Jack Frost. "I didn't feel like I wanted to be overproduced any more," he tells me. "I felt like I've always produced my own records anyway, except I just had someone there in the way. I feel like nobody's gonna know how I should sound except me anyway, nobody knows what they want out of players except me, nobody can tell a player what he's doing wrong, nobody can find a player who *can* play but he's *not* playing, like I can. I can do that in my sleep."

As ever, Dylan is circling, defining what he *is* first by what he *isn't*, by what he doesn't want, doesn't like, doesn't need, locating meaning by a process of elimination. This rhetorical strategy goes back at least as far as "It Ain't Me, Babe" and "All I Really Want to Do" ("I ain't looking to compete with you," etc.), and it still has plenty of real juice in it. When Dylan arrives at a positive assertion out of the wilderness of so much doubt, it takes on the force of a jubilant boast. "This is the best band I've ever been in, I've ever had, *man for man*. When you play with guys a hundred times a year, you know what you can and can't do, what they're good at, whether you *want* 'em there. It takes a long time to find a band of individual players. Most bands are *gangs*. Whether it's a metal group or pop rock, whatever, you get that gang mentality. But for those of us who went back further, gangs were the *mob*. The gang was not what anybody aspired to. On this record I didn't have anybody to teach. I got guys now in my band, they can whip up anything, they surprise even *me*." Dylan's cadences take on the quality of an impromptu recitation, replete with internal rhyme schemes, such that when I later transcribe this tape I'll find myself tempted to set the words on the page in the form of a lyric. "I knew this time it wouldn't be *futile* writing something I really *love* and thought dearly *of*, and then gettin' in the studio and having it be beaten up and whacked *around* and come out with some kind of incoherent thing which didn't have any resonance. With that, I was *awake*. I felt freed up to do just about anything I pleased."

But getting the band of his dreams into the studio was only half the battle. "The records I used to listen to and still love, you can't make a record that sounds that way," he explains. It is as if having taken his new material down to the crossroads of the recording studio Dylan isn't wholly sure the deal struck with the devil there was worth it. "Brian Wilson, he made all his records with four tracks, but you couldn't make his records if you had a *hundred* tracks today. We all like records that are played on record players, but let's face it, those days are *gon-n-n-e*. You do the best you can, you fight that technology in all kinds of ways, but I don't know anybody who's made a record that sounds decent in the past twenty years, really. You listen to these modern records, they're atrocious, they have sound all over them. There's no definition of nothing, no vocal, no nothing, just like—*static*. Even these songs probably sounded ten times better in the studio when we recorded 'em. CDs are *small*. There's no stature to it. I remember when that Napster guy came up across, it was like, 'Everybody's gettin' music for free.' I was like, 'Well, why not? It ain't *worth* nothing anyway.'"

Hearing the word "Napster" come from Bob Dylan's mouth, I venture a question about bootleg recordings. In my own wishful thinking, *The Bootleg Series*, a sequence of superb archival retrospectives, sanctioned by Dylan and released by Columbia, represents a kind of unspoken consent to the tradition of pirate scholarship—an acknowledgment that Dylan's outtakes, alternate takes, rejected album tracks, and live performances are themselves a towering body of work that faithful listeners deserve to hear. As Michael Gray says in *The Bob Dylan Encyclopedia*, the first three-disc release of outtakes "could, of itself, establish Dylan's place as the pre-eminent songwriter and performer of the age and as one of the great artists of the twentieth century." On *Love and Theft*'s "Sugar Baby," the line "Some of these bootleggers, they make pretty good stuff" was taken by some as a shout-out to this viewpoint. Today, at least, that line seems to have had only moonshine whiskey as its subject. "I still don't like bootleg records. There was a period of time when people were just bootlegging anything on me, because there was nobody ever in charge of the recording sessions. All my stuff was being bootlegged high and low, far and wide. They were never intended to be released, but everybody was buying them. So my record company said, 'Well, everybody else is buying these records, we might as well put them out.'" But Dylan can't possibly be sorry that the world has had the benefit of hearing, for instance, "Blind Willie McTell"—an outtake from 1983's *Infidels* that has subsequently risen as high in most people's Dylan pantheon as a song can rise, and that he himself has played live since. Can he? "I started playing it live because I heard The Band doing it. Most likely it was a demo, probably showing the musicians how it should go. It was never developed fully, I never got around to completing it. There wouldn't have been any other reason for leaving it off the record. It's like taking a painting by Manet or Picasso—goin' to his house and lookin' at a half-finished painting and grabbing it and selling it to people who are 'Picasso fans.' The only fans I know I have are the people who I'm looking at when I play, night after night."

Dylan and his favorite-band-ever are just a few days from undertaking another tour, one that will be well under way by the time *Modern Times* is released in late August. I've always wanted to ask: When a song suddenly appears on a given evening's set list, retrieved from among the hundreds in his back catalog, is it because Dylan's been listening to his old records? "I don't listen to *any* of my records. When you're inside of it, all you're listening to is a *replica*. I don't know why somebody would look at the movies they make—you don't read your *books*, do you?" Point taken. He expands on the explanation he offered for "Blind Willie McTell": "Strangely enough, sometimes we'll hear a cover of a song and figure we can do it just as well. If somebody else thought so highly of it, why don't I? Some of these arrangements I just *take*. The Dead did a lot of my songs, and we'd just take the whole arrangement, because they did it better than me. Jerry Garcia could hear the song in all my bad recordings, the song that was buried there. So if I want to sing something different, I just bring out one of them Dead records and see which one I wanna do. I *never* do that with my records." Speaking of which: "I've heard it said, you've probably heard it said, that all the arrangements change night after night. Well, *that's* a bunch of bullshit, they don't know what they're talkin' about. The arrangements don't change night after night. The rhythmic structures are different, that's all. You can't change the arrangement night after night—it's impossible."

Dylan points out that whether a song comes across for a given listener on a given night depends on where exactly they're sitting. "I can't stand to play arenas, but I do play 'em. But I know that's not where music's supposed to be. It's not meant to be heard in football stadiums, it's not 'Hey, how are you doin' tonight, Cleveland?' Nobody gives a shit how you're doin' tonight in Cleveland." He grins and rolls his eyes, to let me know he knows he's teasing at *Spinal Tap* heresy. Then he plunges deeper. "They say, 'Dylan never talks.' What the hell is there to *say*? That's not the reason an artist is in front of people." The words seem brash, but his tone is nearly pleading. "An artist has come for a different purpose. Maybe a self-help group—maybe a Dr. Phil—would say, 'How you doin'?' I don't want to get harsh and say I don't care. You do care, you care in a *big way*, otherwise you wouldn't be there. But it's a different kind of connection. It's not a light thing." He considers further. "It's alive every night, or it feels alive every night." Pause. "It becomes *risky*. I mean, you risk your life to play music, if you're doing it in the right way." I ask about the minor-league baseball[1] stadiums he's playing in the new tour's first swing: Do they provide the sound he's looking for? "Not really, not in the open air. The best sound you can get is an intimate club room, where you've got four walls and the sound just *bounces*. That's the way this music is meant to be heard." Then Dylan turns comedian again, the guy newly familiar to listeners of his XM satellite radio show, whose casual verbal riffs culminate in vaudeville one-liners. "I wouldn't want to play a *really* small room, like ten people. Unless it was, you know, *$50,000 a ticket* or something."

Let me take a moment and reintroduce myself, your interviewer and guide here. I'm a forty-two-year-old moonlighting novelist and a lifelong Dylan fan, but one who, it must be emphasized, *doesn't remember the sixties*. I'm no longer a young man, but I am young for the job I'm doing here. My parents were Dylan fans, and my first taste of his music came through their LPs—I settled on *Nashville Skyline*, because it looked friendly. The first Dylan record

1. So what's Bob Dylan's favorite baseball team, anyway? "The problem with baseball teams is all the players get traded, and what your favorite team used to be—a couple of guys you really lifted on the team, they're not on the team now—and you can't possibly make that team your favorite team. It's like your favorite uniform. I mean . . . yeah . . . I like Detroit. Though I like Ozzie [Guillen] as a manager. And I don't know how anybody can't like Derek [Jeter]. I'd rather have him on my team than anybody."

I was able to respond to as new—to witness its arrival in stores and reception in magazines, and therefore to make my own—was 1979's *Slow Train Coming.* As a fan in my early twenties, I digested Dylan's catalog to that point and concluded that its panoply of styles and stances was *itself* the truest measure of his genius—call us the *Biograph* generation, if you like. In other words, the struggle to capture Dylan and his art like smoke in one particular bottle or another seemed laughable to me, a mistaken skirmish fought before it had become clear that mercurial responsiveness—anchored only by the existential commitment to the act of connection in the present moment—was the gift of freedom his songs had promised all along. To deny it to the man himself would be absurd. By the time I required anything of Bob Dylan, it was the mideighties, and I merely required him to be good. Which, in the mideighties, Dylan kind of wasn't. I recall taking home *Empire Burlesque* and struggling to discern songwriting greatness under the glittery murk of Arthur Baker's production, a struggle I lost. The first time I saw Dylan in concert, it was, yes, in a football stadium in Oakland, with the Grateful Dead. By the time of 1988's *Down in the Groove*, the album's worst song might have seemed to describe my plight as fan; I was in love with the ugliest girl in the world.

Nevertheless, Eighties Dylan was my Dylan, and I bore down hard on what was there. Contrary to what you may have heard (in *Chronicles, Volume One*, among other detractors), there was water in that desert. From scattered tracks like "Rank Strangers to Me," "The Groom's Still Waiting at the Altar," and "Brownsville Girl," to cassette-tape miracles like "Lord Protect My Child" and "Foot of Pride" (both later to surface on *The Bootleg Series*), to a version of "San Francisco Bay Blues" I was lucky enough to catch live in Berkeley, to a blistering take on Sonny Boy Williamson's "Don't Start Me to Talkin'" on *Late Night with David Letterman*, the irony is not only that "bad" Dylan was often astonishingly good. It is that his then-seemingly-rudderless exploration of roots-music sources can now be seen to point unerringly to the triumphs to come—I mean the triumphs of now. Not that Dylan himself would care to retrace those steps. When I gushed about the Sonny Boy Williamson moment on *Letterman*, he gaped, plainly amazed, and said, "I played that?"

So, the drama of my projected relationship to my hero, thin as it may seem to those steeped in the sixties or seventies listeners' sense of multiple betrayals—*He's gone electric! Country-domestic-unavailable! Christian!*—was the one Dylan described to David Gates of *Newsweek* in 1997, and in the "Oh

Mercy" chapter of his memoir, *Chronicles*—the relocation and repossession of his voice and of his will to compose and perform, as enacted gradually through the nineties. Early in that decade it might have seemed he'd quit, or at least taken refuge or solace in the solo acoustic folk records he'd begun making in his garage: *Good As I Been to You* and *World Gone Wrong*. Live shows in what had become "The Never Ending Tour" were stronger and stronger in those years, but new songs were scarce. Then came *Time Out of Mind*, an album as cohesive—and ample—as any he'd ever recorded. When that was followed by *Love and Theft*, and then *Chronicles*, a reasonable Dylan fan might conclude he was living in the best of all possible worlds. In fact, with the satellite radio show beaming into our homes—Dylan's promised to do fifty of the things!—Dylan can be said to have delivered more of his voice and his heart to his audience in the past decade than ever before, and more than anyone might have reasonably dared to hope. "Well, isn't that funny," Dylan snorts when I mention "the myth of inaccessibility." "I've just seen that Wenner Books published a book of interviews with me that's that big." He stretches out his hands to show me. "What happened to this inaccessibility? Isn't there a *dichotomy* there?"

Yet it's awfully easy, taking the role of Dylan's interviewer, to feel oneself playing surrogate for an audience that has never quit holding its hero to an impossible standard: the more he offers, the more we want. The greatest artist of my lifetime has given me anything I could ever have thought to ask, and yet here I sit, somehow brokering between him and the expectations neither of us can pretend don't exist. "If I've got any kind of attitude about me—or about what I do, what I perform, what I sing, on any level, my attitude is, compare it to somebody *else*! Don't compare it to me. Are you going to compare Neil Young to Neil Young? Compare it to somebody else, compare it to Beck—which I like—or whoever else is on his level. This record should be compared to the artists who are working on the same ground. I'll take it any way it comes, but compare it to that. That's what everybody's record should be, if they're really serious about what they're doing. Let's face it, you're either serious about what you're doing or you're not serious about what you're doing. And you can't mix the two. And life is short."

I can't help but wonder if he's lately been reconditioned by the success of the Martin Scorsese *No Direction Home* documentary, to feel again the vivid discomfort of his unwanted savior's role. "You know, everybody makes a big deal about the sixties. The sixties, it's like the Civil War days. But, I mean, you're talking to a person who *owns* the sixties. Did I ever want to acquire the sixties? *No.* But I own the sixties—who's going to argue with me?" He charms me with another joke: "I'll give 'em to you if you want 'em. You can have 'em." For Dylan, as ever, what matters is the work, not in some archival sense, but in its present life. "My old songs, they've got something—I agree, they've *got* something! I think my songs have been covered—maybe not as much as 'White Christmas' or 'Stardust,' but there's a list of over five thousand recordings. That's a lot of people covering your songs, they must have *something.* If I was me, *I'd* cover my songs too. A lot of these songs I wrote in 1961 and '62 and '64 and 1973 and 1985, I can still play a lot of those songs—well, how many other artists made songs during that time? How many do you hear today? I love Marvin Gaye, I love all that stuff. But how often are you gonna hear 'What's Going On'? I mean, who *sings* it? Who sings 'Tracks of My Tears'? Where is *that* being sung tonight?"

He's still working to plumb the fullest truth in the matter of his adventures in the recording studio. "I've had a rough time recording. I've managed to come up with *songs,* but I've had a rough time recording. But maybe it should be that way. Because other stuff which *sounds* incredible, that can *move* you to tears—for all those who were knocked off our feet by listening to music from *yesteryear,* how many of those *songs* are really good? Or was it just the record that was great? Well, the record was great. The record was an *art form.* And you know, when all's said and done, maybe I was never part of that art form, because my records really weren't artistic at all. They were just documentation. Maybe *bad* players playing *bad* changes, but still something coming through. And the *something* that's coming through, for me today, was to make it just as real. To show you how it's real." Dylan muses on the fate of art in posterity. "How many people can look at the *Mona Lisa*? You ever been there? I mean, maybe, like, three people can see it at once. And yet, how long has that painting been around? More people have seen that painting than have ever listened to, let's name somebody—I don't want to say Alicia Keys—say, Michael Jackson. More people have ever seen the *Mona Lisa* than ever listened to Michael Jackson. And only three people can see it at once. Talk about *impact.*"

Conversation about painting leads to conversation about other forms. "That's what I like about books, there's no *noise* in it. Whatever you put on the page, it's like making a painting. Nobody can change it. Writing a book is the same way, it's written in *stone*—it might as well be! It's never gonna change. One's not gonna be different in tone than another, you're not gonna have to turn this one up louder to read it." Dylan savored the reception of *Chronicles*. "Most people who write about music, they have no idea what it feels like to play it. But with the book I wrote, I thought, 'The people who are writing reviews of this book, man, they know what the hell they're talking about.' It spoils you. They know *how* to write a book, they know more about it than me. The reviews of this book, some of 'em almost made me cry—in a good way. I'd never felt that from a music critic, *ever*."

While my private guess would have been that Dylan had satisfied the scribbling impulse (or as he says on *Modern Times*, "I've already confessed / No need to confess again"), in fact he seems to be deep into planning for a *Chronicles, Volume Two*. "I think I can go back to the *Blonde on Blonde* album—that's probably about as far back as I can go on the next book. Then I'll probably go forward. I thought of an interesting time. I made this record, *Under the Red Sky*, with Don Was, but at the same time I was also doing the Wilburys record. I don't know how it happened that I got into both albums at the same time. I worked with George [Harrison] and Jeff [Lynne] during the day—everything had to be done in one day, the track and the song had to be written in one day, and then I'd go down and see Don Was, and I felt like I was walking into a *wall*. He'd have a different band for me to play with every day, a lot of *all-stars*, for no particular purpose. Back then I wasn't bringing anything at *all* into the studio, I was completely disillusioned. I'd let someone else take control of it all and just come up with lyrics to the melody of the song. He'd say, 'What do you want to cut?'—well, I wouldn't have *anything* to cut, but I'd be so beat down from being up with the Wilburys that I'd just come up with some track, and everybody would fall in behind that track, oh, my God." He laughs. "It was sort of contrary to the Wilburys scene, which was being done in a mansion up in the hills. Then I'd go down to these other sessions, and they were in this cavelike studio down in Hollywood, where I'd spend the rest of the night, and then try to get some sleep. Both projects suffered some. Too many people in the room, too many musicians, too many egos, ego-driven musicians that just wanted to play their thing, and it definitely wasn't my cup of tea, but that's the record I'm going to feature."

Now, this may be the place for me to mention that I find Side Two of *Under the Red Sky* one of the hidden treasures of Dylan's catalog. The album's closer, a garrulous but mysterious jump-blues called "Cat's in the Well," in particular, wouldn't be at all out of place on *Love and Theft* or *Modern Times*.

But as he's told me, Dylan doesn't listen to the records. And unlike me, he claims no familiarity with *The Bob Dylan Encyclopedia*. ("Those are not the circles I really move around in," he chuckles when I ask. "That's not something that would overlap with my life.") But just as when he praises his current band as his absolute best—an evaluation supporters of Mike Bloomfield and Al Kooper, not to mention Garth Hudson and Rick Danko, et al., might take issue with—I've come to feel that Dylan's sweeping simplifications of his own journey's story are outstandingly healthy ones. Puncturing myths, boycotting analysis, and ignoring chronology are likely part of a long and lately quite successful campaign not to be incarcerated within his own legend. Dylan's greatest accomplishment since his sixties apotheosis may simply be that he has claimed his story as his own. (Think of him howling the first line of "Most Likely You'll Go Your Way and I'll Go Mine" upon his return to the stage during the 1974 tour: "You say you love me and you're thinkin' of me / But you know you could be *wroooonngg*!"). I take our conversation today the way I took *Chronicles*, and the long journal-song "Highlands": as vivid and generous reports on the state of Bob Dylan and his feelings in the present moment.

In other words, never mind that I think *Under the Red Sky* is pretty good. After that early-nineties disillusionment, how did he decide to record *Time Out of Mind*? "They gave me another contract, which I didn't really want. I didn't want to record anymore, I didn't see any point to it, but lo and behold they made me an offer and it was hard to refuse. I'd worked with [Daniel] Lanois before, and I thought he might be able to bring that magic to this record. I thought, 'Well, I'll give it a try.' There must have been twelve, fifteen musicians in that room—four drummers notwithstanding. I really don't know how we got anything out of that." He pauses to consider the record's reception. Released just after a much-publicized health scare, the album's doomy lyrics were widely taken as a musical wrestling match with the angel of death. "I mean, it was perceived as me being some chronic invalid, or crawling on bleeding knees. But that was never the case." I mention that some are already describing the new album as the third in a trilogy, beginning with *Time Out of Mind*. Dylan demurs: "*Time Out of Mind* was me getting back in and fighting my way out of the corner. But by the time I made *Love and Theft*, I was out of the corner. On this record, I ain't nowhere, you can't find me anywhere, because I'm *way* gone from the corner." He still toys with the notion I've put before him. "I would think more of *Love and Theft* as the beginning of a trilogy, if there's going to be a trilogy." Then swiftly gives himself an out: "If I decide I want to go back into the studio."

In a day of circular talk we've circled back to the new record, and I venture to ask him again about certain motifs. *Modern Times* shades *Love and Theft*'s jocular, affectionate vibe into more ominous territory, the language of murder ballads and Edgar Allan Poe: foes and slaughter, haunted gardens and ghosts. Old blues and ballads are quoted liberally, like second nature. "I didn't feel limited this time, or I felt limited in the way that you want to narrow your scope down, you don't want to *muddle* things up, you want every line to be clear and every line to be purposeful. This is the way I feel someplace in me, in my *genealogy*—a lot of us don't have the murderous *instinct*, but we wouldn't *mind* having the license to kill. I just let the lyrics go, and when I was singing them, they seemed to have an ancient presence." Dylan seems to feel he dwells in a body haunted like a house by his bardlike musical precursors. "Those songs are just in my genes, and I couldn't stop them comin' out. In a reincarnative kind of way, maybe. The songs have got some kind of a *pedigree* to them. But that pedigree stuff, that only works so far. You can go back to the ten hundreds, and people only had one name. Nobody's gonna tell you they're going to go back further than when people had one name." This reply puts an effective end to my connect-the-dots queries about his musical influences. I tell him that despite the talk of enemies, I found in the new record a generosity of spirit, even a sense of acceptance. He consents, barely. "Yeah. You got to accept it *yourself* before you can expect anybody else to accept it. And in the long run, it's merely a record. Lyrics go by quick."

When all is said and done, Bob Dylan is keen that I understand where he's coming from, and for me to understand that, I have to grasp what he saw in the artists who went before him. "If you think about all the artists that recorded in the forties and the thirties, and in the fifties, you had big bands, sure, but they were the vision of one man—I mean, the Duke Ellington band was the vision of one man, the Louis Armstrong band, it was the individual voice of Louis Armstrong. And going into all the rhythm and blues stuff, and the rockabilly stuff, the stuff that trained me to do what I do, that was all *individually* based. That was what you heard—the individual crying in the wilderness. So that's kind of lost too. I mean, who's the last individual performer that you can think of—Elton John, maybe? I'm talking about artists with the willpower not to conform to anybody's reality but their own. Patsy Cline and Billy Lee Riley. Plato and Socrates, Whitman and Emerson. Slim Harpo and Donald Trump. It's a lost art form. I don't know who else does it beside myself, to tell you the truth." Is he satisfied? "I always wanted to stop when I was on *top*. I didn't want to fade away. I didn't want to be a *has*-been, I wanted to be somebody who'd never be forgotten. I feel that, one way or another, it's OK now, I've done what I wanted for myself."

These remarks, it should be noted, are yet another occasion for laughter. "I see that I could stop touring at any time, but then, I don't really *feel* like it right now." Short of promising the third part of the trilogy-in-progress, this is good enough news for me. May the Never Ending Tour never end. "I think I'm in my middle years now," Bob Dylan tells me. "I've got no retirement plans."

3

All the Poets (Musicians on Writing)

An Interview with Rhiannon Giddens

By Scott Timberg

Scott Timberg: Let's start by talking about your songwriting—on the new record, and going back as far as you want. I expect that, as a songwriter, you're drawing from a lot of different sources. From your own life, from the blues, from old-time music, from other songwriters, maybe Dylan. But how important are writers—poets, novelists, short story writers, essayists—to what you do as a musician?

Rhiannon Giddens: Oh, I think they're very important. You know, it's like, if you want to be a writer you've got to read, right?

ST: Right.

RG: So if you want to be a songwriter, you've got to listen . . . and read. You know, I've always been drawn to the word—I'm a voracious reader—and I've always been drawn to lyrics in particular. I mean, I love tunes and everything, but I was a big fan of Tom Lehrer and

Stephen Sondheim, and I loved Sting's early stuff—very poetic songwriting. You know, I'm one of those weirdos and I never listened to Dylan . . .

ST: Never really got into him?

RG: It's not even that I never really got into him, I never listened to him, other than the famous songs that everyone knows—"Blowin' in the Wind" and whatever. I've never listened to a Dylan record in my life. I'll be honest with you—I never have. What I ended up doing was kind of skipping Dylan and going straight to the stuff Dylan listened to, you know what I mean?

ST: Sure, right.

RG: And the people that I listened to from the folk revival were all mostly interpreters—like Joan Baez and Peter, Paul and Mary. So, I didn't really get into that kind of folk writing.

ST: Right, singers and not songwriters for the most part.

RG: Yeah, yeah, so the songwriters that I was really into were, a lot of them, performing for the stage—kind of quirky stuff, like They Might Be Giants. Stuff like that. And I loved, I do love people's writing styles—I've made a study, in my own little way, of words. It shouldn't have surprised me too much that I ended up writing songs, you know? When I look back on it, I'm writing all these lyrics and looking and just appreciating—I really love clever, intelligent writing. I don't necessarily write like that, but I appreciate it.

ST: Now, when you were a kid, which writers or which books were you rally geeking out over?

RG: I mean, I was a big nerd, so sci-fi/fantasy for sure. The writing style of Robin McKinley—I love her writing style, and when I write short stories it's kind of similar to what she does.

ST: And what's her stuff like?

RG: She's a fantasy—like, a magical fantasy writer. There's just a beautiful flow to her writing. It was a lot of her earlier stuff that I read, and I just remember kind of clasping onto these things, like phrases and how words are put together, and how sentences are put together. And I was kind of an obsessive booklet reader—CD booklets . . . Because I have a hard time understanding lyrics fully . . . And I don't have that—like, I don't listen to rap because I don't understand what they're saying, ever. And there's people who can pick it out and they figure it out, but I can't do that, so I always pick up the booklet and look at the words. And that's why I post all my CDs.

ST: Like buying a book of short stories or something, right?

RG: Well, I don't know about that for these lyrics, but I just remember that viscerally: taking the booklet out, and there are all the words . . . [I remember] following and memorizing old CDs that way. And I'd say the first lyricist that I really, really got into was Sting. His early stuff, like—

ST: *The Dream of the Blue Turtles*, right?

RG: Yep, *The Dream of the Blue Turtles* and *Bring on the Night*, and I loved the one after *The Dream of the Blue Turtles . . . Nothing Like the Sun.*

ST: Yeah. Named after the first line in that Shakespeare sonnet, and I think it has a Hendrix cover. "Little Wing" or "Castles Made of Sand" or something like that.

RG: It does, it does. "Little Wing," and it's got "They Dance Alone," which is talking about the women in South America—I can't remember where, I think Chile—who would dance with the photos of the men who had disappeared—as protest, you know? So like that—writing from a protest point of view, writing from a poetic point of view, writing from a historical . . . He worked in shit like Scylla and Charybdis from Greek mythology—

ST: Yeah, that's the first time I ever heard that phrase—I think that's from "Wrapped Around Your Finger." It's from *The Odyssey*?

RG: Yeah, it's from *The Odyssey*. And of course I'd already read that by the time I heard the song and I was like, "Ah, man this is cool! This dude has all this stuff." And his later stuff—not so much.

ST: Let's go back to your reading for a second. You said you were really drawn to science fiction and fantasy, which literally give kids a key to other worlds. What drew you to that stuff, and what did you get from it?

RG: Oh, you know it was its basis—there are so many different worlds and it's kind of like history . . . but like history where women have more power, or where there are dragons, you know? It's so connected to my love of history, but in this weird, kind of shifty way—this fantasy stuff. And then the sci-fi reached for the limits—and they weren't even the limits anymore. I was a very introspective kid. I was overweight, I had low self-esteem, and so I just kind of lived in these worlds. I read a lot.

ST: It's funny that it would come out of your love of history, because a lot of the best science fiction is like a future history. The Asimov Foundation books were kind of a rewriting of *The Decline and Fall of the Roman Empire*, and *Dune* was written like a history . . . You went to Oberlin and studied opera, and you've recorded as a classical singer. With lieder, you're singing poetry. Has any of that stuff spoken to you?

RG: Oh, yeah. I fell in love with lieder in particular. I mean, the operatic stuff is fine, but it's all, "Oh, I'm dying of love for you—don't leave me!" and all that shit. It's fine to act, but when you look at the poetry . . . I mean, with exceptions of course, because there are beautiful moments in opera: the Da Ponte libretti, the Mozart operas are genius—there are these things. But as a general rule, you're there for the emotional content. But lieder, you know, art songs—particularly the German lieder, more than the French—really drew me. And through the poetry—that's where German is beautiful.

ST: Definitely, yeah.

RG: It's Goethe's words set to Schubert's melodies. You can't beat that . . . Elevating the words to something else. You know, I did full concerts in German lieder—

ST: Oh, really—you sung whole concerts of Schubert and so on?

RG: Yeah, I won an art song competition with a full concert of German lieder. A lot of memorization there. But I loved it and I love it today.

ST: Love Schubert.

RG: Have you heard much [Hugo] Wolf? I love Schubert's stuff, and you're right, his melodies are incredible, but when you get to Wolf, it's like the melody is subservient to the setting. You know, I think his stuff is just . . . stunning. Yeah, I highly recommend him.

ST: Let's talk about a whole other side of things—country, Appalachian music, which comes from Scotland and Ireland, and the string and pipe music of the Celts. I know you have a personal and musical connection to that tradition—I wonder if literature from that part of the world—

RG: We've got to back up for a second, because it did not just come straight from Ireland, Scotland, and England. There is music that comes from there and you have musicians from Africa. It's not just the banjo—it's putting together the fiddle and the banjo on plantations—

ST: Right.

RG: And, of course, you've got all these ballads that do survive in the mountains, and there are obviously direct lines from Ireland and Scotland and England, but it's very important to recognize that the string band music is a fusion. And even stuff that ends up in the mountains is coming from Black players, you know what I mean?

ST: Right, you're emphasizing that this as an American mélange, bringing a Gaelic tradition and a West African tradition together.

RG: Kind of. Still, the idea that there's this sort of equal footing is not true. These European strains of music are getting syncretized, and the music becomes a new thing. There's this exchange between Blacks and whites. So when you have these rich fellas—you know, plantation owners—saying, "Learn these tunes so we can play for our dances," we start seeing this exchange. It is eventually a back and forth, but it starts there. It's a history. You know, I'm being pedantic about it because it's a history that has been hidden. It's just important to say that, because that whole idea of either purity from the old country or "the European fiddle meets the African banjo"—it's not that simple. You know what I mean?

ST: And the vast majority of what we're talking about happened before recording, so we're still sort of unearthing it now. Do you know when the flat seven came in as the sort of de rigueur way you would play this stuff? Because I think of that as a compromise between a West African scale and the European major scale—you know what I mean?

RG: Yeah, I'd say it's coming in at this kind of undocumentable time. There are primary sources talking about the weird scale of the Caribbean music. You know, the otherworldliness of it, and the "barbarity" of it. Stuff was going on in the Caribbean, where the European form and the African forms were having their first meeting. It was also happening in Congo Square in New Orleans, and then you get this

American form—string band music—happening on plantations in the South. I mean, I can't tell you "this is where the seven comes in," but that's my best guess, and there's a lot of scholarship that backs that up.

ST: Yeah.

RG: And nowadays, there's just so much stuff coming out talking about these early years—it's really amazing.

ST: Right, I think all we have right now are educated guesses. But we're probably talking the period of Reconstruction where this is happening, right? I mean the blues—

RG: No, what I'm saying is we have guesses, but we also have a lot of primary source material, and we even have some transcriptions and stuff. And we're talking about before the Civil War. The heart of this music goes back to the very first—we're talking about the 1500–1600s in the Caribbean.

This is where African American music starts—it doesn't start in the South, it doesn't start with Reconstruction, it doesn't start with the Civil War. It starts when Africans are first shipped over to the Caribbean. Read *Sinful Tunes and Spirituals* by Dena Epstein. And, like you said, there are no recordings. All we have is writing, but if you put enough of that together, you get a picture of all this music down in the Caribbean. And that's where people were sent to get seasoned. A lot of the people who were sent up to the South went through those ports. And they brought the banjo. The banjo first emerges in the Caribbean.

ST: So, it's a long way of saying there's certainly Celtic roots to what you do. You have, I think, an Irish husband, and you've played Irish music. So I'm wondering, does that tradition of literature, whether Scottish poetry or Irish American novels, speak to you in any way? Have you gotten into any of those writers?

RG: Not really, but I love Gaelic poetry. There's some really beautiful stuff—I guess underappreciated—when you're talking about Scottish culture. Some of the court stuff is amazing . . . Gaelic culture goes back thousands of years. It was one of the first literate cultures in Western Europe. They have everything—court poetry and folk poetry, and it's all really beautiful.

ST: You spent some time working with fragments from Dylan's songs from the New Basement Tapes, which he hadn't recorded. Did Dylan's words strike you as lyrics or poetry, or some mix of the two?

RG: Probably a mix, I guess. Yeah, he's a very poetic lyricist, you know. Yeah. He's cool—it's a cool project. I mean, I'm just not a Dylan worshipper, so I can't speak to his whole body of work. We worked with lyrics he hadn't set to music, so some of them are really cool, some of them are random. He's obviously got a very poetic turn of phrase. He's a supertalented, genius kind of guy.

ST: I wonder if there's a writer of any kind whose work you're either getting into lately or have sort of come back to—someone who's feeding your work these days.

RG: I'm reading a lot of historical writers—you know, people writing actual history. So I'm not reading a bunch of fiction at the moment. But I've always been a huge fan of Neil Gaiman. His writing style's really beautiful. Weird—a little weird, a little cool. But yeah, I'm reading people like Edward Baptist. He wrote this book, *The Half Has Never Been Told: Slavery and the Making of American Capitalism*, and it's just like—the writing in it is just killer.

ST: Do you have a favorite historian or two besides him—a music historian, a historian of, you know, the American experience?

RG: Yeah, Andrew Ward is great—he's written several books. He wrote a book on the six Jubilee Singers and a book of slave narratives called *The Slaves' War*.

ST: Have you learned anything from literature about artistry, that's bigger than just inspiring song lyrics?

RG: Yeah, I mean that's where a bunch of my songs come from—history. Andrew Ward's book—songs came from that. The people who make history live inspire me to write songs about it. That's my whole thing.

ST: It's the larger spirit you get from reading history that makes you want to do it yourself.

RG: Yeah, definitely, yeah.

4

Chronicles: Volume One (Excerpt)

By Bob Dylan

Columbia was one of the first and foremost labels in the country and for me to even get my foot in the door was serious. For starters, folk music was considered junky, second rate, and only released on small labels. Big-time record companies were strictly for the elite, for music that was sanitized and pasteurized. Someone like myself would never be allowed in except under extraordinary circumstances. But John was an extraordinary man. He didn't make schoolboy records or record schoolboy artists. He had vision and foresight, had seen and heard me, felt my thoughts, and had faith in the things to come. He explained that he saw me as someone in a long line of a tradition, the tradition of blues, jazz, and folk and not as some newfangled wunderkind on the cutting edge. Not that there was any cutting edge. Things were pretty sleepy on the Americana music scene in the late '50s and early '60s. Popular radio was sort of at a standstill and filled with many empty pleasantries. It was years before the Beatles, the Who, or the Rolling Stones would breathe new life and excitement into it. What I was playing at the time were hard-lipped folk songs with fire and brimstone servings, and you didn't need to take polls to know that they didn't match up with anything on the radio, didn't lend themselves to commercialism, but John told me that these things weren't high on his list and he understood all the implications of what I did.

"I understand sincerity" is what he said. John spoke with a rough, coarse attitude, yet had an appreciative twinkle in his eye.

Recently he had brought Pete Seeger to the label. He didn't discover Pete, though. Pete had been around for years. He'd been in the popular folk group the Weavers, but had been blacklisted during the McCarthy era and had a hard time, but he never stopped working. Hammond was defiant when he spoke about Seeger, that Pete's ancestors had come over on the *Mayflower*, that his relatives had fought the Battle of Bunker Hill, for Christsake. "Can you imagine those sons of bitches blacklisting him? They should be tarred and feathered."

"I'm gonna give you all the facts," he said to me. "You're a talented young man. If you can focus and control that talent, you'll be fine. I'm gonna bring you in and I'm gonna record you. We'll see what happens."

And that was good enough for me. He put a contract in front of me, the standard one, and I signed it right then and there, didn't get absorbed into the details—didn't need a lawyer, adviser, or anybody looking over my shoulder. I would have gladly signed whatever form he put in front of me.

He looked at the calendar, picked out a date for me to start recording, pointed to it and circled it, told me what time to come in and to think about what I wanted to play. Then he called in Billy James, the head of publicity at the label, told Billy to write some promo stuff on me, personal stuff for a press release.

Billy dressed Ivy League like he could have come out of Yale—medium height, crisp black hair. He looked like he'd never been stoned a day in his life, never been in any kind of trouble. I strolled into his office, sat down opposite his desk, and he tried to get me to cough up some facts, like I was supposed to give them to him straight and square. He took out a notepad and pencil and asked me where I was from. I told him I was from Illinois and he wrote it down. He asked me if I ever did any other work, and I told him that I had a dozen jobs, drove a bakery truck once. He wrote that down and asked me if there was anything else. I said I'd worked construction and he asked me where.

"Detroit."

"You traveled around?"

"Yep."

He asked me about my family, where they were. I told him I had no idea, that they were long gone.

"What was your home life like?"

I told him I'd been kicked out.

"What did your father do?"

"'lectrician."

"And your mother, what about her?"

"Housewife."

"What kind of music do you play?"

"Folk music."

"What kind of music is folk music?"

I told him it was handed-down songs. I hated these kinds of questions. Felt I could ignore them. Billy seemed unsure of me and that was just fine. I didn't feel like answering his questions anyway, didn't feel the need to explain anything to anybody.

"How did you get here?"

"I rode a freight train."

"You mean a passenger train?"

"No, a freight train."

"You mean, like a boxcar?"

"Yeah, like a boxcar. Like a freight train."

"Okay, a freight train."

I gazed past Billy, past his chair through his window across the street to an office building where I could see a blazing secretary soaked up in the spirit of something—she was scribbling busy, occupied at a desk in a meditative manner. There was nothing funny about her. I wished I had a telescope. Billy asked me who I saw myself like in today's music scene. I told him nobody. That part of things was true, I really didn't see myself like anybody. The rest of it, though, was pure hokum—hophead talk.

I hadn't come in on a freight train at all. What I did was come across the country from the Midwest in a four-door sedan, '57 Impala—straight out of Chicago, clearing the hell out of there—racing all the way through the smoky towns, winding roads, green fields covered with snow, onward, eastbound through the state lines, Ohio, Indiana, Pennsylvania, a twenty-four-hour ride, dozing most of the day in the back seat, making small talk. My mind fixed on hidden interests . . . eventually riding over the George Washington Bridge.

The big car came to a full stop on the other side and let me out. I slammed the door shut behind me, waved goodbye, stepped out into the hard snow. The biting wind hit me in the face. At last I was here, in New York City, a city like a web too intricate to understand, and I wasn't going to try.

PART II

Rock 'n' Roll Saved My Life

Writers on Music

5

Banjo Interlude

An Idle Teen's Life Is Saved by Music

By Daniel Wallace

"'Dueling Banjos' saved my life." Without this simple song—and it's hard to think of one simpler, more traditional, easier to understand—who really knows how it all would have turned out. I might have ended up living beneath an old painter's tarp in a grassy lot behind a 7-Eleven, splitting the discarded sandwich I found with the stray cats who took up with me, working an interstate exit until the sugar took one of my legs. I think a life can be saved by a song or a book or by love, the same way it is when you're dragged from a river the moment before you breathe your last breath, or talked down off a ledge. Something or someone has saved my life probably half a dozen times in the last fifty years, but the first time I remember that happening was in 1973. I was fourteen years old.

I tell people I'm from Birmingham, Alabama, but that's not really true. I'm from Mountain Brook, a country-club suburb of Birmingham—"The Golden Ghetto," we called it. It's where most of the white, right people in Birmingham lived, and where I imagine they still do. I wasn't rich myself—my parents were—but as a kid you're in the back seat of the car your parents are driving, literally *and* metaphorically. What a great deal that was. I'd done nothing in the world but get born, and already I'd hit the jackpot: Everything my parents worked half of their lives working for was mine from the get-go. I was just glad I wasn't born to poor parents, because then I'd have been riding in the back seat of a used car, not a long, black Electra "Deuce and a Quarter." It was a sweet ride.

As swell as this all sounds, it's not the best environment for a kid to grow up in. I won't live long enough to feel safe admitting to everything I did back then, to my body and my brain, some of it before I was fourteen years old, because there are other people, and my job, to consider. But if my seventeen-year-old son had done half—no, a fourth—of what I did as I was wandering through the hazy landscape of my high school years, I'd worry for his life.

I just had so much *time* on my hands. Other than go to school, I didn't have anything to do. At all. My lone chore, and this one only in effect half the year, was to clean the pool. We had a housekeeper, Velma, who did everything my mother didn't or wouldn't do, which included cooking, cleaning, washing, ironing, and running errands. She even took us to the fair. When I'd leave for school in the morning, my bed was unmade, dishes and half-empty Mountain Dew bottles were scattered across the floor, the turntable turning, the needle still skipping on that skip in "Stormy Monday" it could never quite get past—They call it, they call it, they call it—and clothes, jeans, T-shirts, gym shorts, socks, underwear—were everywhere: on the top of the dresser, hanging off a bookshelf, in a mound on my closet floor. But when I returned at four, it was model-home clean, as if in Velma we had our own nose-twitching Samantha. I'd call her late at night, brattishly demanding to know where my Grateful Dead T-shirt was, the one with the goof smashing an ice-cream cone into his forehead. If she said "in the hamper" my patience became exhausted, because at its best my patience couldn't make it up a flight of stairs. "Dammit, Velma, that was the T-shirt I wanted to wear to school tomorrow!" Or worse. I was awful. How she, how anybody put up with me is bewildering: looking back now, of all the people I knew, I like myself least of all.

Every so often, someone will ask me, as many of us get asked, "Where were you when Elvis died, the Challenger blew up, the World Trade Center fell?" No one ever asks me where I was when I first heard "Dueling Banjos." But I can tell you: I was in the passenger seat of my mother's black-and-white 1972 Monte Carlo, on my way to Homewood to hang out in a record store/head shop called the Angry Revolt, where I would later buy my first, and last, waterbed. I was wearing the same thing I wore every day: overalls, a white T-shirt, red low-top Converse. I was growing my first anemic moustache, and had long brown tangled hair, parted in the middle.[1] That was when I heard it, one hot afternoon driving down Oxmoor Road, one song probably sandwiched between "Crocodile Rock" and "Tie a Yellow Ribbon Round the Old Oak Tree." I don't have to hum it for you; for better or worse, the introductory notes are as familiar to us as the opening to Beethoven's Fifth. That call-and response, what amounts to a conversation between a banjo and a guitar, tentative at first, checking each other out, finding common ground, gathering speed, and then exploding, the way all really good songs do. Still, it was bluegrass, and it was weird to hear bluegrass on a pop-radio station. Weird to hear it anywhere: as far as I can remember, I never had. A couple of minutes later, it was over. Nothing happened. My life changed without me even knowing it.

It's easy to imagine how happy my parents must have been when, a few weeks later, I asked them to buy me a banjo. Easy to imagine because, up to this point in my life, I had never been interested enough in anything to ask for it. Easier to imagine now that I have my own son, and I'm waiting for him to ask me for anything.

They bought me a cheap one, the strings taut about an inch above the fretboard. Still, I could not stop playing it. I played every single day. I took lessons from a banjo legend, Herb Trotman, who encouraged me, and after about six months or so my mother bought me a real banjo, a Stelling, the swankiest of all swanky banjos, and from there I could not be stopped. After a couple of years I talked with Herb about becoming a professional banjo player one day, and he thought that might could happen, if I kept it up. I played in bars with friends, at bluegrass festivals like Horse Pens 40 in Steele, Alabama. I learned how to play mandolin, guitar, a little fiddle. I was crazy with music. I played before, after, even during school in the parking lot at lunch.

Finally, one Christmas, I was seventeen by then, I asked for an upright bass, and, of course, I got it. It was as big as a tree. I hauled it upstairs to my room that Christmas morning, not an easy task, and stated playing, plucking notes so low I could barely hear them. It took me about an hour to realize I'd

---

1. When I was arrested in an IHOP parking lot later that year, for something I'd rather not go into, my sad and tired father picked me up at the police station and said, "You look the part." As much as I resented him for saying that, and for everything else he said or did, he was right. I could've played the part of the Troubled Teen on an after-school TV special with no help from wardrobe at all.

never wanted to play the upright bass. It was almost impossible for me to play at all. The strings, as big and round and long as a guy wire, hurt the fingers on both hands, and the sounds I made on it, even when I hit them just right, didn't interest me, at all. For the first time in my musical life, I was bored, uninterested, and in a way that's hard to understand or explain, I soon began to feel the same about guitar, violin, mandolin, and, inevitably, the banjo. It was more than boredom, though, and I don't even think it had that much to do with the bass: I'd fallen out of love with music. Sad to think now how all of these lovely handmade instruments found a new dark home beneath my bed. It was not so much that I moved on to something else, because I just went back to my old decadent ways; I merely left them behind. *It's not you, it's me.*

This is the thing, though. Without "Dueling Banjos," I don't think I'd ever have become a writer. That sounds like a stretch, I know. But since I don't believe in fate, or that people are born to be one thing instead of another—whether that's being a writer or an athlete or a farmer—I might as well believe in a song. I think we're at the mercy of, and are the product of, the accidents we live through; in my case, the accident was being in the car with my mother listening to a particular radio station on a particular day on the way to Angry Revolt. I don't know how or why that song did what it did, but it led me toward a new world, and gave me a pinhole view of everything we think of as art. That world was a long, long way from where I was then, but I could see it from there. Maybe it didn't save my life, but it gave me one, which may be the same thing.

6

Tonight We Improvise

From Sag Harbor *(Excerpt)*

By Colson Whitehead

Everybody hated WLNG. It was Sag Harbor's lone radio station, beaming out sentiment at 92.1 megahertz, reverberating through our skins and inner transistors even when the stereo was off. They called themselves a Classic Oldies station, spinning the requisite Motown and Beatles and barefoot singer-songwriters to justify themselves to advertisers, but their specialty was the oddball tune, the one-hit wonders and fluke achievers, the "Popcorn"s, the "Monster Mash"es, the sublimely dreadful "Itsy Bitsy Teenie Weenie Yellow Polka Dot Bikini"s.

Everybody'd heard those goofy songs a million times before, and it was a cold cold heart that didn't hum along for at least a second. What sent people trampling to the exits was a different kind of one-hit wonder, a species of song so cloying and unashamed that the soul shivered in recognition. They came to WLNG to die, these misfit ditties: feverish declarations of affection, tearjerkers about magical last-chance afternoons, odes to the everlasting that were thinly veiled bids for restraining orders. Rented-by-the-hour string sections sawed away at our resistance, lonesome sax solos paraphrased heartbreak. I can't tell you the names of the songs because I don't know, can't say who got the songwriting credit and who cashed the royalties. All I could do was succumb to the LNG Effect when these songs came on.

It proceeded thusly: out of the speakers emerged a song you'd heard only once before in your life, one that left such a faint record in your brain that it was a memory of a memory. Paralyzed by confusion, you wondered, *Where have I heard this before?* The answer was, Nowhere important. Far from scoring some significant life passage, it was most likely the soundtrack of an anti-event—searching for the matching sock, wiping tartar sauce from your lip—but the deep sense of familiarity and loss was unshakable. That was the LNG Effect—a feeling of nostalgia for something that never existed. It creeped people out. And maybe you'd never even heard the song before, only thought you had and completely invented the connection, so nimble the song's persuasion. There was a quality to the voices of the singers, these faceless warblers and sweater-vested harmonizers, that made their corny scenarios and schmaltzy pleas hypnotizing, transporting. For a few verses, that was you trotting along by the departing train car, coming around to tell the truth after all this time, that was you in the foxhole begging your girl back home to stay true, that was you standing there without defenses for once, in the pouring rain, saying what had to be said. You can't say *longing* without the *l*, *n*, and *g*.

At some weak moment these songs had hit the pop charts, mingling with the more likely pop creations for one brief, glorious instant. Out of place at the party, digging their elbows in the wall and nervously chugging punch before they were found out. They fell out of the Top 40 and tumbled down the rankings, plummeting away from most people's consciousness . . . out of our universe and into another, welcomed into the WLNG firmament the second they hit 41, twinkling in their bygone constellation. I imagine that the LNG Effect was exactly the opposite for the singers. For them, hearing their songs come on wasn't the reinforcement of an illusion but the affirmation of reality—if someone was playing their record after all this time, then they actually existed and it wasn't just a dream, their moment onstage. They heard their words again, restored after being stripped by Muzak-makers and elevator composers, and were made whole.

Everybody hated WLNG because WLNG fucked you up. They turned the station in a New York minute. My friends had no time for it, fiddling for rogue, clear-day broadcasts from KISS FM in the city. My brother was entering a big reggae phase. My mother liked classical music, zooming past 92.1 on the way to all that public radio wine and cheese at the bottom of the dial. And while my father had a well-known weakness for Easy Listening, he loathed the voice of LNG's afternoon guy, Rusty Potz—Rusty Potz!—whom he referred to as "that man" before shutting off the little Panasonic boom box in the corner of the dining area.

So of course WLNG was (one of) my secret shame(s), indulged when I had the house to myself. The songs were too mawkish to be anything other than solo pleasures, savored in private while tickling invisible ivories or fondling a phantom microphone. The furtive way I scoped out the premises, slowly turning up the volume on the radio, wary of every increment, setting it a little higher and higher as I grew bolder, certainly echoed universal porn protocols. Sometimes I forgot to clean up after myself and hours later I'd hear "Who's been listening to WLNG?" from the living room, whereupon I'd walk out and declare "I hate that station!" like a proper citizen. In fact, my father asked the question the same way he asked "Who's been watching Channel J?" in the city, when the dial on the cable box pointed to the local red-light district. Channel J, home of Ugly George and *Midnight Blue*, the porny public-access shows that had been many a Manhattan boy's and girl's introduction to naked moving parts, a stretch of shabby Times Square in the TV lineup. Sometimes I was the culprit, sometimes not. It says a lot about the world that being walked in on with your hands down your pants while Al Goldstein played some grainy action clip of Seka was preferable to getting caught singing along to "Who Put the Bomp (In the Bomp Bomp Bomp)."

I bring all this up because one late afternoon toward the end of the season, I was double-dosing on masturbatory pastimes—listening to WLNG and touching myself. Not touching myself like that, but running my tongue over the mounds and crevices of my teeth and gums. I'd gotten my braces off a few days earlier and was in complete ecstasy over the feel of my new mouth. Look on my Works, y'all, and Despair! Which is not to say that in all probability I hadn't partaken of the more conventional form of self-gratification in the last twenty-four hours, I just wasn't doing it right then. I held masturbation in high esteem, for without it we'd never have developed the opposable thumb, and from the opposable thumb flows all of civilization, the shaping of rudimentary tools, creation of fire for warmth and food preparation, cave paintings, cuneiform, and eventually the Betamax. Think about that next time.

I probed, I polished, I tickled the smooth and lovely surfaces of my naked choppers. They'd never been like that: level, even, sans gusty gaps. Half the reason the braces went on in the first place was to correct my magnificent overbite, which I'd helped buck out when I was a kid. I sucked my thumb well into grade school, popping that little fucker in my mouth at every available moment of alone time. Sucking on the tit that never gave milk. I see I'm going way back with you today, down memory lane where the asphalt stops and it's just dirt leading off, to the origin of this love of solitary consolations. Holy cow, it winds its way back to the crib, this self-pleasuring bent, in the all-too-frequent onanism, the zoning out to sad-sack narcissistic ballads, sucking my thumb—the various strategies of getting a little comfort in this cold mean world. If you had these things, you didn't need anyone else.

I finally started leaving my thumb alone when chicken pox ripped through my second-grade class and I got little white blisters all over the inside of my mouth from sticking my tainted digit in there. I had the pox on the outside like everyone else, but inside, too, where no one could see. I looked in the mirror, and thought, *Cursed!* Or whatever word second-graders use to nail that feeling of being singled out for a ghastly and specific doom. *Snaked! Goblin'd!* Some say that it's an old wives' tale that sucking your thumb will mess up your teeth, but give me a sandwich board and I'll shill for this theory up and down Broadway. Surely something that felt so reassuring needed to be punished, by deformity, blindness, by a plague of white blisters visited upon the wicked territory of my mouth.

The braces were supposed to come off freshman year, but I never went to my appointments so the treatment stretched on for an extra year and a half. That spring I finally got my act together and started fulfilling my half of the bargain, snapping the rubber bands around the spikes and hooks, showing up at the right time to Dr. Henderson's office. He was an okay guy. I liked the way he said, "You might feel a slight pressure," as if this were a rarity and not a constant state of being.

"How's Sag?" he asked when I clambered into his chair that last time. The summer before, he'd rented a condo in Baron's Cove behind town, and when I ran into him on the beach or whatever, this specter rose before me, him looming in his smock and mask, spiny and serrated implements glinting in the summer sunlight. On those occasions I hummed hello to him, keeping my lips tight.

"The usual," I said.

He got to work with his mallet and monkey wrench and unshackled my teeth. A gruesome funk drifted away from the accumulated microscopic and not-so-microscopic food bits that had been rotting under the metal for years. He cleaned my teeth and my tongue danced over them.

He handed me a mirror. "You're going to be kissing a lot of girls now."

I didn't mind being patronized by Helpful Hints form the back of the *Orthodontists' Handbook*. It made sense to compliment the recently straightened on their new look, to help them appreciate the end result of all their suffering. What ticked me off was the implication that braces were what held me back from age-appropriate shenanigans, the fabled Frenching, bra-fumbling, and blue balls. Obviously, it would have been hard for me to kiss fewer girls, basic mathematical properties of the number zero being what they are. In order to improve my portfolio, I needed to dump the braces. But what of the essential me beneath everything? In the logic of my affection, those who would love or kinda like me could see beyond the Iron Maiden embracing my teeth, my incompetent presentation and chronic galoot-ness. None of that mattered. There was something good under there. I had to believe hat. If you couldn't see it, you weren't worth being with, right? Not worth kissing. So what people saw of me was a test.

Back at the apartment, I grinned and sneered at myself, practicing with my mouth. I looked at my new smile and wondered what it meant.

I was in the city for four days. On the way in from the island, a perfect orange dome of smog covered Manhattan. The dome kept in the August heat and hoarded the stenches of the city, the decaying garbage and car exhaust, the evaporating essences of those trapped inside. I stepped off the Jitney at Eighty-Sixth Street and waded into the bog. It hadn't rained in a while, and miserable puddles fermented along the sidewalks, dark objects bobbing in them and multicolored oil trails hovering on their surfaces. It was late enough in the summer that people were too beaten down by the heat for rage and violence. They gave in, slumping up the sidewalks, martyrs to the choices they'd made.

Reggie had been back a few times to buy records or clothes, but this was my first trip back to the city. My room was a snapshot of my brain circa two and a half months ago, a picture of the mess left behind by the evacuation. Yellowing *Village Voices* lay open to the concert pages, listing the names of bands I hadn't seen and venues I'd never been to. All spring I memorized their addresses and situated them in the amorphous downtown that existed in my head. One day I'd make it down there after dark, below Fourteenth

Street. The hip murk. The records I marathon-taped the night before I left were strewn about, half out of their sleeves, the Birthday Party's *Mutiny*, the first two Stooges records. Stuff I bought because I'd heard it on the mix tape my older sister played when she came back for spring break. Who's that? What's this? Elena was spending the summer away from us, working at a movie theater in her college town. My father made a fuss about that, but what was he going to do, go up there and drag her down?

No one was around in the city, my few friends from school. I wanted to get back to Sag as quickly as possible. I had two more weeks of summer left. I wasn't done with it yet.

When I got back out, the stagehands had moved everything around. Most people, they leave a place for a few days and are reassured on their return that despite their worry, they hadn't missed anything. The legendary party, the life-changing late-night hangout. Not in my case. Not ever. The world really ramped up its carousing when I wasn't around and I had to listen to all the details when I got back. This was especially true toward the end of summer, when things accelerated as they got drawn into that September gravity. Just four days, and Clive was gone. I didn't care for sports, watching or participating, but Clive's fabled basketball camp impressed me as a special calling—he had a higher purpose, going off to fulfill his dunking destiny. In the tradition of Sag friendships, I wouldn't see him until next year. Bobby was in the city, for a few days or for good, it wasn't clear. His grandfather had gotten sick again, so they were all back in Westchester dealing with that. Which left us without a car, as Randy was working double shifts at the Long Wharf to top off his tuition war chest. It might have been December, the desolation we saw when we walked around.

We had one late arrival to replace those we'd lost, Melanie. She used to come out when she was a little girl, according to NP. NP had inherited the nosy-historian gene from his father, who maintained an extensive mental database on everyone in the developments. How long they'd been coming out, which parcels their family had bought and traded over the decades, where their kids and grandkids were going to school, and how much they were or were not raking in from their big jobs. Melanie's family was first generation, NP told me one day as we were wiping down the vats in Jonni Waffle, but they'd sold their house on Cuffee Drive ten years ago. "My dad said her daddy made some bad business decisions." Getting rid of your Sag house, that was unforgivable. Like selling your kids off to the circus for crack money. Mr. Downey was an outsider, you see, and did not understand our ways. How else to explain losing his family's most precious possession?

Now the Downeys were divorced and Mom was trying to reconnect with her heritage. The story was an easy sell in the developments—the wayward daughter back in the bosom and the impostor back where he came from, selling used cars in a cheap suit somewhere. Melanie and her mother rented a house in the Hills, back out for the first time in years. Everyone called her mother "Peaches," a childhood nickname now reclaimed. Peaches put on a good show, insinuating herself into the little klatch on the beach in front of our house. She climbed up on the Franklins' motorboat and water-skied, the only middle-aged lady brave enough to do so when Teddy Jr. was at the helm. The ladies rose from their beach chairs and watched from the shore as the boat hoisted her from the water. Peaches waved at them like a teenage beauty queen showing off during the talent portion, wobbling only a little on the turn. She even got a letter printed in the *Sag Harbor Express* bitching about the weekend traffic, a gesture of righteous outrage that won over anyone still reluctant to welcome her back into the fold.

Her daughter was similarly adept. She hadn't yet claimed her birthright as a proper Black American Princess, the sartorial markers and debilitating stares, so it wasn't until the following summer that Erica and Devon welcomed her into their gang, but Nick quickly scooped her up. So to speak. She became a familiar sight at Jonni Waffle, poking her head in to coax Nick out for a break on one of the Long Wharf benches and lingering outside at end of shift so that they could walk back in the dark. Her little wheezing laughter signaled her approach, around development corners and the stoops of houses, and then she came into view. She walked in a style halfway between an amble and a sashay—she was edging toward the sashay, getting it down, learning how to put her big hips into it. Next year, whoo-boy.

I first saw her on NP's back patio, early August. She was straddling their old green-and-white lounger and sipping Country Time lemonade. The unmixed bits of the flavor packet swirled around each time she tipped the glass to her plush lips, her long, curly hair corkscrewing into the air. Melanie was soft and round in a sweet, baby-fat way, with this remarkable ability where she converted everything she wore in her legs into hot pants, the press of her thighs turning prim white tennis shorts into Daisy Dukes, the zipper tab of her acid-washed jeans standing at attention like a needle on a pressure gauge.

I didn't remember Melanie from when were little, but she pulled off a convincing display of insider knowledge like a well-briefed spy. She talked about the "Dancing Popcorn Box and Hot Dog" ads that used to run between features at the old Drive-In, hypnotizing you into a trip to the concession stand, and name-checked Frederico's and the Candy Kitchen with authority, as if she'd enjoyed an unbroken line of hallowed summers. With Devon and Erica making only strategic appearances in our scene After the Breakup, she was usually the only girl around and wasn't bothered by it. The Nick thing helped. I guess she didn't mind that he was technically a townie, or maybe the fact that her own credentials were out of order brought them closer. She feigned interest in his hobbies like a pro, like she'd been married a couple of times and knew how to tolerate the feeble enthusiasms of men. She watched patiently while he adjusted the graphic equalizer on his monstrous radio, furrowing her brown with concentration during his lectures on how this particular setting really enriched the beatboxing in "The Show," but the B side of the single, "La-Di-Da-Di," benefited from a little more treble, to foreground Slick Rick's vocal dexterity.

Although, right, there was that one afternoon of foreshadowing. The gang was eating slices at Conca D'Oro, the orange drops of grease turning the paper plates opaque. "That's not a sample," Nick said, "they did it live in the studio." You didn't want to get Nick started on Melle Mel's studio acumen. I guess Melanie sensed I was looking at her and she turned to me and surgically flicked her eyes to the ceiling. Then she returned, rapt, to his dissertation on "Funky Beat," the old-school master text. But I saw her.

That's where things stood that day I was alone in the house listening to the radio. It was the weekend, so Reggie was pulling a double at BK, and it was the third cloudy day in a row so the beach was empty except for the one-weekenders, who had to make the best of it. My parents were off at some function in Nineveh. I was killing flies with rubber bands. I snuck up as close as their hundred-eyed heads allowed, then drew back the rubber and let 'em rip. I'd gotten pretty good at the hunt over the summer, leaving tiny red smears on the windows and walls. My charnel house o' horrors. The light was fading, but I spotted one unlucky dude lingering by the handle of the glass door and I stalked over, my tongue tickling my upper right bicuspid . . . when I suddenly got really depressed. A sadness pumping through my branching capillaries, suffusing my limbs, splashing into the furthest hideaways in my pinkie toes and lumps of earlobe. It was such a profound incident that I imagine the intensity of it left chemical markers in my hair that a high-tech lab could identify, like I'd been smoking some serious reefer, that back-row uptown-theater shit. The fly flew away. I put my hand on a chair to steady myself.

I became aware of the music and understood. I got dinged by LNG, but good. The lyrics carouseled in my head:

> Have I a hope or half a chance
> To even ask if I could dance with you, you-oo?
> Would you greet me or politely turn away
> Would there suddenly be sunshine on a cold and rainy day
> Oh, Babe, what would you say?

Had I heard this song before? Surely I must have in another life. Another house. The singer croaked out his proposal. His was no velvet instrument, but he made up for it in intensity. The desperation that is cousin to passion. I was there with him at the English seaside resort at the end of summer. The coastal retreat past its heyday. It's the last night at the Dime-a-Dance before they demolish it, the last big concert of the season before they shutter the boardwalk. There he is in his one good suit, seersucker, with shiny elbows and stains from twenty wakes, the widower who has been standing along the wall all night, watching her, looking away when she turned her head toward him. This angel in white with her dark eyes and glowing skin. He saw here at the first dance at the start of the summer—he'd gone on a lark, usually he stayed away from such things—and returned every Saturday night to get a glimpse. Working up his nerve. To risk love one more time. Tonight is his last chance and he gathers himself, rubbing the rim of his old derby with his thumbs and digging his winnowed soles into the dance floor.

Had I heard this song before? I didn't know. Was that a clarinet, that farting sound? I listened to the words and tried to go back. When was it? The phantom when. No, it was a saxophone. The sax player waltzed through his solo, he was up on a tenement roof at midnight, playing for all the lonely ones, who drifted from their beds and moved to their windowsills to hear this more clearly. They couldn't see him. It was the moon itself playing those luscious notes. In the morning they weren't sure if they'd dreamed it. They tried to remember the melody all day and couldn't for the life of them. By lunch, they were thoroughly ashamed for letting him down.

The song ended and the volume spiked up to showcase a commercial for Allen M. Schneider Real Estate. I heard my parents' car in the driveway and dove for the radio, spinning the dial to my mother's Nothing But the Classics. They came up the stairs, and when they got inside my father resumed. It was an argument from inside the car that they'd paused in between closed spaces. Who knew what started it. By then it was deep into the ancient grudges and unforgivable failures. The usual.

I hadn't made any plans. But I did what I normally did not do. I left the house. It was funny—as soon as the door closed, I couldn't hear it. Maybe the wind carried it in another direction. It got windy at sunset that time of year. I was always tormented by the knowledge that the entire developments must have been listening to us, but the screen door wheezed shut and those sounds were gone.

Walking out of the driveway, I tried to get the song out of my head. It didn't work. What if someone came along and heard me humming it? Picking up a ditty from WLNG was hard to explain, like claiming you got VD off a toilet seat in a bus station. You walked around with it to your shame. There were songs that were guilty pleasures, like "Fernando." That ABBA shit. Everybody had 'em. Then there were songs that betrayed fundamental ideas you had about yourself. *Have I a hope or half a chance.* There could be no accommodation for such exposure. My friends wouldn't understand. Reggie would punch me in my face. Certainly my sister wouldn't approve, but I saw her so rarely that I no longer worried about what sarcastic remark she'd throw my way.

I haven't talked about Elena much because she wasn't there. I haven't talked about her because she went off to college and never came back. I've mentioned the great migration, when you stop coming out to Sag except for the occasional visit. You got a real summer job in the city, or something on campus, or an internship in the office of a family friend. Common rite of passage. *Enough of this bourgie shit.* You left the place that made you to take your chances in the wide world. But Elena did more than outgrow Sag Harbor. She went off and we saw her on Thanksgiving and Christmas, and sometimes she came back down to New York if she had a longer vacation, but it was never the same. She hasn't been in here much because she'd already moved on.

Elena was three years older than me. Growing up, she was our babysitter, buddy, and bully, according to her needs. Tugging us out of traffic, turning the oven on to 350 degrees so that me and Reggie could slide our Swanson's in there side by side, keeping Mondays at 8 P.M. in a stranglehold for her beloved *Little House on the Prairie.* Those hard-won frontier lessons. When we destroyed her nerves, she threatened to tell our father, which shut us down like that.

She slimmed down and hipped up when she hit high school, unveiling a cool downtown persona that made the most blasé private-school deb seem like a Kentucky rube. She came home after everyone was in bed and tossed glossy invites from the Peppermint Lounge and Danceteria onto the table in the foyer, where they accumulated like exotic stickers on a steam trunk. At night, strange sounds emanated from her room, bruised melodies wrung from Mission of Burma 45s and ink-black flexis out of British music magazines. There were Friday evenings where she'd psych herself up by playing *Sandinista!* cut for cut, all six sides, and then tromp out of the house in Day-Glo boots to wrestle down the night. Leaving me and Reggie alone in the house with a stack of splatter flicks from Crazy Eddie's, fascinated by ideas of our future, high-school selves. Suckers!

The last few summers, she'd been in charge when our parents were in the city. Now that it was my job, I knew what her expression had meant when our parents' friends asked when our folks were coming out. She was a camp counselor at Boy's Harbor, bossing those kids around all day, which made things easier for us as she was all out of fascist directives by the time she got home. I listened to her sneak out of the house after me and Reggie went to bed. I heard the car door slam as she went off on her secret missions and I put myself in charge of us in the empty house until morning. Her final summer, she was too hip and strange and "white-acting" for the Sag Harbor boys and girls she'd grown up with, and went out to find others like her, her fellow unlikelies. She never brought them around, but she must have found her tribe.

I only saw her once that summer. The week before I got my braces off. Bobby was still out, and we were driving down Main Street, South Hampton, rushing to catch the 7:20 show of *Beyond Thunderdome.* We'd seen it before, but we had nothing else to do. We were about to turn into the parking lot behind the theater when Bobby said, "Isn't that your sister?"

She was across the street, smoking a cigarette in front of one of the fancy restaurants reserved for grown-ups. If our parents took us out to dinner, it was to the Lobster Inn or the latest one-season home-style fried-chicken joint or takeout place. The grown-ups kept the shiny, written-up restaurants for their nights away from the kids. Or away from the wives. She was talking to a German-looking guy with long blond hair and bright white teeth that gleamed from all the way across the street. He had a Eurotrash demeanor I will forever associate with the high-tech terrorists of *Die Hard*, and yeah, I know the movie didn't come out until three long summers later, but what do you want, the movie made a big impression on me, and it is hard to accept the notion of a pre-*Die Hard* world. The cruel efficiency of those guys. She patted his arm and smiled at some little witticism of his, tracing down to his elbow. They were fucking.

They were still there after we found a parking space. Which was good, because I didn't want to have to go inside the restaurant and tell the garçon or whatever that I wanted to look for someone. Her companion spotted me approaching and watched me over her shoulder. His face had that expression I've seen many times, when I'm walking down the street and there's a white person sitting alone in a car. The look on his face was the one they always get before they lock the car doors. Click, click, click up the street as I pass. We were in South Hampton.

"Elena?"

She gave me her hug—I'd forgotten how good it felt—and introduced me to Derek. He lost his squint and shook my hand with a big big smile.

"What are you doing here? When did you get out?"

"I just popped in for the weekend," she said. "I'm visiting Derek."

Bobby checked out her friend, raising a skeptical eyebrow.

I said, "Oh, I didn't know."

"It was a last-minute thing."

"When are you coming over? 'Cause I work—" I began to say. Because I didn't want to miss her.

"I'm probably not going to have time to make it over there," she said. "Probably. It's just a quick visit."

"Oh."

The traffic rushed in the street. Bobby told me he was going to buy tickets and that I should meet him over there. Elena nodded her head toward Derek and he slunk into the restaurant. She had a lot of training with delivering nonverbal directives, working on me and Reggie all those years.

Elena took a drag and exhaled through her nose. "Do me a favor and don't tell Mom and Dad you saw me, will you?" she said. "They wouldn't understand."

"You weren't even going to see us."

"Don't start pouting. Of course I want to see you and Reggie." She squeezed my shoulder. "I'm going to try and come out for longer before I have to go back to school. This was a spur-of-the-moment thing." She stamped out her cigarette and said, "You know how it can be in that house."

"What do you mean?"

"You know what I'm talking about."

She looked through the window of the restaurant after Derek. "Just do me a favor, Benji, and get out when you can," she said. "Work hard and get into a good school. That way you're out of the house and that's it."

"I don't understand."

"Yes, you do."

The next time I saw here was Thanksgiving. She stayed one night and then went to a party in Connecticut some friend of hers from school was having. She was meeting all sorts of new people, she said.

No, I didn't have to worry about running into Elena with that song in my brain. Those cornball words on my lips. I was out in the middle of the street, a few houses up. Far enough away that I didn't have to pretend I didn't live where I lived. It could go on for five minutes or five hours. This time I was going to stay away.

"Ben." Melanie stood at the corner of Meredith. She was on the grass by the curb, her fingers splayed out on her hips. She wore a white button-down shirt tight enough that it made her look like she'd jumped a cup size. She'd twisted her hair into two long braids that danced on her shoulders when she moved her head. I didn't see Nick.

She prodded something on the ground with her foot. She said, "That's gross." It was a yellow centipede of plastic, clumped with dirt.

"Yeah, you shouldn't litter," I said.

"It's a jimmy hat."

"Right." I hadn't seen one outside the packaging before. Sometimes guys I knew opened their wallets to show off their expectations, and amateurs like me gawked at the outlines of the ring. Now I realized I had seen them before, out in the woods behind the park or deflated on a sidewalk among the other fucked-up New York confetti.

She scraped it with her sandal up the grass and into the woods.

"Nick's at work?" I said.

"I don't know where Nick is. I'm not his keeper."

"Okay."

"What are you doing?"

"Nothing."

"Right," she said. We took a few steps down Terry.

"I can't believe it's almost September," I said.

"Yeah."

I asked her when she was going back. She told me, next week. It was that time of year. At night we started closing the windows. The breezes woke you in the middle of night or startled you at dusk with their sudden lacerations. You remembered packing at the beginning of the summer and trying to figure out how many long-sleeved shirts and sweaters to bring, and realized you chose the wrong number like you did every year. It was almost over. The city rose higher and higher on the horizon.

"You must be glad to be coming out here again," I said. I had a roll of non sequiturs in my pockets and I was just tossing them out across the water trying to get a good skip going.

"It's nice out here," she said, "but it's not all that. Too quiet, you know?" I knew she lived in Queens, and in my provincial head the Outer Boroughs were a hotbed of licentiousness. Sag Harbor people who lived in Queens and Brooklyn were simply cooler. No ifs, ands, or buts. They didn't cage themselves in private school. Their parties ripped the weekend asunder. The standard projections of the repressed. But hearing confirmation from Melanie, who was like a year younger than me, just a freshman, made me feel like more of a stiff than usual.

She kinda squinted at me as we rounded the corner and I remembered the phone call. See, something out of the ordinary had happened the day before. We were at NP's house, me and Marcus and Nick. NP's mother was at a luncheon in the city, so we availed ourselves of his house for a change. We were out on the patio, talking shit, when NP went to answer the phone. He poked his head out of the back door. He looked puzzled. He said, "It's Melanie."

Nick took his radio off his lap. NP said, "She wants to talk to Benji."

Now we were all confused. Nick sat back down, not looking at me. NP shrugged.

The phone was shaped like a banana, a sad, bright-yellow relic of early-'70s design whimsy. The coils of the handset cord were so gnarled and incestuous that I had to pull for every inch. "Hello?"

"It's Melanie."

"Hi." The handset tried to spring away from me.

"What are you doing?"

"Hanging around with NP and Reggie. What about you?" I don't know why I didn't mention Nick.

"Just watching TV."

I looked out the window into the backyard, but I could only see the old tire swing. I fell off it when I was little and scraped up my face and still hated it for chumping me out. "Not much happening here." I cleared my throat.

"It's a boring day." I heard a voice in the background. Peaches. "I gotta go," she said. "We're going to Caldor for slippers."

"Okay."

I went back outside. NP said, "Oh, Heavenly Dog."

"She just wanted to see what was up," I said.

Nick said, "She's all . . ." swatting his hand at an invisible gnat. He wrinkled his face into a well-known expression of male aggravation at the opposite sex, so instantly recognizable that it could have been an international sign for such a thing, hanging in airports and train stations. He didn't seem pissed with me and, in my way, I forgot about the phone call a minute later. She wanted to say hi. It wasn't that weird.

Except for the reliable haunted houses Azurest was filled up. Every weekend the new arrivals buzzed their hedges into shape, turned the faucets until the rust ran out, exchanged their old mildewed doormat for the latest offering from the Hardware Store in Town. Cars were bumper to bumper in the driveways and clotted the curbs, the vehicles of spectators assembling for the Main Event. The big fireworks show before they had to head back to the city. I realized I was humming that song again and stopped. How long had I been doing that? Had she heard? I said, "You called me Ben before."

"I thought that's what you wanted people to call you?"

"That's right."

"Benji is cute, but I know what you mean. I used to always go, 'Ben-ji! Ben-ji!' whenever you came down the beach with Reggie."

Huh. "When were you last out?" I asked. "I know you used to come here all the time, but I must have been really little because I can't remember."

She shook her head and smirked. "Just until I was five. But I remember it all. You used to stay at that red house on Hempstead. We all ran around playing red light, green light in the backyard. And there was that old pump that used to be home base."

"You remember that?" I saw it, me and the rest of the gang zigzagging across the grass, saw all their faces but did not see hers.

"You remember that time I kissed you?" she asked.

"What?"

"I was like five or something and I told you we should get married."

"Really?"

"Yeah."

"What did I do?"

"You ran away screaming."

"Really?"

"My mom had to apologize to your mom because I kept following you around trying to kiss you all the time."

"That's weird." Was she fucking with me? That's all I could think. There was that phone call yesterday, and then her telling me this. This was a plot, a conspiracy of city-style, private-school cruelty. No other explanation.

"I thought you were the cutest boy out here," she said. She stopped. "What happened to you?"

"What happened?" I cocked my head back because I felt that was the appropriate response to such a statement. Insulted, etc. What a normal person would do.

"No, I don't mean it like that," she said, chuckling. Her fingers brushing down my arm. "I mean, you just always seemed so happy all the time. You had that *Planet of the Apes* pajama top you liked to wear as a shirt even though it was the daytime, and you were always laughing with Reggie at everything."

"Now I'm all angry and mad?"

"I didn't say that." She bumped me with her hip.

Huh.

We were outside Marv's house. It was a rancher with a long flat roof, painted a robin's-egg color that was what radiation would look like if you could see radiation. Light came from the basement window, through the dirt splashed on by the rain. I thought about Rusty Potz, the WLNG afternoon guy. He coated his voice with so much reverb it sounded like he worked underground, only getting fresh air during one of their remote feeds from the Sag Harbor Mason's Annual Fish Fry. ("Tickets are still available at the Municipal Building on Main Street.") From his hepcat rock-'n'-roll patois, I pictured him with a white beret and satin baseball jacket, standing in front of a few signed photographs of him shaking hands with Bill Haley and His

Comets, the Yardbirds, and sundry crooners dressed in matching cardigans. He worked alone in his dungeon, stirring the cauldron, concocting longing for his listeners.

WLNG didn't play hip-hop, of course, outside the occasional spin of "Rappin' Rodney." That's where Marv and his underground operation came in, down in his basement. Marv was an inbetweener, a few years older. He was "street-smart," wielding the latest styles with the unself-consciousness that came from actually being that elusive thing: unimpeachably down. Once he hit high school he stopped coming out, to commit himself to the B-boy lifestyle. He was the first person I met with two turntables. One turntable, you liked music. Two turntables, and you were an artist. In the summer of '81, he cut up "Good Times" like a true acolyte of Grandmaster Flash, slashing the fader back and forth in a three-card monte panic, rubbing out a few tentative scratches, zip zip. The famous bass line strutted like a hustler around the room in a beige jeans suit, with an Apple Jack on his head: What can I get up to now? He didn't have that many records in his milk crate, but they all had the name of the song blacked out with Magic Marker. "That's so no one bites me," he explained. We crowded around, watching his magic. After a while he'd say, "I'll see you later—I gotta practice," and he was alone again in the cement room, working solo in his bunker like the WLNG guy. You deliver the news and you do it alone.

Marv's mother still came out. She'd probably covered his DJ tables with second-home basement crap, old sewing machines and spiderwebbed boogie boards. The stuff you keep around because you convince yourself that one day you might use it again. We all know how that ends. Melanie remembered Marv from the old days and I told her that he didn't come out anymore because he thought Sag was for kids. She told me about her cousin, who was a big DJ at some clubs in the Bronx, and then said she remembered when Marv's mother threw a birthday for him and invited all the kids. One of the big kids started chasing Marcus around the picnic table trying to noogie him, and Marcus slipped and crashed into it, sending the birthday cake flying. "It went all over the place."

I remembered that day. Everybody wearing some form of multicolored striped article of clothing, that was the rule. Reggie attempted to salvage a clean chunk of cake from the ground. It was something he might do, gather what he could from the mess. Make sure he got his. But I didn't remember Melanie. I tried to put the scene back together, picture the faces under the cardboard party hats. I couldn't see hers. But she had to be there. Was that the day she kissed me? Hovering at my side all afternoon, brushing her arms against me by accident. Then leaning over. I was her husband. It must have happened. Where did it go?

That fucking song scrabbled in the cage of my head, shaking the bars:

For there are you, Sweet Lollipop
Here am I with such a lot to say, hey hey
Just to walk with you along the Milky Way
To caress you through the nighttime
Bring you flowers every day
Oh, babe, what would you say?

Like I said, I'd been dinged, but good. Now it stirred up all the silt at the bottom. Bringing me around. It was my first kiss I was remembering, that lost day I recovered. I saw it clearly. The song must have come through the kitchen window that day, the radio set on WLNG when Marv's mother checked the weather report. She left it there at 92.1 and the enchantments followed. The big kid tormenting Marcus was Big Bobby, no, it was Neil, Neil the pervert who one time climbed up the roof of our porch to peep on Elena and got caught. My parents and his parents didn't talk for two summers. He was premed at Morehouse now, that was the word. Marcus smashed his skull into the table and things went into slow motion as the Carvel cake and Dixie plates and Hi-C tumbled through the air. Someone pulled on my arm, whispering, "Benji."

It seemed impossible not to remember something like that. The first time a girl put her lips on yours. What kind of chump forgets being a five-year-old mack? I would've coasted on that for years if I'd known. But I did know. I was there. What put it out of my mind? I looked at Melanie's profile, the coast of her nose and mouth and chin. She was one of us. A Sag Harbor Baby.

We were at the corner, the end of Richard Drive. The natural destination was town. Where we'd run into somebody and then it wouldn't be just me and her anymore. There was nowhere else to go.

Melanie said, "There it is," I turned and saw the old place up the street and I knew it wasn't her at all.

I will take the world at its word and allow that there are those who have experienced great love in their lives. This must be so. So much fuss is made over it. It follows that there are others who have loved but came to realize over time that what they had was merely the shadow of a greater possibility. These settled, and made do, or broke things off to continue the search. There are those who have never loved, and they walk through their days grasping after true connection. And then there is me. Ladies and gentlemen and all of you at home just tuning in, the angel of my heart, my long lost love, was a house.

There she was, my Sweet Lollipop. Posing coyly behind the old hedges, just a wedge, a bit of thigh, visible behind the trees. When people were inside at night, the light from the windows splashed through the leaves and branches, diluting the darkness. It was always a comfort rounding the corner and seeing that after you'd been running around all day. Soon you'd be inside with everyone else.

The windows were black. Since the swap, where we got the beach house and my aunt kept the Hempstead House, she rarely came out. Occasionally she gave the keys to friends for the weekend, and it was disturbing to see an *alien vehicle* in our driveway. Ours, even though it wasn't anymore. My mother would call her sister to double-check that everything was okay. I hadn't seen anyone there all summer.

"Let's go see," I said. She walked with me without hesitating. The house my grandparents built was a small Cape Cod, white with dark shingles on the roof and red wood bracing the second story. It was made of cinder block, stacks of it hauled out on the back of my grandfather's truck. Every weekend he brought out a load, rattling down the highway. This was before they put in the Long Island Expressway, you understand. It took a while. Every weekend, he and the local talent put up what they could before he had to get back to his business on Monday. Eventually he and my grandmother had their house. Their piece of Sag Harbor.

The hedges out front were scraggly and disreputable, but the lawn was grazed down to regulation height. The house looked like it did at the start of every season, ready for us to open it up. "Do you want to go inside?" I asked.

"Will we get in trouble?"

"No one's using it."

She said, "Okay," and the way she said it zipped my groin, pushing my dick up against my jeans. It was almost dark.

The driveway led to the back patio. Weeds and low flowers sneaked through the cracks in the decaying concrete between the paving stones, and it was still light enough to see some anthills in there, too, the telltale volcanoes of orange dirt. In former days Reggie and me knelt over them with magnifying glass from the Wharf Shop, tilting the incinerating beam on any unfortunate critters popping out for a hive errand. It was where we had arranged the doomed radio men and bazooka guys from our plastic platoons into the path of Tonka bulldozers, and, farther back, filled bright plastic buckets with water from the hose. The toddler games we found meaning in. We spent drawn-out afternoons transferring water from container to container, spilling some each time until the cement was drenched and we were all out and we cried for a refill. Crawling around like ants ourselves, doing nonsense things like that. Behind the patio, the backyard sloped up, and the pump still stood there like a rusted scarecrow, its underground pipes leading nowhere. I don't know if they ever led anywhere.

The patio furniture was piled on the screened-in porch, a rickety contraption that kept the sun off us on hot days and the rain off us on cloudy ones, the water rolling off the roof into worn-away hollows as we swung on the old rocking couch, watching this and kicking our feet out. The roof of the porch was directly under the upstairs windows and Reggie and me used to sneak out onto the tarpaper in Alcatraz breakouts. Not that we had anywhere to go. Eventually we got big and bold enough to jump over the side, that long seven-foot drop. We wasted a lot of time doing that. Wishing, Maybe this time we'll break something.

I told Melanie to wait there and scuttled through the furniture. We left the window to the junk room unlocked when we lived there. Maybe my aunt did, too. What was there to steal? We were more likely to be accidentally locked out than robbed. I shoved the window open, clambering onto the lumpy guest bed, which was covered with our old board games and my aunt's spy thrillers. Stained shades from thrown-out lamps and busted Weedwackers, fishing poles and plastic boxes full of screws. I walked around to the back door and let her in.

The house looked small from the outside. That was its trick. Step inside and it went on for miles. We were in the kitchen, where the pale green General Electric appliances hummed, the matching dishwasher and fridge and range nestled among the pink Formica countertops. The electricity was turned on and they sparked to life; the electricity was turned off and they shuddered into comas for nine months. The door creaked as I closed it, as it always did. You never forget your first creak. It was the original creak, the creak standard that I would compare all other creaks to. Everything in that house was my model for things out in the world. This is what a doorknob looks like. This is what a drain looks like. The first chair I called a chair was there in the living room, next to my one and only and ever lamp. My feet dangled for years until the floor finally reached up to meet them. Window. Couch. Coffee table. My everlasting objects.

"Cobwebs," Melanie said, scraping her face.

A seafaring sort, my grandfather had paneled the living room in broad, brown planks of knotty pine that made it look like the belly of a ship. A buoy from his old sailboat hung over the couch, the name arcing across it in weathered black paint: MY GLORY. The old horseshoe crab was still there, the dried shell hanging on the nail my father had hammered into the wall after I brought it back from the beach. The only thing I noticed that was different was the TV, but I couldn't believe that the old black-and-white still worked, so I forgave its replacement. It took five minutes to warm up, making all sorts of frantic sounds, like you'd startled the people inside from their dozing. A white dot finally materialized in the middle of the screen. A white dot in a sea of blackness. The first star in the universe on the first day. It grew and spread and the sound came on and eventually the comedian hit his punch line, the weatherman told the future, the monster stepped out of the fog. You had to wait for it to come around.

"Nick's working tonight you said."

"I'm not his keeper," she said.

"Do you want to go upstairs?" I asked. Our eyes were getting used to the dark and a car came up Hempstead, illuminating the room and us in a lighthouse sweep.

"Okay."

This was my old house where all the good things still lived even though we had moved on. Everything as it was. Even the boy, the one who always seemed happy. He had to be here. This was where he lived. Haunting the place in his polyester pants and fucked-up Afro. Was the same bottle of hydrogen peroxide sitting in the medicine cabinet? The grisly white foam. He was always running around and not looking where he was going. It all bubbled up. I saw it clearly. I thought it had been the kiss that the song retrieved, but it was this place. My lost love's face was the two windows facing the street, the front door for a nose, and the three brick steps for a mouth. Darling. I hummed the chorus and I didn't care if Melanie heard. Certain songs got you like that. You could make fun of them, ignore them, try to tune them out, but the verses still got inside. People you'd never meet offered the words you were unable to shove past your lips, saying what you felt about someone once, or might become capable of feeling one day. If you were lucky. They spoke for you. Gather the small, rough things you recognized in yourself.

The kids' rooms were on the second floor. I walked up ahead of her, my fingers lighting on the banister made smooth by all our hands, finding the nail heads raised by the settling wood. I anticipated each one before my fingers discovered it. I'd fallen down the stairs plenty when I was learning how to go down stairs. Slamming my stupid head across the steps and finishing in a bruised heap at the bottom. This was the place where I learned to pick myself up, because when I fell the house was always empty.

Elena's room was on the left, me and Reggie's was on the right. The shades at the back of our room were open, enough ambient light sneaking in for us to make out the two beds, the dresser, and the weird vanity table that had been moved up there before I was born, for lack of a better place. The mirror of the vanity was flanked by two mirrored wings on hinges—if you moved them into a triangle, leaving a slot for you to peek inside, the mirrors retreated into endlessness, tossing images of themselves back to themselves in a narcissistic loop. It looked like a tunnel burrowing through the back of the vanity, through the wall, and into an extradimensional beyond. It was amazing how long I could stare at that. The shouts of my friends playing with Reggie came up through the window, or my sister yukking it up with her girlfriends in the next room and I stood there staring.

"This was my bed," I said. I sat down and spread my palm out. The bloom of rusted springs spotted the mattress. She sat down next to me. She said something and I responded, drawing up sentences from a reservoir. I hadn't been on my bed for years. The last time I slept in it—the night of that summer's Labor Day party—I hadn't known it was going to be the final time. A car crept up Hempstead, the headlights casting a window-shaped trapezoid across the ceiling. I knew the circuit—the light traversing the wall next to the vanity, creeping up the white ceiling tiles, then elongating and disappearing in the middle of the room. If the trapezoid blinked off there, the car contained strangers, revving up to 114. If it continued across the ceiling, it was my parents returning after a night out, turning into the driveway, driving the diamond into its home berth above my bed before my father shut off the engine. When that happened, I was safe from all the night sounds that had unsettled me since we were sent to bed. I couldn't sleep, even then. I followed each transit of light, hoping. When the light hovered and stopped, my parents were home and everything would be okay.

"It's quiet up here," she said. Her knuckles rested against my thigh.

"It is, isn't it," I said. She looked into my face. Her eyes glistened in the dark. Then she shut them, screwing them down like she was concentrating very hard, and she pursed her lips.

Why me? She was going out with Nick, but maybe she wasn't anymore. Certainly all the evidence pointed to the conclusion that she wanted me to kiss her. The tale of the childhood smooch, the phone call yesterday, her current pose—oh, let's stop there, I think we have what they call a preponderance, good people of the jury. But why? I reviewed our recent encounters. Had I been cool or said something funny? Accidentally brought forth the winning parts of me? I couldn't think of anything outside of my usual shtick. Maybe my Bauhaus T-shirt was finally kicking in, advertising my sophisticated musical tastes. Did she like Bauhaus, too? It was unlikely. She seemed pretty New Edition. It occurred to me that Nick looked a lot like Bobby Brown. Was she trying to get back at Nick for something? I wasn't the person you made out with to make someone jealous. I was the person you made out with to make someone pity you, like, look how fair I've fallen since you left me, what with the far-off stare and general air of degradation. I was missing something. My braces were off. But that seemed such a trivial thing. I was a dummy for skipping my appointments. I could have been doing stuff like this all the time, apparently. I thought of Emily Dorfman sliding her long fingers around mine and now Melanie Downey perched on my bed like a nymph in a painting by one of the Old Masters or like one of the buxom camp counselors in *Friday the 13th*, about to burst out of her cherry hot pants. The girls had to reach out to me. I was too involuted. They had to pull me out of myself. Pull me where? As if it were better outside, with the rest of the world. I needed people to be able to see past my creaky façade in order to prove their worth, but when they did see past it, I refused to accept it. If people looked inside, surely they'd quickly discover there wasn't much to see.

She said, "Uh?"

All this thinking! You understand the impediments I faced back then. Everything came to a halt before this relentless grinding-over. A normal person would have concentrated on the matter at hand, but I came from a degenerate line. I was at a party chatting up a high-probability but got foolishly distracted by the long-shot lovely across the room whose smile kept me on the hook. In this case, the bewitching lass wasn't even a lass at all, but a two-story part-time home with a leaky roof and periodic squirrel infestation. I was part of a dead-end tribe of human beings twiddling our thumbs for extinction. We picked the wrong line in supermarkets, sitting like bags of cement with our meager foodstuffs in our basket, counting and recounting to make sure we had less than ten items, and when we finally resolved to switch to the faster line, it was too late and now that was the slow line. In fact, the act of us joining that line made it the slow line. We peered into the doors of packed buses and decided to wait for the next one, like we had all the fucking time in the world, and looked up the street for twenty minutes for the next one, finally deciding to walk, and then the next bus zoomed past as we galumphed between stops. We sat like idiots as gorgeous girls with big, patient lips offered themselves to us while we reveried over bygone cobwebbed things. We never know when we have it good, and we forget so easily. We will die out. Not that this particular occasion was a chance to pass on my wretched genetic material and extend my kind's useless reign on this earth, but you understand where such behavior leads—eventually the accumulated missed opportunities, shortsighted decisions, and wrong turns will overtake us. We are too stupid to live. It's amazing we made it this far.

Just kiss her. I kissed her. Leaned over, every adjusting spring in the mattress zinging in loutish commentary. It was the house. I could be the real me because this was where I lived, free from what happened and who I came to be. No matter what people saw when they looked at me, there was this man inside.

Did I mention my eyes were open? I watched her eyes rove under their shadowy lids. Her tongue was soft. Softer than my tongue, or were all tongues the same degree of softness and mine was soft, too? I lifted a hand and rested it on her tit. I squeezed it. Gingerly, like a sailor who'd been thrown overboard and woke to find sand under him. Is this real, the soft stuff between my fingers? She exhaled through her nose. This was a real feeling. The chorus went like this:

> 'Cause oh, Baby I know
> I know I could be so in love with you
> And I know that I could make you love me too
> And if I could only hear you say you do, oo oo oo oo
> But anyway, what would you say?

I know that I could make you love me too. I was wrong again. It wasn't the house I was in love with, either. It was what I put in it. I saw it clearly now, the day I first heard the song, as if I were peeking into the vanity to find the scene unfolding in infinite truth. It was in this very house, many years ago. The sun was bright and every color dazzled. Me and my brother were on our knees on the cement in the back of the house, ramming our toy eighteen-wheelers into each other. Everyone thought we were twins because we were never apart. CB radio was king, and we talked in misapprehended CB lingo. "Breaker One Night, Breaker One Night." I had a red rig and my little brother had a blue one—when our mother took them out of the shopping bag, it was my turn to pick first, so I got the one I wanted. "We got a Smoking Bear on our tail." My sister was lying on the faded green chaise, painting her toenails a brain-splitting red with small, delicate strokes. She and her friends had just discovered nail polish and eye shadow and stuck to a strict practice regimen. She said, "Come here, Reggie, let me do your nails," and he said, "No, no!" My mother flipped the pages of a magazine at the patio table, wearing the white sweatbands that were always on her wrists that one summer she played tennis. "It's good for the heart." She looked so young. She said, "Elena, leave your brothers alone," and turned the page. My father upended the bag of Kingsford and shook a mound into the grill. He said, "The first batch will come off in approximately fifty-five minutes." And I said, "Yay! Yay!" because there was nothing better than barbecue. We were a family. This was the scene the song gifted to me. The radio played in the kitchen, the black transistor radio sitting on top of the green GE fridge. The man sang through static, "I know that I could make you love me too." The perfect day so long ago when we were all together. The beautiful afternoon before it went wrong.

Of course it never happened. But that was WLNG for you. Got you every time.

I was sucking on her neck. My stomach growled. My eyes were still open. That's how I saw the headlights. The lights moved across the wall, tracing the distance like a needle sweeping across a record. But the lights didn't disappear where they were supposed to. They kept going, to my parents' place, and we heart the tires snapping pebbles and stones in the driveway.

"Oh, shit!" I said, jumping up as if the house were made of glass and we were suddenly visible up in the air, floating.

"Who is it?"

We scrambled to the side window, which gave us a steep angle on the driveway. It wasn't someone pulling in to make a U-turn. The headlights extinguished and the door opened.

"We gotta get out of here," I said. I was having an action-flick moment, quoting the hero after he discovers the ticking time bomb.

"This sucks!" she said.

I unlatched the windows. She said, "Are you crazy?"

"No, look—the roof." I saw her frown at me. "It's totally safe." Then whispering: "Me and Reggie used to go out here all time."

We heard the front door creak open. That creak! I threw a leg outside and pulled my body through. Melanie banged her head on the frame and said, "Ow!"

"Shh!"

"Ooh!"

"Shh!"

We stepped over the twigs and acorns lobbed from the trees. I led her to the side of the porch away from the driveway. "Now what?" she whispered, looking over.

"We gotta jump for it," I said. More action-flick dialogue. The edge of the canyon, the mercenaries' jeep bouncing closer. The kissing jostled something loose, some he-man narrative.

"I'm not doing that." A hand downstairs discovered the lamp in my parents' former bedroom, throwing light onto the grass.

"We have to," and I jumped. It really wasn't that far and my legs knew what to do after so many rehearsals. I'd seen myself jumping off the porch to escape a raging fire or a mass of zombies moaning up the stairs but never thought I'd be looking up at a girl, saying, "I'll catch you."

I didn't. She knocked me into the dirt like an Acme anvil. She yelped. Loud enough for the person inside to hear. Then we ran. Along the side of the house, dashing across the front yard and into the street. I heard someone yell after us, and snuck a glance back to see a silhouette on the front stoop. But we were around the corner with a quickness.

The next day I saw Melanie through the window of the ice-cream store, the lookout by the waffle grill. I took my break. She sat on one of the benches, rubbing her sandals in the dirt, pretty toes poking out. She watched me walk over. A limousine prowled up the lane between us, a slow black shark, and I waited for it to pass. Her expression did not change. I gave her the ice cream I'd scooped for her. Mint Chocolate Chip in a Waffle Cone with Rainbow Sprinkles, what I'd heard her ask for all those times when she came in to see Nick while my head was down in the vats. She said, "Oh, thanks," and extended her soft tongue to the ice cream. "It's hot out today."

I told her that my aunt had let one of her employees use the house for the weekend. She said, "That's okay," and looked past me and Nick materialized and slid up next to her, circling his arm around her and slipping his fingers into the tight pocket of her jeans. He didn't ask about the cone. That was that.

My aunt sold the house a few years later. When I asked her why she'd do such a thing, she told me, "I never went out there. What was the point of holding on to it?" I was appalled, but you know me. I was nostalgic for everything big and small. Nostalgic for what never happened and nostalgic about what will be, looking forward to looking back on a time when things got easier.

She sold the house to that brand who keep it up, diligently mailing checks to the lawn guy and the guy who turns on the water at the start of the season, but who never seem to come out. They haven't done a thing to it, repainted it or anything, so it looks like always did. When I walk by there now, I could be staring at a photograph of when my grandparents just finished it, them stepping out into the street to admire what they'd accomplished. Or the first time I saw it when I was a baby, aloft in my mother's arms. Far away, then getting bigger and more real the closer we get to it.

It looks like it's waiting.

7

Ubu Lives!

Remembering Punk and Its Stories

By Rick Moody

The Pere Ubu of the later seventies, from 1975 to 1979—from the singles of their early period up through *New Picnic Time*—was one of the most interesting bands of the seventies, perhaps one of most formidable rock and roll bands ever.

Tom Herman on electric guitar was truly a great player, part garage rock riff machine, part noisy slide-free jazz guy. Mostly integrated like a bass player, with impeccable rhythm and groove, but then occasionally really breaking out with the caterwauling.

Allen Ravenstine on analogue synthesizer and occasional sax also brought abstraction and free jazz chops to the Ubu sound, an eruption of white noise and squawls that bent out of shape the rock forms that the band used as a starting point. He created the spiderwebbery, the menace.

And then the rhythm section of Tony Maimone and Scott Kraus that was exploratory, atavistic, locked in.

What Pere Ubu did was like going into the sub-basements and firebombing any carbon-based life form in order to preserve (in ash) what was poignant.

They restored the feeling of early rock and roll by repurposing it, and making it new again by seeing it from a different spot, namely from Cleveland.

Pere Ubu is a band that does not have a convenient beginning and no ending, like an expansionist multiverse. The beginning is in Rocket From the Tombs, the band that preceded them, and which generated some of their early material. Eventually the legacy of Rocket From the Tombs was reabsorbed into Pere Ubu, like a partial twin, in that this predecessor was re-created as a re-performance, thirty years later, and continues to exist as a trace, an implication.

The debate early on in Pere Ubu was about one guitar or two guitars and for a long time one guitar was sufficient, and revisiting the question now is to lose the thread. In early Pere Ubu, melody could happen in surprising spots, in the bass register, where the guitar was more closely linked with the rhythm section, except when it was closely linked to defoliation.

I haven't mentioned David Thomas's voice yet, which is both singular, pre-rock, and proto-punk. It's one of the greatest voices I know of. Sort of half "Winchester Cathedral," and half Albert Ayler, and especially the way he can use different spots to frame his voice, not always out front, but sometimes inside the songs, like another instrument. Lots of range too. He can go to the falsetto.

Thomas is inarguably one of the great lyricists in the punk and postpunk periods. A period which has some great lyricists. "Non-Alignment Pact," for example, is a masterpiece. "Humor Me" is a masterpiece. And so on. He's a better and more prolific lyricist than Patti Smith, for example, and a better lyricist than Michael Stipe. More outwardly and metaphorically inclined than self-expressing. Self as a metaphor for the world. Only Mark E. Smith compares.

Early Ubu/Rocket singles seemed to come from nowhere. They were *sui generis*. "Final Solution" and "Sonic Reducer" (written in the same batch) are brutal songs, and both about teen alienation in a way that rock songs had simply not managed to be. Teen alienation is *the* subject of rock and roll, but no one had described it with the appropriate figurative language until these songs: "The girls won't touch me 'cause I've got a misdirection."

Misdirection is a remarkable word here. Surprising, original, evasive, with a faint double entendre. What is the manifest content, the expressed purpose in *misdirection*? That there is a direction that could *not* be missed and is thus the sort of thing so as to be rewarded with a touch? How do *touch* and *direction* correlate?

And how does this surprising word choice attach to the ominous slow-motion version of "Summertime Blues" that is "Final Solution." Maybe mishearing *misdirection* is the purpose of the word, as mishearing is the purpose of the music, the re-purpose of the music, as decaying Cleveland is an instrument in the ensemble.

My theme is the ravages of time. At the point at which I was originally pondering this series of analects I asked David Thomas if he would make a short series of dialectical pairings about Cleveland at the dawn of Pere Ubu versus Cleveland *of the present*, no longer a rust belt town, perhaps, or at least a town that has transcended the injurious rust belt designation, while remaining homely, desperate, beautiful, feral.

Thomas replied to my inquiry with the highly poetical (in terms of density and form) scattering of lines that I will place precisely in the middle of this assemblage.

I think of hearing "Dub Housing," the song not the album, as the beginning of Pere Ubu for me, which happened in a cinderblock dormitory in Providence, Rhode Island, in 1981. The circumstances were not as scary as the song. But the terror constructed in the song was reinforced in that dehumanized setting.

I was used to thinking that certain things, certain moves, certain bits of business, gesture, were enough in music to convey terror and isolation, certain kinds of minor chords, a certain swell of synthesizer or organ, a guitar at the lower end of its feasible scale, but "Dub Housing" did none of these things and got more mileage out of a wind instrument being played in a free jazz mode against a very simple riff, and a piano that kind of wanders off, and a singer who wails some phoneme on the ones.

Why so terrifying? "Dub Housing" is about collectivization, about the horror of urban living, perhaps, and it accomplishes this by being such a tautly composed band outing, an entity without a front-person, without the need of a front-person, that it incarnates the fear of collectivization, which is the fear of the trivialization of the individual ("in the dark a thousand insect voices chitter-chatter").

If there's a misheard *misdirection* in this lyric it's that, depending on the day, I sometimes hear the above quotation as a "a thousand *innocent* voices."

It was a cinder block dormitory, and a lot of drinking was taking place. I remember shattering a wine bottle there accidentally one time, breaking the bottle on a railing in the stairwell, and rushing into the nearest dorm room, busting on some guy doing his homework, to try to find a strainer so we could *strain out the glass* from the wine, and continue drinking.

It's poignant and awful that alcoholism on the scale that I practiced it then can take place in a dorm room with one roommate defenestrating, while another roommate is just sitting there trying to read, I don't know, *The Organization Man*, or *Critical Theory Since Plato*, while on a turntable there was "Dub Housing."

Soave Folinari in those days cost about $2.50 a bottle (a "fruit forward wine of outstanding value"). Or thereabouts.

I can remember the song "Dub Housing" like it's a work of fiction, a story that has already been made into a novelizing of life lived, and I can't see it, and I don't have access to it, though I could easily check it with the guy who played "Dub Housing" for me on this occasion.

It's the *lost qualities of the past,* alluded to in the David Thomas syllogism on time to be found below, that makes clear how inaccessible and impacted memories really are.

And it happens, in part, that I write these lines in the very same city, Providence, with its history of religious protest, and could easily walk there, to the cinder block dormitory to see what is being listened to there now, though I'm willing to bet that "Dub Housing" and its catalogue of terrors has not been played there regularly since. Maybe Kendrick Lamar.

I have written elsewhere about how the album that followed *Dub Housing*, viz., *New Picnic Time* is the most terrifying rock and roll album ever recorded, and I will not belabor that argument at any length, except to say that it is an album of religious dread, and nothing is more terrifying than religious dread. On Wikipedia, *New Picnic Time* is referred to as the band's "crowning achievement."

Crowning achievement is a lofty coinage in this context. What could it possibly mean on an album that imagines and feels out the idea of religious vulnerability in a way that is both full of awe and sad. As an example of same, I adduce the incredible and overpowering song titled "The Voice of Sand." Truly among the most affecting songs of the punk era for me.

"The Voice of Sand" consists only of a few tracks of EML synthesizer, in a sprung, nonrhythmical context, and some whispering by David Thomas. The lyrics go like this: "This is the voice of sand / The sailors understand /

There is far more sea than sand / There is far more sea than land." And they are based on a poem by Vachel Lindsay, whose own story is every bit as dark as *New Picnic Time.*

This is the voice of sand. The image is deeply moving and important, for giving voice to such an elemental and neglected thing, such a ubiquitous feature of our daily geological lives. But sand, and its fractal shoreline, for marking the edges of the oceans, serves as a delimiting agent, an invitation to immensity, and, as a marker of time, a thing that can be broken down limitlessly in the grinding and eroding action of time.

The jackhammering of the Ravenstine synthesizer, along with some detuned swoops, sounds more like industrial shuddering than oceanside, and it prefigures an electronica that would emerge in four or five years in popular music, but what arrests in the song in question is Thomas's whispered vocal. As with the voice of God, which briefly appears in Bergman's *Fanny and Alexander*, Thomas's vocal definitely locates the numinous.

It's infinitesimal, it's minute, it's faceless, it's collectivist, it's beyond scale, it's unobservable, it's as old as the formation of the planets, it's as old as asteroid strike. It's the calling card of the origin of time. It's a trace of the first cause. "Sand" is a crowning achievement, as *New Picnic Time* is a crowning achievement, and maybe it's a crowning achievement as a *misdirection.*

After *New Picnic Time,* there was this other band that in certain ways sounded like Pere Ubu—it still had David Thomas singing in it, and it still had Allen Ravenstine making stranger synthesizer noise in it, but otherwise it was completely different. The name of this band was also Pere Ubu. The secret was Mayo Thompson, from the Red Krayola, who had a completely different guitar sound from Tom Herman. Herman left because of the tension in the room during *New Picnic Time.*

It would be hard to say exactly what Mayo Thompson's guitar sounded like. In a way it didn't sound like a guitar very much. It sounded more like a desert wind, as conjured up in a contemporary automobile name. Or like an industrial washing machine of some kind in a Laundromat that plays *smoove jazz.* Maybe it made a sort of a leaky faucet sound. It definitely was doing things that a guitar could not traditionally do.

But the one thing that Mayo Thompson's guitar didn't seem to be doing was reconstructing primeval rock and roll parts. Tom Herman sounded like he was concealed within a rockabilly preacher yearning to be free. He had a forked tongue. But Mayo Thompson sounded more like some combination of the 13th Floor Elevators and Ornette Coleman and the rhythm guitarist from the Ohio Players.

I was living in San Francisco in 1984, and I knew this guy from Providence, his name was Tom, and he is tangentially related to these recollections. Tom had moved to San Francisco, and he had nowhere to stay, so my roommates told him he could live with us for a while. Tom was a big Pere Ubu freak. I think he had written a final paper for a Brown class in surrealism on Pere Ubu.

Tom got a job working at the De Young Museum, which was where I was working too, and I can still remember him sitting in the gift store, maybe doing *bag check* with the headphones in, and then I asked him what he was listening to, and he said it was *Song of the Bailing Man* (1982), or *The Art of Walking* (1980), and I remember listening to this album through a single ear of a headphone, and thinking it sounded pretty great.

I sort of let go of the Pere Ubu legend for a while, until *The Tenement Year*. This is a superior album, *The Tenement Year*. Circa: 1986. You can tell it's important, because the title evokes Cleveland, and the indigo disrepair of the Midwest. One thinks of the flaming Cuyahoga.

The Tenement Year, which has a different guitar player on it (Jim Jones), features some slightly poppy stuff, like "We Have the Technology," but it also has superior placement of Allen Ravenstine's EML synthesizers, which sound as though they were recorded in the room with the band, and accorded a helping of reverb. They didn't record him straight into the board.

When saying *Tenement* was "poppier," what we mean, I expect, is that it had some really good melodies. Some of the really good melodies were because of new guitar player Jim Jones. He could really play lead guitar. In a way, he was probably the best lead guitar player the band ever had, and that's saying something. Thomas had also become more adroit as a writer of vocal lines and hooks.

Also: two drummers. The whole two-drummer thing, you know, in the jam band world, I can never quite understand it. (King Crimson has three now!) How do people not step on other people's parts? At least in this case, the extra drummer was Chris Cutler, from the unimpeachably excellent band Henry Cow, the second drummer was more a creator of accents in the percussion section than a timekeeper. It's amazing that *The Tenement Year* is as clean and spacious as it is.

I can also remember, about the time of *The Tenement Year*, listening to all the David Thomas solo albums, and really getting hung up on a song called

"Song of Hoe," in part because of the following line: "Woe to the weeds when they meet me."

This line is associated with a welter of painful memories from that time, a myriad of my own grim biographical asterisks. For example, when my partner lost her mother. Or when we didn't keep the baby. Later, the baby visited my partner in her dreams, spoke to her, and kept doing so. Woe to the weeds.

David Thomas's reply to my inquiry about making pairs of words about how Cleveland had changed, supplied the following:

> Time is a river.
> Upstream is the unknowable yesterday.
> Downstream is the undeniable tomorrow.
> Locked in place between the two is a boat.
> The banks of the river rush past. The boat is static.
> The world changes. Pere Ubu doesn't.
> The bank ahead looks similar to the bank behind until it moves
> into memory, the upstream unknowable.

I find this phrase deeply moving: "The bank ahead looks similar to the bank behind until it moves into memory." In the present I am interacting with people and institutions and landscapes while confusing this present with the past. Or vice versa. The past misdirects its narratives into the present. There are people who so closely approximate people in the past that I feel I could recite their stories, their jokes, conundrums, paradoxes, grief.

"Until it moves into memory." This process in which the events of the future become less numerous and less impressive than the events of the past is a slow one, like radiation from solar flares. It happens unbidden. You cannot exert action upon spacetime, you are only subjected to it. The tendency upon beholding these particular facts is the weeping tendency. Woe.

We pause briefly over my MFA thesis at Columbia University. Everything about that particular project was futile. My alcoholism was extremely bad in the second year of graduate school, and I was drinking earlier and earlier in the day, and not really working as well as I would have liked, seeing double at the typewriter, crippling myself with hangovers. I had some systematic inability to understand what a *story* was.

So what is a story? Since the time of my active alcoholism, I have had occasion to think carefully about what a story is, and my idea of story is that it is a thing that happens *in time.* It is a sequence of events in time, generally acted out on a body or a group of bodies. Sometimes it is narrated by a consciousness, and consciousness acts a drag on a hurtling of time. But time wins in the end.

I came to understand these things about time ("Upstream is the unknowable yesterday") only by living out beyond the time of graduate school and mental illness. Alcoholism probably prevents the actual understanding of story and consciousness in anything like deep engagement. But: I did in fact finish a thesis at Columbia, and I used as one of my epigraphs this line from David Thomas: "Harry had a notion to bail out the ocean."

It's revealing that there was a song called "Song of the Bailing Man" on the solo album called *More Places Forever*, some five years after the Pere Ubu album of the same name. I think the music for this recording, the song called "Song of the Bailing Man," was entirely new and had nothing to do with the earlier album by Pere Ubu. Was there a lyric floating around that got reused? And what accounts for the reuse of the image, if not? Did two narratives collide? Or was a thought repeated because it was not yet depleted?

My workshop instructor in spring of 1986, the venerable experimental writer William S. Wilson, wrote "image of futility" in the margin about my epigraph from David Thomas, and that was probably without his knowing one thing about David Thomas. This, of course, got me thinking about whether "Harry had a notion to bail out the ocean" was an image of futility or not.

I played *Dub Housing* in a car on the way back from my fifth high school reunion, with some friends from high school in the backseat of the car, and at a certain point they were all yelling at me: *What the fuck is this music! Turn off this music! Why are we listening to this music! It's not even music!* To which the correct response is: *You don't understand the sublime.*

The furnace of the sublime, the alchemical furnace of things converted into their opposites, through or against similitude, is like the beginning of spacetime, when there are not words for all the things, because it is the time before the names, and sometimes the words in David Thomas are like this; they are obverses of themselves or seem to mean other things, or don't mean anything at all, so much as they mean to suggest a feeling, a feeling in reverse, the dread responsibility of naming.

And: I had a break from Ubu after the sort of *popular* period of the band, the years on the Mercury label, and some of the songs of the popular period were kind of great, but were just not what I wanted or expected, and even when they rose from the grave of that commercial time and started performing in the original way again, the uncompromising way, they were different.

I was more interested in the reunited Rocket From the Tombs, which was happening simultaneously. By the turn of the century there was no longer just Pere Ubu for David Thomas, there were often multiple projects happening at once, and one of them was this very well curated Rocket From the Tombs, the risen-from-the-dead version of the band.

Both things are true: the music of the mid-seventies was miraculous and perfect, and there will never be anything better, and time doesn't work this way, and there are periods of explosive growth in music in every era, and all the eras are happening at the same time, rushing away from each other toward steady state.

My tendency in the early 2000s was to be interested in work made between, say, 1973 and 1978, and having read a lot about Cleveland, and the way that a lot of the greatest work in Cleveland was made without undue contamination by the business, few things could have generated as much excitement for me as the retooling of Rocket From the Tombs.

The label called Smog Veil released the Rocket From the Tombs tapes from the seventies in 2002. A lack of tightness, guitars all over the place, strangled vocals! It was more punk than punk, because it didn't have a name yet, and the lyrics were reflective of an actual way of life, instead of being shoehorned into a movement. *The Day the Earth Met Rocket From the Tombs* is a great shocking blast of a thing. It's in your face, like a sullen teenager, shouting at you, "Ain't it fun when you know you're gonna die young!"

When the band tried to re-create the magic in 2004 with *Rocket Redux*, wherein they recorded all the old songs, they were maybe trying to get a piece of the publishing, or maybe they were just trying to tighten up what were really very badly recorded masterpieces. They added Richard Lloyd on guitar, one of the greatest guitarists in rock and roll, whose violent changes of direction in mid-solo flatter the intensity of the original material. And then David Thomas and Cheetah Chrome sang the songs anew, the latter with a voice pocked by the decades. Like John Mellencamp run over by farm equipment.

I saw Rocket From the Tombs play live, as I have said, in 2004 or 2005, and they were very memorable. David Thomas, who was perhaps at his most unhealthy period, now much in remission, sat for most of the gig, and it was great to see such incendiary music played not only by a bunch of old guys, but sung by a guy who sat, and who complained before the encore that there was no way he was going back down those stairs to the green room just to come back up again. No way! Punk rock! Rocket From the Tombs were therefore of the present and of the past. They shimmered between eons.

I should admit: I take issue with a Pere Ubu recording called *Why I Hate Women* (2006), just because, even if the meaning of the title is precisely the opposite of its manifest content. The official explanation of the title, which I interpret as both an indulgence and a desire to cast responsibility elsewhere—the title of a Jim Thompson novel "he never wrote"—just reminds me why I dislike Jim Thompson.

But because of the title, *Why I Hate Women*, I didn't pay much attention, erroneously, and was indeed more interested in the Rocket From the Tombs phenomenon, the total commitment to minimal melodic material, two guitars, and abrasion. I even liked some of the "new" Rocket From the Tombs material, new songs (from *Barfly*, 2011), because of the bludgeoning.

What I missed out on, by not paying attention, was that Pere Ubu, in the interim, had again become a really extremely compelling band. That is, the band had started to have the qualities that the "classic" lineup had. It had, and has, band qualities. There's the drummer Mehlman, and there's the bass player Michele Temple, who has a lovely understated presence. The two of them now interacting in very interesting ways. Robert Wheeler on synthesizer has completely recreated the Allen Ravenstine chair of pointillist serpentine wisps. He plays theremin too. Keith Moliné on guitar brings a very experimental energy to the instrument. The band has become a thing that can bend its collective energy around any new conceptual interest, whether stage play, or collision with dance music.

And this brings us to *20 Years in a Montana Missile Silo* (2018). In many ways, it brings together all the threads I've been describing. Or maybe *20 Years in a Montana Missile Silo* is a crossing of moments in a secular crisis, a folding over of historical epochs and thematic obsessions, and with them the different orchestral flavors of the different eras all in one.

For example, *20 Years in a Missile Silo* has three guitar players on it. And two keyboard players, and a clarinetist. So it has a feeling more like a Pere Ubu *orchestra* than a rock and roll band, and indeed I have read that this is the point, that Pere Ubu in Thomas's conception has now become infinitely expandable.

Bits of *arrangement*, which is the sort of word one might not presume to use about early Ubu albums, are so sophisticated on *20 Years*, here and there washes of assault, and then outbursts of guitar noise that come and go, appear and disappear. What does it mean for a recording to be guitar-based now? I am not even certain that some young people of my acquaintance know what an electric guitar is *for*, much less what it might sound like on a recording.

But I want to talk about "Cold Sweat." "Cold Sweat," the last song on *20 Years*, is the preeminent example of the cinematic and painterly aspect of the whole here: "Hold me close / I feel the time is running out / I know you must / feel it too." The song rhymes "notion" and "ocean," like "Song of the Bailing Man." And the play of ideas, gentle, unfolding, is counterposed against a recollection of James Brown's song of the same name, which is itself about the presence of a certain cathected love object causing an auto-cooling episode. Pere Ubu's "Cold Sweat" is about intimations of mortality, and the immensity of creation.

Pere Ubu's "Cold Sweat" is about the same things that *New Picnic Time* is about, but without the consolations of a reliable spiritual scaffolding, with which to fend off immensities of scale.

"Cold Sweat" by James Brown slaughtered melody. But David Thomas builds in melody, really sings into it, so as to reintegrate melody, and the song likewise includes big developmental moments, keyboard progressions, that remind me a bit of another great threnody on the subject of mortality, viz., "Decades," by Joy Division ("Here are the young men, the weight on their shoulders . . .").

20 Years in Montana Missile Silo, as a recording project, also coincided, or nearly coincided, with the untimely death of Pere Ubu's longtime engineer Paul Hamann, whose father, also an engineer and studio owner, recorded the band initially. If a sense of making a legacy in a particular location, Cleveland, in a particular room, with a particular engineer, is at the heart of Pere Ubu, it's conceivable that some portion of that legacy is now in question.

"Cold Sweat" forecasts this anxiety. And it's the anxiety that I feel writing these lines, no longer a college student hearing Pere Ubu for the first time, but now a middle-aged music critic and college professor looking more backward at music than looking forward.

Have we arrived at an ending? That the upstream is unknowable, excepting in its repetitions? That the downstream and upstream helix around one another? The iterations of the past and future are pulsations in the music-making of the present, and in the acute observations of this band, continue on, emanations of singularity, out of time and fashion, like a flickering of emergency lighting in the disused warehouse of a former industry. Thousands were once employed there.

8

By Heart

From Eat the Document *(Excerpt)*

By Dana Spiotta

It is easy for a life to become unblessed.

Mary, in particular, understood this. Her mistakes—and they were legion—were not lost on her. She knew all about the undoing of a life: take away, first of all, your people. Your family. Your lover. That was the hardest part of it. Then put yourself somewhere unfamiliar, where (how did it go?) you are a complete unknown. Where you possess nothing. Okay, then—this was the strangest part—take away your history, every last bit of it.

What else?

She discovered, despite what people may imagine, having nothing to lose is a lot like having nothing. (But there was something to lose, even at this point, something huge to lose, and that was why this unknown, homeless state never resembled freedom.)

That unnerving, surprisingly creepy and unpleasantly psychedelic part—you lose your name.

Mary finally sat on a bed in a motel room that very first night after she had taken a breathless train ride under darkening skies and through increasingly unfamiliar landscape. Despite her anxiety she still felt lulled by the tracks clicking at intervals beneath the train; an odd calm descended for whole minutes in a row until the train pulled into another station and she waited for someone to come over to her, finger-pointing, some unbending and unsmiling official. In between these moments of near calm and all the other moments, she practiced appearing normal. Only when she tried to move could you notice how shaky she was. That really undid her, her visible unsteadiness. She tried not to move.

Five state borders, and then she was handing over the case for the room—anonymous, cell-like, quiet. She clutched her receipt in her hand, stared at it, September 15, 1972, and thought, This is the first day of it. Room Twelve, the first place of it.

Even then, behind a chain lock in the middle of nowhere, she was double-checking doors and closing curtains. Showers were impossible: she half-expected the door of the bathroom to push in as she stood there unaware and naked. Instead of sleeping she lay on the covers, facing the door, ready to move. Showers and bed, nakedness and sleep—she felt certain that was how it would happen, she could visualize it happening. She saw it in slow motion, she saw it silently, and then she saw it quickly, in double-time, with crashes and splintered glass. Haven't you seen the photos of Fred Hampton's mattress? She certainly had seen the photos of Fred Hampton's mattress. They'd all seen them. She couldn't remember if the body was still in the bed in the photos, but she definitely remembered the bed itself: half stripped of sheets, the dinge stripe and seam of the mattress exposed and seeped with stains. All of it captured in the lurid black-and-white Weegee style that seemed to underline the blood-soak and the bedclothes in grabbed-at disarray. She imagined the bunching of sheets in the last seconds, perhaps to protect the unblessed person on the bed. Grabbed and bunched not against gunfire, of course, but against his terrible, final nakedness.

"Cheryl," she said aloud. No, never. Orange soda. "Natalie." You had to say them aloud, get your mouth to shape the sound and push breath through it. Every name sounded queer when she did this. "Sylvia." A movie-star name, too fake sounding. Too unusual. People might actually hear it. Notice it, ask about it. "Agnes." Too old. "Mary," she said very quietly. But that was her real name, her *original* name. She just needed to say it.

She sat on the edge of the bed, atop a beige chenille bedspread with frays and loose threads, in her terry-cloth bathrobe, which she'd somehow thought to buy when she got her other supplies earlier in the afternoon. She had imagined a bath as bringing some relief, and the sink into the robe afterward seemed important. She did just that, soaked in the tub after wiping it clean. Eyes trained on the open door of the bathroom, and careful not to splash, she strained to determine the origins of every sound she heard. She shaved her legs and scrubbed her hands with a small nailbrush, also purchased that day. She flossed her teeth and brushed her tongue with her new toothbrush. She tended to the usual grooming details with unusual attention: she knew instinctively that these details were very closely tied to keeping her sanity, or her wits, anyway. Otherwise she could just freeze up, on the floor, in her dirty jeans, drooling and sobbing until they came and got her. Dirt was linked to inertia. Cleanliness, particularly personal cleanliness, was an assertion against madness. It was a declaration of control. You might be in the midst of chaos, terrified, but the ritual of self-tending radiated from you and protected you. That was where Mary figured a lot of people got it wrong. Slovenliness might be rebellious, but it was never liberating. In fact, she felt certain that slovenly and sloppy attention to personal hygiene surrendered you to everything outside you, all of the things not of you trying to get in.

The TV on low, she looked but barely watched, hugging her knees toward her. Unpolished clean nails, uniform and smooth. Legs shaven and scented with baby oil, which looked greasy but smelled powdery and familiar. She inhaled deeply, resting her face on her knees and drawing her legs closer. She was a tiny ball of a human, wasn't she? A speck of a being in the middle of a vast multi-highwayed and many-sided country, wasn't she? Full of generic, anonymous, and safe places just like this one.

She thought of famous people's names, authors' names, teachers' names, the names she made up when she was eight for her future babies. Abby, Blythe, Valeria. Vita, Tuesday, Naomi. She put on an oversized T-shirt and clean cotton bikini briefs decorated with large pastel pansies, size 4. She thought of girlfriend names and cheerleader names. Names of flowers and women in novels. She ate peanut butter on white bread and drank orange juice directly from the carton. She was ravenous, very unusual for her. She took a large bite and a big swig, the sweet pulpy taste mixing into the glutinous, sticky mouthful. She didn't finish swallowing before taking another huge bite. Maybe I'll be a fat person in my new life. She started to laugh, and the peanut butter-bread-orange juice clump stuck momentarily in her throat, cutting off the airway. She imagined, indifferently, choking and dying in this motel room. She swallowed and then laughed even harder, out loud. It sounded crazy, her short sudden laugh against the quiet mono sound of the television. She could hear her breath squeeze in and out of her lungs and throat. She turned up the volume on the television and stared hard at it.

Jim Brown was talking to Dick Cavett. Brown wore a tight white jumpsuit with beige piping and a wide tan leather belt through the high-waisted belt loops. They both sipped something out of oversized mugs, also white, and placed them on a mushroom-shaped white metal table between then. Brown smiled handsomely and kept declaring—with exquisite enunciation—his respect and support for his friend, the president.

A piece of lined paper in a spiral notebook, a ballpoint pen. Karen Black. Mary Jo Kopechne. Joni Mitchell. Martha Mitchell. Joan Baez. Jane Asher. Joan isn't so bad. Linda McCartney. Joan McCartney. Joan Lennon. Oh, good, sure. Bobby would appreciate that. She almost waited for him to contact her—but she knew he would not, not for a while anyway. At eleven o'clock she turned the channel to watch the news, tried to see if he, or any of them, had been identified or arrested. Jane Fonda, Phoebe Caulfield, Valeria Solanas. She liked these names. Mustn't reference her real name in any way. Brigitte, Hannah, Tricia. Just don't get cute. Lady Bird. Pat. Ha.

"You are no longer Mary from the suburbs. You are Freya from the edge," Bobby had said. They sat cross-legged on a handwoven rug Bobby had bought in Spain. She spent many nights getting high kneeling on that rug; she could examine it needlessly. Moorish Mobius patterns took you in dervish circles back to where you started but done in incongruous, rainy European colors—muted greens and yellows—next to imperial, regal and regimental looking banners and shieldlike things. The rug wasn't authentic, but whoever made it had worked meticulously to evoke something authentic, studied relics of conquerings, exiles, and colonies. It clashed and conflicted in the way real things often did. It was the most beautiful thing either of them possessed, and they often sat on it, next to their bed, which was just a mattress on the floor with no frame or even box springs. All the kids she knew slept on the floor; it softened the distinction between their bed and the rest of the world. She felt safer, nearer to the ground. What did it mean, a culture where people sat cross-legged on the floor, on beautiful rugs? Were there horizontal and vertical cultures? Was living closer to the earth free and natural, or was it simply meager? Was it good, or better, or just different for someone?

"And what will *you* call me?" she had asked, leaning her head against his back. He often wore sleeveless undershirts, very thin and slightly ribbed;

when she pressed against him he smelled both tangy and sweet. Pot and incense and sweat.

She tried to conjure him, with her eyes closed, in her midnight bed. She thought Bobby looked exotic, handsome not so much in the total as in the details. The closer in she was, the more attractive he became. His skin had a faint yellow-green undertone that was the opposite of ruddy: skin so smooth under her touch that she could feel every tiny rough spot on her own fingers or lips; skin so clear and fine she could see his blood pulse at wrist and temple and neck. And although she wasn't ever crazy about the random curliness of his long black hair, which grew out rather than down, she adored the silky way the hair slipped through her fingers when she pulled her hand through it, and the tension in his shoulders when she pressed against them, and how in candlelight she would see her white skin—her slender hand, say—against the dark skin of his broad back, and it would catch her off guard always, the contrast between them. She felt then exquisite and even fragile, which she liked. She wasn't supposed to, but she did. Perhaps because they spent so much time together, and dressed alike and spoke alike—even laughed alike—it was great to in some palpable way be unalike.

"Will you call me Mary, at least when we're at home, in bed?"

"Only Freya. And you have to call me Marco. In these sorts of activities you can't use your real name. Ever. If you want to change your life, first you change your name."

"A nom de guerre? Isn't that sort of ridiculous?"

"All cultures have naming ceremonies. You have a given name, but then you get a chosen name. It's part of a transformation to adulthood. They tell you who you are, and then you decide who you are. It's like getting confirmed, or getting married."

"But I didn't choose that name. You did."

"I'm helping you. The first thing we do is make up a new name. A fighting, fearless name."

"A Bolshevik name?" Mary said, frowning.

"It's a Nordic goddess name. A towering priestess name. A lightning bolt name. A name to live up to."

She closed her eyes and rested against him. "Okay."

"A name that exudes agitprop. These are always two syllable names that end in a vowel. Freya, Maya, Silda, Marco, Proto, Demo. If you don't like that name, come up with another." They never did use those names except in the press communiqués and on the telephone. Now she was choosing another name, its opposite—a hidden, modest, meek name—but truly choosing.

The next morning (was it morning?), when she woke after hardly sleeping, she sat down in the one chair, a molded plastic affair in mustard yellow, next to the motel bed, in the dead time between showers and sleep, with nothing to do but indoctrinate herself into her new life. She could not leave until it was done. She wrote it all out on a piece of spiral notebook paper. Her age: twenty-two. Birthplace: Hawthorne, California. Name: Caroline. Hawthorne was just another suburban town in California, which you could bet was more like all the other suburban towns in California than it was different, and it would do just fine even if her favorite band was also from Hawthorne. And Caroline is a pretty girl's name that also happened to be the name of the girl in one of her favorite songs. Okay, there was no point in being witty about any of this, encoding it or making it coherent in any way, except if it helped her remember. But as Bobby had warned her, if it is legible to you, then it gives you away. But everything, of course, means something. However hermetic and obscure, it can't fail to signify, can it? Unless, of course, she wanted it somehow, however quietly, to be legible and coherent. Unless, of course, she wanted someone, at some time, to figure it out.

Caroline. Caroline Sherman. Okay?

She, my mother, apparently walked by my open bedroom door as I was blaring "Our Prayer." I'd just gotten my hands on the Beach Boys' three-disc *Smile* bootleg—you know, the kind of bootleg where there are like ten versions of the same song in a row? All these versions are usually just alternate takes that vary only slightly from the other versions. Say, for instance, on this take, Brian stops singing two bars from the end. Or the harmonies get muddled slightly. Or somebody says, "One, two, three, four," at the beginning in a soft, defeated, boyish voice. So these aren't versions, per se, these are screwups.

There are plenty of other bootlegs featuring actual different versions of Beach Boys songs: they occasionally have an extra verse, or a different person singing lead. Or different harmonies, different arrangements. Sometimes completely different lyrics. What my extended-box-set-bootleg packing of *Smile* offers though is almost exclusively alternate takes. Ten, fifteen, twenty takes that are nearly identical to each other. They have already worked out how it is going to go, exactly how it will sound, and the takes are all about executing it. Now, you might ask, why the hell does someone want to listen to all that? And in truth, when I realized what I had bought (ninety dollars, no less), at first I was disappointed. But, and this is a big but, there is something amazing about hearing the takes. It is as if you are in the recording studio when they made this album. You are there with all the failures, the intense perfectionism, the frustration of trying to realize in this world the sounds you hear in your head. Sometimes they abruptly stop after someone says "cut" because they lost it, it didn't break their hearts enough, they just couldn't feel it in the right places. Or someone starts laughing, or says suddenly, "Could you hear me on that?" What happens is you jump to a new level in your obsession where even the most arcane details become fascinating. You follow a course of minutiae and repetition, and you find yourself utterly enthralled. Listening deeply to this kind of music is mesmerizing in itself; the same song ten times in a row is like meditation or prayer. So it is quite apt to listen to a song like "Our Prayer" in this manner. I'm on listen number three of the full ten versions, at about version seven, and I am peaking—my desire to listen is being satisfied but hasn't been entirely fulfilled, fatigue hasn't crept in yet, I still yearn for more, and it is a premium experience at this point, the blast of wall-to-wall harmonies, five-part, singing no words but just beautiful, celestial ahhs, the voices soaring, pure instruments of sound. Really, the Beach Boys at their acid choir best.

She, my mother, stopped by my door, which, as I said, was open, in itself a very unusual thing. I must have just returned from the kitchen or the bathroom and not yet closed the door. Maybe I was so into the music and wanted too much to be back next to it that I didn't even notice the door. I think actually I had a sandwich and a soda in my hands and I was arranging them on my desk, and that's why I hadn't closed the door yet. I noticed her leaning slightly against the doorjamb. I thought perhaps she mistook the open door as some sort of invitation. But then I noticed this tiny smile creeping across her lips, and how she wasn't really looking at me, and then I realized she was listening to the music, that was why she was standing there.

Okay, it was about eight o'clock, and by this time in the evening—I've noticed this, really all the time and without really intending to notice—by this time she was a little drunk. I knew this because I occasionally go to the living room to watch TV. Or I go to the dining room to eat dinner with her. She does this thing where she pours like a third of a glass of white wine and then she pours club soda into the glass to top it off. A wine spritzer, I guess. A corny suburban housewife kind of drink. She thinks it's a light aperitif, I imagine. You might call it that, an aperitif, if you wanted to make it sound reasonable and almost medicinal. Thing is, she soon finishes and then does the third of a glass and spritzer routine again. Thing is, she does this all evening long. It's not like I'm counting or really even paying attention, but it is hard to miss when she does this all evening long, every evening. I'm not even saying there is anything wrong with it. She never seems drunk—she doesn't get all slurry and drop things. She just seems increasingly placid and bit dulled by bedtime. She is already the sort of person who seems constantly to be half-way elsewhere. So this habit only makes her more and more absent or indifferent to the vagaries or boredom of being in this house. I'm not judging here but merely describing what it is she does. I am just observing her. I think maybe the whole third of a glass plus seltzer thing indicates she isn't quite admitting to herself how much she drinks, but surely at some point she goes to refill and she realizes she's down to the last third of a glass in the bottle (and we are sometimes talking a magnum here, a big economy jug) that started the evening full, and she must realize, then, that she is drinking quite a lot. But by then she must also be placid enough, plied enough by the countless spritzers where perhaps this empty magnum doesn't weigh on her too much at all. She is by then, well, whoever she is, in her private silent thoughts, and I don't really mind as long as she doesn't interfere with me, which she usually doesn't.

So she was feeling no doubt buzzed by eight o'clock, and this song caught her as she walked down the hall. She was lost in it, faintly smiling. She looked really young standing there listening, and sort of uncovered, which was unusual for my mother. She is generally so creepily guarded and cryptic in odd, sunny ways. Like she isn't really entirely sure she is in the right house or the right life. Like she's a guest here. I guess she lacks the kind of certainty one expects in a parent. She seems to lack the necessary confidence. The song ended, there were a few seconds of silence and then "Our Prayer," take number eight, kicked in. during the break, she smiled at me—a flirty, sheepish smile, disarmingly unmomlike.

"Great song," she said. Then it began again, and I lowered it reluctantly.

"A teenage symphony to God," I said, quoting the liner notes that quoted Brian Wilson.

"Yes, that's right," she said, nodding. "They always sound most like that when there aren't any words. When they use their voices as instruments. Just pure, perfect form."

So she said this kind of smart thing about the Beach Boys and then wandered off to refill her glass or something. That's the first time I remember thinking, How can that be?

After our introduction, our brief paragraphs of biographical detail, we segued effortlessly into our obsessions. We have spent the last few weeks together in an orgy of listening. I was relieved to discover that Gage was no don't-touch-the-record collector. He was passionately into listening and playing things for you to listen to. We sat in his room—which has a black light, I kid you not, and the appropriate psychedelic posters to go with it—and we had listening jags, hours of intensity. Jumping promiscuously from "You have that?" to "Wait until you hear this!" But very shortly the novelty began to wear off. We quickly grew less patient with one another's interests. He was deeply into this '70s thing, particularly a lot of deep listening to Roxy Music's mid- to late-70s albums. I was cool with that but I had been through it all two summers ago. Naturally he tried to fly the rather perverse opinion that Roxy's late '70s discoish period was really the best stuff, rather than the avant-pop and math-fizz of their earlier experimental stuff. Something along the lines of the "glorious dance music of 1979" (a hyperbolic assertion, which is just so typical of Gage and his ilk, and so utterly false).

"Dude, listen, check out the percussion on this track. Totally conjured on a Jupiter 8. That is all of '80s dance music in a nutshell," Gage said to me.

"Yeah, *dude*. That's quite a legacy to claim."

"That it is. Nothing like those late '70s thick-as-a-brick analog synths, synthesizers that had no shame!"

It was the trend—unspoken but somehow felt everywhere at once—among some music freaks to be into synthesizers, but only the spaceship-landing, proudly precise and artificial vibrato of early- to middle-period pre-digital synths. Roland Jupiter 8s. Minimoogs. Yeah, sure.

"I don't know. The production is really flat. Like airless."

That was my bullshit response, to call the production "airless," because it just means this music is not flying my flag right now, and I've got several choice albums on deck, all without synthesizers save perhaps a theremin and with production that could supply enough oxygen to feed an army of asthmatic smokers for life. And of course Gage was being totally fascistic about what we had to hear next. But the thing is the guy was in the thrall, so deep into his obsession, his Roxy freak, that he meant it. He was drowning in the circular mess of relativity, in the mindfuck of repeated listening, the loss of perspective that comes with looking at something too closely. I know. I've been there. Don't even get me started on the Beach Boys. As I am writing this, it's there. As I was sitting at Gage's trying to listen to his records, I was fondling an original issue 45 of "God Only Knows." I was humming, no, vibrating, *Pet Sounds*'s songs in order. And I couldn't wait to satisfy my jones for it. So I knew exactly where Gage was at, but Gage didn't have much perspective for a guy his age, did he? He didn't have a clue how deep in he was, how tragically without perspective. I know the day will come when I won't feel this way about the Beach Boys. I know, at least intellectually, that day will come. Then perhaps I will be all gooey for the genius of early Little Feat or late Allman Brothers or something. And when I realize this I feel a little sad. I could be reading a great book, couldn't I? Or going for a bike ride or meeting a girl at the pool or hacking into someone's bank account. (Or even bathing more often, for God's sake.)

As I sat at Gage's feet—black light hurting my eyes, listening against my will to the perverse whispers of Bryan Ferry—I wondered if my life was going to be one immersion after another, a great march of shallow, unpopular popular culture infatuations that don't really last and don't really mean anything. Sometimes I even think maybe my deepest obsessions are just random manifestations of my loneliness or isolation. Maybe infuse ordinary experience with a kind of sacred aura to mitigate the spiritual vapidity of my life. But, then again, maybe not.

As soon as I got home from Gage's, I threw on the record I longed to hear. Listening, I reconsidered my earlier despair—no, it is beautiful to be enraptured. To be enthralled by something, anything. And it isn't random. It speaks to you for a reason. If you wanted to, you could look at it that way, and you might find you aren't wasting your life. You are discovering things about yourself and the world, even if it is just what it is you find beautiful, right now, this second.

I am a person, I think, who feels comfortable in my isolation. Even someone like Gage (who is someone with whom admittedly I have a lot in common, a person with whom you might think I would enjoy keeping company) doesn't alleviate my feelings of loneliness. The effort it required just to be around him and tolerate him made me even more lonely. I am at home only in *my own personal* loneliness. The thing of it is I don't necessarily feel connected to Brian Wilson or any of the Beach Boys. But I do, I guess, feel connected to all the other people, alone in a room somewhere, who listen to *Pet Sounds*, on their way headphones who feel the way I feel. I just don't really want to talk to them or hang out with them. But maybe it is enough to know they exist. We identify ourselves by what moves us. I know this isn't entirely true. I know that's only part of it. But here's what else: Lately I find I wonder about my mother's loneliness. Is it like mine? Does she feel comfortable there? And if I am comfortable with it, sort of, why do I still call it loneliness? Because—and I think somehow she would understand this—you can have and recognize a sadness in your alienation and in other people's alienation and still not long to be around anyone. I think that if you wonder about other people's loneliness, or contemplate it at all, you've got a real leg up on being comfortable in your own.

9

Precious Resource (Rock and Our Generation of Novelists)

An Interview with Jonathan Lethem and Dana Spiotta

By Florence Dore

Florence Dore: Can you say something about why people your—our—age are bringing rock and roll so explicitly into novels? You two are important in this shift, but there are so many novels bringing rock explicitly into novels at the turn of the twentieth century. What's this about, in your opinion?[1]

Dana Spiotta: For me—and maybe this is also true for other writers in our generation—it is wanting to write fiction that engages with the cultural moment in multiple ways, particularly when I am writing about the past. Music is going to be a big part of that, as well as movies, books, technology, advertising, and historical events. How is 1978 different from 1968? Music is clearly a

1. Email interview with the authors, May 2018.

place we might detect a big change. What is popular reflects and colonizes the consciousness of the moment. Which is to say, a song of the summer or an ad tagline will change how language is used, even how we think. Most of the people I know, including myself, have music and movie and book references running through their minds all the time. These artifacts are part of how we make sense of the world, and it is part of how we build our identities. A character in my first novel says that if someone saw all the films she had seen in the order she had seen them, someone might truly understand who she is. The same is true for music. It is deeply tied to technology as well, as our generation grew up with LPs and mix tapes. We collected records, or many of us did, and the objects held meaning and that has changed pretty dramatically in the last thirty years. I guess I write so much about music because it is a part of the culture I can read in a compelling way.

As far as using cultural referents in novels, there is a long history of that, of course. *Ulysses* is full of popular song references from Dublin in 1916. We don't need to know the songs to get it, but it makes it more real, more alive, to have them in there. I have also been influenced by the wit with which Jonathan Lethem uses cultural artifacts. Like Doctorow, he is very adept at mixing imaginary references with real references. In *Fortress of Solitude*, for example, we get the real cultural references (Superman, Dylan, Eno), but we also get Barrett Rude Jr., a very persuasive imaginary soul musician, and we even get the elaborate liner notes for his boxed set—the ne plus ultra of how to pull off hybrid imaginary/real artifacts in fiction.

Jonathan Lethem: Thanks Dana, it's a thrill you feel that way. And your answer to this question is extraordinary, and speaks for me beautifully. What I'd add is that for me, after dwelling with them so long as a reader and writer, the area of mysterious energy for me in the novel has to do with their property of being both inside and outside individual consciousness, at a number of levels. They're machines for exploring the way solitary minds and voice plunge and plummet through collective social and political realms—they do the self-and-others in different voices. So, while novels are always personalizing the wide-screen cultural and political stuff—seizing it for examination as eccentric individual sensation and emotion—"What was it like to grow up and fight to become a person in such-and-such era of collective experience?"—they're also charged in the opposite direction: to use individual voice, subjective emotion, and interiority to say something about society and history, about the outer world the characters inhabit. I think that even when novels *try* to restrict themselves to individual subjectivity, they fail at that restriction. Even if they don't try to capture externalities—historical and cultural context, ways people were thinking about being people at a certain time and place—they do so anyhow. And, mostly, they don't avoid this assignment, but take it aboard at least half-willingly.

So, then you get rock 'n' roll and also the movies, which—putting aside treacherous notions of "the popular arts," or high v. low stuff—are unmistakably collective and outward arts, in the way they're received in the culture, in the way they take up space. For most, any personal, subjective intimate characters moving into collective space, coming of age inside it, they mark the wider and more collective experience one measures individuality against. If I'm wrong in speaking for anyone beside myself here, then at least you know how it feels to me.

Lastly, and not to get too Camille Paglia on you, but rock and roll is specifically a repository for Dionysian yearnings in a broadly anti-Dionysian culture, so it's a precious resource. Yes, I'm saying we're losers who don't know how to have fun!

FD: Dana, in the first two paragraphs of *Eat the Document* [excerpted above], a novel for which you lift your title directly from the documentary of the Bob Dylan tour, you make reference to "Like a Rolling Stone" and "Me and Bobby McGee." Can you say a little bit about why you chose to plunge readers into this character's consciousness as she thinks about her life in terms of rock lyrics? And generally about the choice of title?

DS: In writing *Eat the Document*, a novel about an antiwar activist who must live underground, it felt essential to the cultural context of 1972 to include the music of the era. The spirit of the antiwar movement was located in the music scene—more so than in books, for instance. The fact that the Weathermen got their name from "Subterranean Homesick Blues" shows the way music of the era shaped how the activists saw themselves. I chose *Eat the Document* because it has the sound of the language used at the time—like "Steal this Book"—but also because of Dylan, and because it was for many years an underground/lost film, which fits with the novel's interest in the cryptic history of American resistance. When the novel opens, she has just run away from her life, so I thought those lyrics would come to her.

But despite the Dylan and Kristofferson references you picked up on in the opening and throughout the book, the Beach Boys dominate. One of the contemporary characters, Jason, is a music collector, and obsessed with lost albums and obscurities. Through his obsession with the Beach Boys lost—at the time—album, *Smile*, he figures out his mother has had a different past than he realized. Dennis Wilson, the lost Beach Boy, even makes an appearance in the book. It fit the book that the Beach Boys had this very popular, innocent surface but they also had an unpopular, dark, tragic side. It seemed to line up with ideas I had about American identity. I needed the music references to make Jason's obsessiveness believable—I wanted to show what one gets out of listening to something over and over. Also, there is something exciting to me in writing about obsessed people. The challenge of it, maybe.

There is an American literary tradition of obsessive characters. In the ur-obsessive text *Moby Dick*, not only is Ahab obsessed with MD, but Ishmael is obsessed with whales and whaling. Ishmael's obsession necessarily becomes the novel's obsession, and Melville really had to go there with the details and specifics—the cetology, the sperm oil, harpooning, etc.—for it to express the weird paradox of worthy obsessions—they are both a constraint and a capacity. That is my model—I am very interested in that kind of excessive character in fiction. In Jason's case—and in Nik in *Stone Arabia*, my other music-centric book—writing required a willingness to nerd out.

FD: Jonathan, your character in *Fortress of Solitude* is literally a Dylan namesake—his parents were fans. At first he feels no connection to the artist, but by the end of the novel he's thinking in terms of the lyrics from Dylan's "Chimes of Freedom." Similar question to the one for Dana: Why does your character think in terms of Dylan lyrics—and Brian Eno lyrics, and Wild Cherry lyrics, etc.? Or why, even in your most recent novel, your surgeon must operate listening to Jimi Hendrix?

JL: I adore Dana's use of the rock references in *Eat the Document* and identify with them wholeheartedly, precisely because they were in part the stratum of the parents' culture, into which her character was born and involuntarily immersed and had to negotiate—and which requires of him that he become a kind of retrospective detective or archivist, as so many of us do in relation to the lives of our parents, whether in childhood or later on. This is precisely the situation of Dylan Ebdus in *Fortress*: he's surrounded with his mother's LP collection, the talismanic clues to her own self-invention in counterculture, long after she's flown the scene—I should say that, of course, I grew up with kids named Dylan, and there were many more who came along shortly after. I also knew a Miles and a Coltrane. So, Dylan, for Dylan, is a part of the air he's breathing before he knows it, but isn't, at first, an object of direct identification—he's associated not with himself but with his mysterious absent mother. Identification only creeps upon him gradually, when he realizes how directly and continuously Dylan's language and expressivity remains available, and isn't bounded to "the '60s."

FD: How important has Dylan—or for that matter any other of the architects of rock and roll you so clearly admire—been to your development as a novelist?

DS: I grew up listening to records alone in my room. The lyrics of the big icons, from Lou Reed to Dylan to Bowie to John Lennon—and on and on—certainly made me more playful with language. But it was the sensibility, maybe, that influenced me the most. The refusal to play nice in punk rock, the lyrical nihilism of Television, the irony in Bryan Ferry, the perversity mixed with resistance in Dylan, the combination of authenticity and artifice in Gram Parsons, the soulfulness of Big Star—I could go on and on—all certainly help shape my idea of what stance an artist should have toward the culture.

JL: Again, I get to stand on the shoulders of Dana's terrific reply. Me too, alone in my room. Poor us. And I'd underline a lot of those specific identifications for what Reed and Dylan and Bowie and Lennon and Tom Verlaine and punk et al. had on offer—but I'd also take what Dana says about Gram Parsons—"the combination of authenticity and artifice"—and let it cover the entire field. This connects to the Dionysian remark I made before: in a culture where Protestant values of earnestness and utility and industry have invested even into our art milieus (and heavily in our literary traditions), rock and roll generally emphasized and empowered a sense of theatricality, of the value of artificiality and self-invention, of *play*.

For me, as it happens, Dylan's lyrics made a kind of cornucopic resource of the kind of literary references that I *wasn't* stumbling upon—yet—by the operation of my own teenage reading impulses. Later I'd know the Beats, and Verlaine and Baudelaire, and the Lomax-type American blues lyrics, and these would all mean plenty to me. But I wasn't going to get there from my parents' bookshelves—though these were splendid in other resources—or by the public-school library offerings—though I did find J. B. Priestley and Alan Drury and, mercifully, Franz Kafka novels there—nor by reading crime and science fiction stories or either Marvel or Zap comics. So, Dylan was a kind of pocket index for voices that were either romantic, symbolist, or demotic.

FD: Would you care to comment on Bob Dylan winning the Nobel Prize in Literature? Do you think all of the rock and roll emerging in literature written by folks born in the 1960s contributed to his win? Are you pissed that Dylan got it over a novelist? What do you make of his win generally, in terms of this moment in time?

DS: I honestly don't have strong feelings about this. I'm fine with it! Plus Dylan's speech was all about *Moby Dick*, so it all ties together in the end.

JL: For me, it seemed natural, and a total gas. By chance I was listening to WNYC the morning it was announced, and my old colleague Claudia Rankine was being interviewed by Brian Lehrer—an interview that hadn't originally had anything to do with Dylan's Nobel, of course, but Lehrer brought it up since it was in the news that morning. Claudia gave it the simplest blessing, one I began to quote immediately: "His words are in everyone's mouths." She meant that he changed the language for poets and for all writers—which is different from claiming that his lyrics *are* poetry, which they're not, because they're lyrics. It never seemed in the least controversial to me, and I was startled when it became so. At first, disappointed that other writers were being so picayune. Not everyone is going to get a Nobel, but the point is for us to be excited about who does! Later, I saw this as a funny and appropriate response—the controversy. Dylan had become so gentrified, after the albums of the early aughts, and I'd assumed his ability to provoke and outrage, which had been one of his essential properties for decades, was finally exhausted. By giving him the Nobel, they renewed it.

10

Whack Fol the Daddy-O

How I Learned to Hate Irish Music Slightly Less

By Roddy Doyle

I hated Irish music. All of it. And it wasn't just the sound of it, the fiddles and the bodhráns, the whooping and wailing and the diddley-eye. It was everything about it, even the name of it, the "Irish", the label, the insistence on its purity and superiority, music as an arm of the state.

I hated a lot of things when I was seventeen—my teachers, my country, my religion, myself—but, especially, I detested the music. All the songs I'd been taught in primary school, the songs that told us that we weren't just different to, but better than, the English, the bad men from across the water who'd oppressed us for eight hundred years. *From Tassagart to Clonmore, there flows a stream of Saxon gore.* And the hymns, the dreary pleas to the God I didn't believe in anymore, and to his nonexistent mother—*Mother of Christ, Star of the Sea, pray for the wanderer, pray for meeeeeeeeee.* The hymns weren't strictly Irish—but they were.

But it wasn't just the rebel songs and the laments and the hymns that I hated. Anything with Irish-language lyrics, anything that mentioned a town that wasn't Dublin, any song that had the words "fields" or "curlew," or "lassie" or "lad," or "praties" or "whiskey" or "Amerikay," or "foe" or "river," or any of the mountains that sloped down to the sea, or any "boy," including, and especially, Danny Boy and the Minstrel Boy. I spat on any boy who ever popped out of any Irish song.

There was a sponsored show, *The Walton's Programme*, on RTE, the state radio station—on Saturday mornings, I think. The presenter, Leo Maguire, finished up with the same words every week: "If you feel like singing, do sing an Irish song." "Fuck off," I answered, silently, every Saturday.

My father was born in December 1923, a year after the foundation of the Irish state. He loved *The Walton's Programme*, and so did my mother, who was born two years later. My father was born an Irish citizen. If my grandmother had given birth to him a year earlier, he'd have been born a British subject. He arrived less than a year after the end of the Civil War. The death toll in that war was small, but the divisions were deep and bitter. My father grew up on one side of that division—the Republican side. So he was Irish, but Irishness was a brand new thing. And he grew up with people who felt that the new state wasn't Irish enough.

My father's name was Rory. He was given that name because he was born on the first anniversary of the execution of the Republican leader, Rory O'Connor. Rory O'Connor himself hadn't always been Rory O'Connor. He had changed his name from "Roderick" to a Gaelic version, "Rory," as an expression of his Irish nationalism. The change of name was a declaration of independence.

My father was born in the Rotunda Maternity Hospital, at the top of O'Connell Street, which had, until a few years before, been called Sackville Street—again, the name change as declaration. The General Post Office, or G.P.O., the site of the 1916 Rising, is on O'Connell Street. This was where, in the words of W. B. Yeats, "all changed, changed utterly—a terrible beauty is born." The street still showed signs of the damage inflicted during the British bombardment in 1916, and the more recent Civil War. Independence, the break from the British Empire, is easy to mark—the 6th of December, 1922. But how do we know when a Civil War is over? Rory O'Connor had been on the side that lost the Civil War, so my father's name was a quiet act of sedition.

This was the man who listened to *The Walton's Programme* with my mother. Every note he heard was a declaration of independence. For much of his life, to be Irish meant to be "not English." When asked by a French journalist if he was English, Samuel Beckett answered, "*Au contraire.*" My father would have nodded; the answer, while funny, would have made perfect sense. My parents grew up in a state determined not to be English. For many of its founders, the new state would be rural, Gaelic-speaking, and Catholic. Its geographical insularity would also become economic, cultural, and moral insularity. This was understandable but damaging. The nationalists were fighting the popular depiction of the Irish as charming but unreliable, stupid, drunken, scheming, incapable of feeding, let alone governing, themselves. The new Ireland would be a pure thing. Protestants and Jews would be less Irish than the real Irish, who were Catholic; Dublin, once the second city of the Empire, would be suspect, less a part of Ireland than the rest of Ireland; people who couldn't speak the Irish language would be barred from Government work. Sports such as soccer and rugby were foreign "garrison" games, left behind by the British. Ireland would have to live up to this new ideal—rural, Gaelic, and Catholic. *If you feel like singing, do sing an Irish song.*

The towering figure in Irish politics for much of my father's life was Eamon de Valera. He had vivid memories of the 1932 general election when de Valera and his party, Fianna Fáil, swept to power after ten years of, first, boycotting the Dáil, the national parliament, and then sitting in opposition. My father remembered helping his own father to grind glass, to put into the poster paste, so that anyone—supporters of other parties, or the police—trying to tear down the Fianna Fáil posters would have the skin torn off their fingers. (He claimed he saw the remains of one of those posters, still clinging to a wall more than thirty years later, in the early '60s, when he was visiting his mother.) He remembered a torchlight procession the night of the election count, as the victorious Fianna Fáil candidate was carried through his village, Tallaght, in South County Dublin. Fianna Fáil had been described as "slightly constitutional"—by one of its own supporters. There were guns in jacket and coat pockets when the newly elected Dáil convened. There was no need for the guns. Fianna Fáil and de Valera remained in power, only occasionally interrupted, for decades.

On Saint Patrick's Day, 1943, when my father was nineteen and serving his time as a printing apprentice, and the rest of Europe was at war, de Valera, the

Taoiseach, or Prime Minister, gave a radio address to the Irish people. Here's an extract:

> The ideal Ireland that we would have, the Ireland that we dreamed of, would be the home of a people who valued material wealth only as a basis for right living, of a people who, satisfied with frugal comfort, devoted their leisure to the things of the spirit—a land whose countryside would be bright with cozy homesteads, whose fields and villages would be joyous with the sounds of industry, with the romping of sturdy children, the contest of athletic youths and the laughter of happy maidens, whose firesides would be forums for the wisdom of serene old age. The home, in short, of a people living the life that God desires that men should live.

De Valera's ideal Ireland was a place of "homesteads," "fields," and "villages." There were no towns and cities. God, apparently, didn't desire that men should live in Dublin. In the ideal Ireland, youths were to be "athletic"; young women were to be "happy" and maidens; and the elderly were to anticipate encroaching dementia and incontinence with serenity. Given what had been happening on mainland Europe, words like "athletic" and "sturdy," presented as signals of the ideal, are almost sinister—and daft. And the word, "bright"—what window was de Valera looking through as he wrote that speech? In Ireland, it rains. Brightness isn't an ideal; it's an occasional meteorological occurrence—a rare fact between rain showers.

"If you're trapped in the dream of the other, you're fucked," said the French philosopher Gilles Deleuze.

"Not if you like Nat King Cole," my father might have answered.

Because he did.

I grew up in the shadow of that speech, or in the dying attempts to make that dream be true. I was eight in 1966, the fiftieth anniversary of the 1916 Rising. I learned the Proclamation of Independence—*Irishmen and Irishwomen, in the name of God and the dead generations*—off by heart. Every night of Easter Week, my family watched the TV drama *Insurrection*, a brilliant reenactment of the Rising. I died for Ireland every night and in the schoolyard the following morning. We sang the rebel songs that were a strong part of the curriculum. The opportunity to roar ourselves into battle was overpowering.

> The Minstrel Boy to the war has gone,
> In the ranks of death you find him.

There were fifty-three other boys in my class and there were no deserters; we were up to our knees in English blood as we sang and marched time beside our desks.

Many of the men who had fought in 1916, the men who had founded the State, were still alive, still in power. (There were women too, but we only found out about most of them decades later.) De Valera was the President; Seán Lemass, who was only sixteen when he fought, was the Taoiseach. I didn't really know it when I was eight, nine, ten, but my country, the Republic of Ireland, was a new one and the old men in their black coats and boots were still dreaming of a country that never came into existence—rural, Gaelic speaking, everything that wasn't English. I lived in a city, Dublin, I learned Gaelic only because it was a compulsory subject in school, and I was already listening to the Rolling Stones and the Beatles.

Actually, Sean Lemass had already abandoned the protectionist policies that had been in place since the 1930s, and the First Programme for Economic Expansion, introduced in 1958—the year I was born—encouraged investment from abroad. He also started the process that would result in Ireland joining the European Economic Community, now called the European Union. De Valera's ideal Ireland was going to be smothered by economics—and music.

My father brought home a record player. He carried it in from the car. The car was another recent acquisition; he was thirty-seven before he drove one, or could afford one. He put the record player on the floor and plugged it in. It was a simple box—grey and pink, I think.

Now let's see.

He'd also bought two records, the soundtrack of *South Pacific* and *The Best of Nat King Cole.* These were LPs, I learned. He showed us the small lever beside the turntable, which adjusted the speed for 33s, 45s, and 78s. He put *South Pacific* on the turntable. We watched the arm hover over the record, and descend—and we discovered the joy of listening to music at the wrong speed.

I discovered the joy of listening to music at any speed. My sisters were older than me and they started coming home with 45s—the Beatles, the Stones, the Tremeloes, Gary Puckett and the Union Gap, Desmond Decker, Glen Campbell, the Who, the Walker Brothers, the Monkees. My father came home with old box sets of Mario Lanza records and 1930s big bands; I don't know where he got them. He brought home Paul Robeson records—*Old Man River*, *The Peat Bog Soldiers*, *River Stay 'Way from My Door.*

My Uncle Joe had to retire young due to ill health and he returned from the USA. He lived with us and brought an incredible collection of records into the house—Smithsonian boxes of them. Woody Guthrie, Leadbelly, Muddy Waters, Lightnin' Hopkins—great names for an Irish boy to ponder, surrounded as he was by Patricks, Johns, and Marys. He brought home Irish American records too, America's idea of what Ireland was and should be. There were records by the McNulty Family—*A Mother's Love's a Blessing* and *When Rafferty Brought the Rumba to the Town of Aughnacloy*. I remember when I realized—*we* realized—that the noise we were hearing was feet. It was Irish dancing—on a record! And the split second of silence was all the dancers in the air, before they landed and got going again—*tappy tappy tappy tap tappy*. It was the only time I ever laughed at Irish dancing.

We got a better record player when I was fourteen or fifteen. The dog leaned against one of the speakers—always the left one—while I played Wishbone Ash, Stephen Stills, Pink Floyd, and Yes—records I bought myself, with money I'd earned working in a nearby hotel. The dog vibrated and I retreated into a world made up of the music and the cover art.

I sneered at everything Irish. I don't know when I stopped being the boy who wanted to die for Ireland and became the young man who hated everything about the place. In school, the Christian Brothers—bastards, all; I curse them nightly—were brutal and stupid, and especially brutal and stupid in their attempts to bully a love of Ireland into us—the language, the music. Irish literature didn't get much of a look in; a few poems by Yeats and Patrick Kavanagh were as much as we glimpsed and the poems did little to wobble my conviction that all things Irish were shite. I bought Joyce's *A Portrait of the Artist as a Young Man* with my own money, and I loved it; it didn't feel Irish. I bought *A Day in the Life of Ivan Denisovich* the same day and, to me, both books seemed to come from the same country, a language far, far away.

I roamed my patch of suburban Dublin with my friends and fellow haters. Dylan, Springsteen, and Lou Reed were our men. Their words shaped our heads. Van Morrison is brilliant too but—and I almost gasp writing this more than forty years later—he wasn't really Irish. He was a Protestant from the North, a place that seemed farther away than Springsteen's New Jersey, and he sang about things that, thank Christ, had nothing to do with what we saw. The North was where the Troubles were, the bombs and killings. Belfast is eighty miles away from my front door but, back then, it was on the dark side of the dark side of the moon. And Van Morrison had escaped.

The Wild, the Innocent and the E Street Shuffle—I climbed into that record. And *Blood on the Tracks*. And *Transformer*. And *Can't Buy a Thrill*. I sat in the classroom with my friends, Ronnie and Paul and Mick, and our other friends, Spanish Johnny, Holly, Candy, Little Joe, Dylan's Jack of Hearts and Steely Dan's other Jack—*wheel turnin' round and round*. I read somewhere that Irish music had Dylan's imprimatur, but I didn't believe it and I didn't care. The Bob I knew could never have liked the Clancy Brothers. The Dylan I listened to in bed, the Bob who sat beside me in the classroom, the man who sang—and sings—*Desolation Row* for me, would have vomited after the first few bars of *Brennan on the Moor*.

I don't trust what I'm writing here. I suspect it's dishonest. It's certainly selective. I won't be listing off the drivel I was listening to at the time; there are embarrassing sounds and haircuts hiding behind the stacks of Dylan, Lou Reed, and Steely Dan records. And I remember the thrill of watching Phil Lynott and Thin Lizzy play *Whiskey in the Jar* on *Top of the Pops*. Irishmen on the BBC, playing a traditional Irish song—*musha ring dum a do dum a da*—it was brilliant. But it was brilliant, I think, because they weren't simply playing the traditional Irish song: they were shredding it, converting it into rock 'n' roll, kicking the Irishness out of it. It was another act of sedition, years before I knew what "sedition" meant. I sat on the floor in our sitting room and watched Phil Lynott, and watched to see what my parents thought of it. My father got in behind his *Irish Independent* and muttered; my mother went into the kitchen. That's not true, by the way. I've no idea what my parents did, or if they were in the room. But I know: they wouldn't have liked it. More importantly, they wouldn't have approved of it and that made it—Phil Lynott on *Top of the Pops*—one of the key moments in the cultural and political history of Ireland. Lynott, a Dubliner, a *Black* Dubliner in leather trousers—the only Black Dubliner as far as I knew—singing an Irish song like he'd found it on the South Side of Chicago; it wasn't what de Valera had had in mind. Lynott's *Whiskey in the Jar* was some sort of exception that proved the rule: Irish music was shite. I didn't *know* that at the time. But I felt it—I think.

It was a book, not music, that started to nibble away at my hatred. As well as all the records, my Uncle Joe brought home hundreds of books. One of them was a hardback edition of Flann O'Brien's *At Swim-Two-Birds*. I hadn't heard of Flann O'Brien; it sounded like a made-up name. (I was right.) It was a name that poked fun at Irish names and it was enough to encourage me to open the book.

At Swim-Two-Birds was hilarious and wonderful. It lampooned Irish mythology and all of the official Irishness. But it did something else too: it made me fall in love with the words and the accent that I heard every day. It seemed that great literature didn't have to be Russian or French or American. *At Swim-Two-Birds* was great literature and it came from up the road. I remember laughing at phrases and rhythms that I hadn't realised were funny. And I was surrounded by them—at home, in school, everywhere. I didn't know it at the time but *At Swim-Two-Birds was* why I didn't emigrate.

I remember the afternoon I decided that the band would play soul.

I started to write my novel, *The Commitments*, in January 1986. It would be about a bunch of Dublin kids who form a band, and the idea, the decision—they'd play soul—came to me one evening as I waited at the station for the train home from work. It wasn't love of the music that steered me to the decision; it was the numbers. A soul band would be big—there'd be a horn section, there'd be women. I wanted a big band, I wanted a big gang of characters. Then it occurred to me that superimposing the Black American form on Dublin would be fun. I'd be able to mess with the lyrics; I'd be able to make the characters dance. I actually remember the moment, the decision, the ideas, as I watched the train—the Dart—come slowly toward me from Howth Junction.

By 1986, I'd been a secondary school teacher for more than six years. I was twenty-seven. The school was Greendale Community School, in Kilbarrack, on the northside of the city, a ten-minute walk from the house I grew up in. I remember the first day, and the first class. The room was quickly full of twelve-year-old boys and girls, and it was like opening *At Swim-Two-Birds* all over again. The words, the voices, the rhythm. The numbers. And that was the way it was, every day. I loved it. I loved being from this part of the world; I loved the way the English was spoken.

I wanted to write. I'd been messing around at it for years; I'd written what I quickly knew was a dreadful novel. It took a while to realize, and to accept, that I could write, somehow, about the things I witnessed, the voices I heard every day. I didn't want to write about a school, or a young teacher in a school, but I wanted the numbers and the voices. Most bands were three or four young men. I wanted more, and I wanted women in the band too. Soul would give me that, so my Dublin lads, the Commitments, became a soul band ten minutes after I got home to my flat in Clontarf that same evening. Soul was the excuse that gave me the numbers; the music came later.

They couldn't play their instruments at first. So it was their manager, Jimmy Rabbitte—I found the name in the Dublin area phone book—who gave them their direction. He, not unlike me, would have read a lot about soul, its history and personalities. So he fed this education to the band members as they learnt to play, and he recruited new members, including the three women who would become the Commitmentettes.

I remember: I was enjoying myself. I spent most of my time working on the dialogue—the extra letters, the deleted g's, the added apostrophes, the shortcuts. I was trying to get the Dublin accent onto paper. The music—the actual songs—could wait. And by the time I got to them, after I'd conquered the dialogue, and I started choosing the songs that I thought would work and began to transcribe them, I knew that the lyrics would have to be given a Dublin accent too. "What becomes of the broken hearted" became WHA' BECOMES O' THE BROKEN HEARTED. "What" is "wha'" and "of" is "o'"; just two dropped letters, but I thought I was inventing something. And I was: Dublin soul. It was fictional music but it was music and, somehow, it was Irish. Urban Irish, Dublin Irish, English language Irish—but Irish. Ireland was there to be heard in the folk music of America, and Black America was in the contemporary music of Ireland. Because, within the confines of my novel, I put it there. I'd found an Irish music that I could accept and love. I could calm down now.

But I didn't. Not for a long time.

Years after I'd self-published *The Commitments*, years after the movie, directed by Alan Parker, had been released, I was at wedding and the band started to play *Mustang Sally.* There was uproar, delight. Arguments stopped, flirting was put on hold. Pints were put back on tables, trousers were hitched. Everyone stood up. Everyone sang along. Everyone. *Mustang Sally* had become a traditional Irish song.

I hate *Mustang Sally*, but that's a different story.

PART III

Rock's Literary Identity

Musicians on Literature

11

Dear Dylan

An Interview with Lucinda Williams

By Florence Dore

Florence Dore: I am really just interested in hearing you talk about the relationship that you see between literature and music, and there's a few ways that I thought we could talk about it. One is Flannery O'Connor—I remember a long time ago reading in an interview that someone had complained about your music as dark and you said, "well, nobody ever complained about Flannery O'Connor being dark." Which is a good point. But since then, you've talked more about her, and said that you sometimes felt like a character in a Flannery O'Connor story—which I can relate to—and that he was your dad's biggest influence. So perhaps you could talk about your reading, and the relationship between your experience of literature and your experience as a songwriter.

Lucinda Williams: OK. Well, I discovered her writing when I was a teenager, and also the works of Eudora Welty and Carson McCullers, and I really delved into Southern short story writers.

FD: Southern women.

LW: Yeah. She was my dad's mentor; to quote him, he said, "Flannery O'Connor was my greatest teacher" when he was starting out. And even as a kid, reading that stuff, there's so much realism in it, oddities and weird people and all that, but to me it just seemed pretty, y'know, normal. Because I guess growing up in parts of the South, and there were all of these exaggerated characters, I learned the meaning of Southern Gothic. And realized that I had relatives—both my grandfathers were Methodist ministers. My dad's father was a Christian in the true sense of the word. He was for equal rights and was a socialist democrat, and he was involved in the Southern Tenant Farmers' Union struggle. My mother's father, on the other hand, who was also a Methodist minister, was more like hellfire and brimstone. So my mother's family, some of them were more like the type of people you'd meet in [a] Southern Gothic. So I saw a lot of different sides of the South. My father being a writer, I grew up with really open-minded, literary, progressive people.

FD: What year was your dad born?

LW: I was born when he was twenty-one; I was born in '53, and I'm sixty-six now, so he would have been born in '32 or something.

FD: Okay, so he'd be in his eighties. And the reason I ask is that he's a little older than my mother, who took the last class that John Crowe Ransom ever taught, so he's of that generation that literature and folk music were really blended together.

LW: Oh yeah. I was getting excited with all this stuff going through my head when you mention John Crowe

Ransom, because my dad knew him. Because that whole writers' world is really small. I never got to meet John Crowe Ransom, but there were always people that would, because my dad taught college, creative writing—

FD: Mine did, too.

LW: —they would probably have a lot in common.

FD: Faculty brat. But my father was an asshole; your father sounds like he was a nice guy.

LW: Well, he could be pretty critical; he described himself one time as "Yes, I could be a little prickly at times." But we moved around until he achieved tenure at the University of Arkansas in 1971. We lived a year or two here, a year or two there; he taught at different colleges around the South: LSU in Baton Rouge, Loyola in New Orleans, Millsaps in Jackson.

FD: Wow, he sounds peripatetic like a songwriter. I have a book I'll have sent to you because I think you'll like it a lot. One of the things I discovered is that Cleanth Brooks and Robert Penn Warren, when they were at Vanderbilt in the 1930s—and they still kind of continued their influence in the 1950s—they put together an anthology called *Understanding Poetry*, which probably influenced your dad and generations of writers and literature teachers. And in that anthology you find Shakespeare and John Donne and T. S. Eliot, who you would expect, but you also find a bunch of ballads, which is fascinating, including "Frankie and Johnny," which Lomax recorded Lead Belly singing four years before that book came out. So there's this really deep overlap among people in your dad's generation; they were the inheritors of that overlap.

LW: You're so right, that's so spot on. Because that's the stuff I started out with. When I first started taking guitar lessons, which was in 1965, I had the John and Alan Lomax *Folk Song USA* book.

FW: So you're learning those songs?

LW: I'm learning those songs, and I'm exposed to poetry and poets who come through town and give readings and hang out with my dad, like James Dickey—he was on the staff at the Bread Loaf Writers' Conference. We went there a couple of summers, and all the writers would be there, and everybody would gather in the big barn in the evening. I was about sixteen or seventeen, and my dad would say, "Go get your guitar" and I'd bring my guitar and sing songs. The director at Bread Loaf was another one of my dad's mentors—his daughter was a folk singer; this would've been in like 1968, '69.

FD: Right around when Dylan is doing all the folk stuff. And hanging around with Allen Ginsberg.

LW: I discovered Bob Dylan, the first album I heard was *Highway 61 Revisited*, in 1965, which was the year I started taking guitar lessons. A student of my dad's, that was the other crossover thing, because he had students who would be listening to Bob Dylan or Leonard Cohen, so I would be exposed to stuff at an early age that I might not have been otherwise. I remember a student of my dad's came over with *Highway 61 Revisited* and waving it in the air and saying, "This is the new Bob Dylan album, it's amazing!" He set it down and literally went into another room, into my dad's office to talk with him, and I looked at it and threw it on the turntable, and it basically changed my life. Not changed my life, but even though I was only twelve and a half years old, there was something on that album I could connect; I could see the connections between the traditional folk music like Woody Guthrie and the literary world. Which were the two worlds that I came out of. So I heard what Bob Dylan was doing and I went, Wow, I really like this—something in my little twelve-year-old head went "I want to try to do this somehow." It was all just happening so fast, but I connected with it.

FD: In my book I have a chapter on William Styron's novel *Set This House on Fire*, which I guess he published in 1960. And I was looking through his letters, and that connection goes back further than I knew, before I started doing research for this book. Styron wrote to his writing teacher, I don't know what college he was at, said to his writing teacher, "You really have to listen to Lead Belly." This was like 1942, William Styron to his literary mentor, basically. So that connection that you were experiencing in the 1960s, I think it's amazing that it went back even further. And I'm going to come back to asking you about your first record in a second, but the other thing I discovered is that John Lomax went to Harvard for a year and worked with this guy George Lyman Kitteridge who was a Shakespearean and a Chaucer scholar. And his mentor was Francis James Child, who put together the ten-volume Child Ballads.

LW: Oh yeah, the Child Ballads. That's interesting.

FD: So Child was into Chaucer and Shakespeare. And Lomax worked with them.

LW: Wow. I knew about the Child Ballads, but I didn't know the history, about the person. That's what's missing now, I think, in the whole music world, is that connection with the literary world. Because the whole folk music scene was so literarily alive, it was developed on the college campuses, everybody was reading, a lot of them were going to Harvard, y'know, Kris Kristofferson, wherever he went, they were well read, educated, politically aware, and all of that.

FD: Have you seen the new Bob Dylan movie that's on Netflix [*Rolling Thunder Revue*, 2019]?

LW: I haven't seen it yet.

FD: You'll love it, and that's one of the things, what you're just describing comes through really clearly—that they're poetic, they're into it as a way of life. It's really quite striking to see—like, Patti Smith gets onstage, and she starts talking and she's weirdly grabbing something on her shirt and you can't tell if it's part of the performance or if she's just kind of on drugs or free associating, but then it's clear it's part of her thing, and then the band kicks in. So it's this whole merging of stream of consciousness and poetry and rock and roll. It's cool as shit.

LW: I know, and that's what I started making a connection with, not just with Bob Dylan, but with Jim Morrison of the Doors, and Patti Smith, and later David Byrne in Talking Heads, that whole thing. Now I'm into this guy Atmosphere, who's a poet, like hip-hop, I don't even like to use the word hip-hop, but for lack of a better word. He's out of Minneapolis, and he's an amazing writer, lyricist, the whole thing.

FD: So how this makes me think about your first record, I always thought it was interesting that it came out on the Smithsonian label.

LW: I know, and of course I had this really romantic vision of Folkways. Because a couple of the earliest Folkways albums I heard were at a friend if my dad's house, probably another writer, his wife, and their family, they had these two Folkways albums and they were the really heavy vinyl, in between a 45 and a regular-sized album, and the album covers were heavy, they were this heavier cardboard. Anyway, they were called *Songs to Grow On*, volumes 1 and 2. And it was Woody Guthrie and Pete Seeger, and it was all, like, kids' songs. So the whole Folkways thing was so strong back in the midsixties, when I started playing songs. And I guess it was in 1977, or something like that, I'd been playing for a few years, a friend of mine from New Orleans had moved up to New York City and had done an album for Folkways. And we were talking on the phone, and I was still living at home at that point, and his name was Jeff Ampolsk—I can't believe I can remember his name—and he did an album called *God, Guts, and Guns* for Folkways. Mo Asch was still running it, little Jewish guy, little flirt y'know, and he was getting up there. He was kind of hard of hearing, did that kind of New York thing—that old New York folkie thing that I just revere. I'm thinking, Folkways, y'know, this is like. . . . So anyway, my friend Jeff said, "Well, you can make a record on Folkways too." And I said, "Really?" And he said, "Yeah, just make a cassette tape of the songs and send it to him."

And so I did, and at the time I was writing a little bit, but I didn't really consider myself—I figured this is Folkways, they're not going to want to hear original songs. So I sent 'em some stuff and they sent me back this one-page contract and a check for $250. Because as far as they were concerned, they were doing all those field recordings and it didn't really matter, you didn't have to go into a studio. But this friend of my dad's who was a civil rights attorney in Jackson, Mississippi, one of his clients was an engineer at Malaco Studios in Jackson. So Tom Royals—you'll see his name, a thank-you to him on that album—he got us an afternoon in that studio. And I went in with this other guitar player from Houston, and just recorded everything, two tracks, in one afternoon.

And then I got to do that second album, and I had all my own songs, that was the first time. And for that album they sent me $500. I had some friends in Houston . . . and we ended up going into Sugar Hill Studios and doing that one there.

And then I went up to New York, I moved up there. I was of course always too late—I was too young to go to Woodstock, I just missed the scene everywhere, by the time I got to New York the punk scene was over. It was kind of a weird time to be up there, the late seventies. But anyway, that's kind of my Folkways story.

FD: It's great, it's incredible the legacy that represents. Because Mo Asch is the one who recorded Lead Belly, all of 'em. And it's really that approach, that way of I guess marketing and understanding southern and Black folk music at the time that made it seem like literature to some of these other people, some of these literary types. So you're right in there—that to me is part of that same legacy.

LW: Yeah.

FD: And when you recorded the one with "Passionate Kisses" and everything on it . . .

LW: On Rough Trade . . .

FD: . . . yeah, that one changed my, I was like woo-hoo, I can play country music now. I was living in Boston and playing music. Anyway, when you did that, can you talk about the relationship between that and the Folkways stuff? Were you trying to be like, y'know, I don't want to be a folk artist exactly, or were you still tied to that, or . . . Because I think that record was really innovative for the moment, first of all it was a woman's voice, but also bringing that Dylan thing, that kind of folk rock overlap but into a different era. There's something different about it.

LW: I had been playing around after those Folkways albums, I moved back to Texas from New York, and was living in Houston, and then Austin again, and then went out to L.A. in 1984. I was playing around there, and was writing more, and I got a development deal, they used to call them, with Sony Records, which meant I got a salary, which was enough to live on for six months, and I was like, oh my god I don't have to work a day job. And I had a little apartment in Silver Lake, and I didn't have any credit cards, and I didn't have all this debt stuff. So I was happy—all I had to do was work on songs. And the idea was that I would write songs and then do a demo tape and turn that into the label, and then they would decide if they were going to sign me or not. So I did that, I had all these songs, including "Passionate Kisses"—pretty much all the songs on the Rough Trade album were on this demo tape, which was produced by this guy Henry Lewy, who had worked with Joni Mitchell, Leonard Cohen. He brought in all these amazing guys to play on it: some of the guys from NRBQ, David Mansfield, Garth Hudson from the Band played keyboards. Anyway, we got all that done, but then the label passed on it. And I was being courted at that time by like every label, every major label and all the small labels. They all noticed something, and they were interested, but nobody knew how to quote-unquote market me. Now we're already into the age where, it's not the sixties or seventies anymore, it's gotta be called something, we don't know what it is, it's not really country, it's not really rock, it falls in the cracks. That's what they told me when Sony heard the demo tape. First they sent it to Sony in Nashville, who said it was too rock for country. And Sony in L.A. said it was too country for rock. So all these labels passed on me, just one after the other after the other. And I was just about ready to go back to Texas, and somehow a copy of the tape wound up with this guy who was working for Rough Trade Records. He heard it and liked it and talked to me about, "Do you want to make a record? We love the songs." It took a European punk label to take a chance on me. So that's how that came about.

FD: Great story. In relation to all this, I would be really interested in hearing what your take on Dylan winning the Nobel Prize is. I know it's old news.

LW: When I was in New York, Bill Flanagan does this radio show, I can't remember what station, but I was invited to come on the air with D. A. Pennebaker, who did *Dont Look Back*, the Bob Dylan film, and these other two writers who I'm embarrassed that I can't remember their names but I can find out, one of them is a really well-known Irish writer, but anyway, it was to talk about that. And I kind of had mixed feelings about it, and I think it's just because I hear my dad's voice in my head, because I looked up to him and wanted to please him all the time. But I remember distinctly, back in the sixties when everybody was falling in love with Bob Dylan, his writing students would come over to the house and they'd stay up late drinking and discussing literature and music, and they'd get into these debates about whether Bob Dylan was a poet or a songwriter. 'Cause in my dad's world, those were two different things. And the younger generation, his students, would say "Bob Dylan's a poet," and my dad would say, "No. He's not a poet, he's a songwriter." So that was going on around me.

FD: It was already a conversation in your house.

LW: It was already a conversation in the house, and then when he won the Nobel Prize, I could hear my dad saying, "Oh my God, I can't believe he won the Nobel Prize." I was actually asked at that thing with Bill Flanagan what my dad would think, and I told them he probably would have said, "No, he's not a writer. What's he doing with the Nobel Prize?" But on the other hand, Bob Dylan's a poet, but that's a tough one because my dad always differentiated between the two. I tell you what really hit home with me was when I took one of my dad's poems and made it into a song. It was something that'd I wanted to do for a long time, and I was working on this one really favorite early poem of his called "Why Does God Permit Evil?" It's this long, rambling poem and really hard to put into a song. And when I was working on songs for, I think it was *Down Where the Spirit Meets the Bone*, my husband Tom actually suggested "Compassion": "Why don't you take this and see what you could do with this?" And it was very challenging, because in my mind you don't just stick a melody on a poem. So I had to rearrange it and make it into a song. So in that regard, poems and songs are completely different.

Songs have melodies to carry them; poetry doesn't have a melody, it's carried in a different way. But at the same time, yes Bob Dylan is poetic, but there is a difference; poetry and songs are different. I think that he's a literary songwriter. Probably what pissed me off is he didn't show up! That's the real issue. Patti Smith had to go, bless her heart, and try to memorize—I don't know why to this day that she didn't just write the words down and have them in front of her. I never would've tried to do that song without it. And then she forgot some of the words and she felt horrible. . . . I've read the whole article she wrote about that. But you know, anyway, bless Bob's heart. I got to meet him briefly one time when I was living in New York that one year I was there, I was playing at Folk City, I got to get up and play a couple of songs, and he came by. Because he used to come by to see Mike Porco, who was the original owner of Folk City. Little Italian guy. And Bob dropped in, he was sitting at the bar, Mike Porco introduced us. And I thought I'd . . . it was the strangest . . . I'm not kidding when I say that there was an aura. It was like meeting my . . . I mean I was madly in love with him in my little teenage world. I used to write in my diary, "Dear Dylan . . ." I don't tell too many people that because it's embarrassing, but to me he was like those two worlds, the perfect blend.

12

Iambic Pentameter and the Blues

An Interview with Steve Earle

By Florence Dore

Florence Dore: Steve, you're a songwriter. But let's talk about your relationship to literature, your history with it.

Steve Earle: Do you remember when we recorded? You were around for the sessions of *The Revolution Starts Now* and *Jerusalem*, a lot of them.

FD: Yeah, I remember that.

SE: When we recorded "Warrior," the way it happened was . . . I had the idea that I was going to do this spoken word piece in iambic pentameter on purpose. It was me, right before I turned fifty, deciding that I was going to . . . learn to do some stuff that I didn't get quite far enough in high school to learn how to do. I'd become fascinated with theater, fascinated with Shakespeare again, all over again. I was at a point where I got to see more plays . . . but I first became interested when the Globe opened in London.

FD: Which was what year? It was in the '90s, wasn't it?

SE: It opened in '94, I think, because I missed Mark Rylance's *Hamlet* because I was homeless and in jail that season. I went to England after I got sober in '96—and I went the first time then, and I saw basically every all-male cast Shakespearean production that Rylance did over the years.

FD: How old were you in this period, when you started going to Shakespeare plays in London?

SE: Back when I was seeing that stuff . . . I was forty. You know, so that whole decade—forty to fifty—was a lot of catching up. I stopped taking drugs and [when you do that you] feel like you have all the time in the world [because] you don't have to find, you know, several thousand dollars' worth of narcotics every day. So I took up a lot of stuff. I started writing prose, which began as my journals that my sponsor made me keep. And that sort of morphed into short stories and became a book. Then I immediately started talking about writing a novel and started dabbling with that. I wrote a play . . . and then . . . poetry had become more important to me. I started reading a lot of poetry.

FD: Like what kind of stuff? Like Allen Ginsberg? And that kind of . . .

SE: Oh, that stuff I already knew chapter and verse. I read *Howl* the first time when I was fourteen.

FD: Oh, really?

SE: It was written the year I was born. You know—

FD: Is that through Bob Dylan?

SE: Probably . . . I mean, I became aware of, it's weird, everything for me is backtracking.

FD: Me too, but in music.

SE: I knew who Allen Ginsberg was. I knew who Jack Kerouac was. But, in 1969, I read *The Electric Kool-Aid Acid Test* by Tom Wolfe. And just like I backtracked from the Creedence Clearwater version of "That's Alright, Mama" to the Elvis Sun Records, I backtracked in literature. . . . It all begins with Kerouac and Ginsberg. So reading poetry for me, and what got me to the Beats was *Electric Kool-Aid Acid Test*. Neal Cassady was a Prankster, and I got fascinated with that character. And Allen pops up in the narrative in a couple of places. And several people who are my friends now, Wavy Gravy is throughout that book, and, he's one of my best friends. You know, I've been really lucky. I've been able to meet a lot of my heroes, and only two have been assholes, so far.

FD: Ha, that's pretty good. Well, alright, you're into poetry, you're reading Ginsberg, you're reading Kerouac—

SE: I was also reading Carl Sandburg because around the same time I'm reading all this Beat poetry . . .

FD: And this is when you're how old? Remind me.

SE: Fourteen, fifteen. So, I'm in high school by that time, and I have a drama teacher whose name is Vernon Caroll, and he and a biology teacher named George Chambers—who also had one of the best local country bands and still plays around San Antonio, and he's eighty-five or eighty-six now. He lives next door to Johnny Bush, and he and Willie Nelson are old, old friends. He never left because he was teaching school, he was single . . . and he took care of his mother and he went to Nashville to make records, but he never could make the commitment to leave his mom. She lived to be really old, so he was the only teacher at our school who drove a Mercedes convertible because he made more money playing around town on the weekends than he did at school. But he and Vernon Caroll were younger, and they knew what they were looking at when they saw me. I was doing terrible in school and I was in trouble all the time, and the only two classes I wasn't kicked out of were biology and drama. They made sure they gave me the right records and the right books.

FD: What did they give you?

SE: There was this really kind of high level musicianship in country music in south Texas, and George turned me on to that . . . Vernon Caroll gave me the first copy of *The*

Freewheelin' Bob Dylan that I ever had. Backtracking again: my first Dylan record was *Highway 61.* I knew about the other records, I'd learned to play "Don't Think Twice, It's All Right" out of a book. And I think I learned it from the Peter, Paul and Mary version. 'Cause it was just—*Freewheelin'* was the only Bob Dylan record that's ever been out of print. It was out of print all through, like, the second half of the '70s and up to the '80s and I had to go buy a copy—my first trip to New York to do press when *Guitar Town* came out I went to Bleecker Bob's and bought a copy of *Freewheelin'* because the only way you could get it was to find it on vinyl at a shop like that.

FD: So you're doing that, your drama teacher and your teachers at school are like "Here, you should have *The Freewheelin' Bob Dylan*." Were you writing songs during that time?

SE: I started writing songs around that time, most of them had girls' names as titles, but yeah. I started trying to do it, yeah. I started the first song that I ever wrote at fourteen. Er, no, I take that back, I was thirteen. I was thirteen. I started that before I was in high school. It was terrible, but I wrote it.

FD: And so, you're listening to these records and just sort of reading on your own, and you drop out of school but you keep reading.

SE: I . . . dropped out; every English teacher I got except one was a fucking football coach, so there was no help. But it was kind of logical the way I went about it. I knew what I was missing. There was like, like, the thread from Tom Wolfe, right-wing cocksucker that he was—great writer though, you know, years later, *The Right Stuff* is still one of my favorite books. But I backtracked to Kerouac and Ginsberg from that and then, as I'm reading, you know, by the time I was fourteen I was hanging out in this coffeehouse called the Gatehouse, and you know people that were older than me talked about books and I would go out and try to find them. Tried to read Dostoyevsky and failed.

Just couldn't get my head around it. And I discovered Hemingway, and I went from Hemingway to Graham Greene. It was sort of a logical thing when you were doing it yourself. There's logical threads you can follow. . . . I read some Dos Passos because I got ahold of Hemingway's letters, and half of them are to John Dos Passos.

FD: So you're a writer at that point, you're a songwriter, you're young, but you're writing songs, and you're reading this stuff. Are you reading Hemingway's letters because you want to know, you want to be a writer?

SE: I'm still writing songs because I'm trying to get girls to notice me, I'm still emulating the Beatles, and you know—

FD: But you're looking to literature and Bob Dylan for your inspiration?

SE: They don't merge until a few years later. I don't come to the understanding that . . . oh, wait, I'll tell you what happened. I was in San Miguel de Allende, I'd been writing songs for several years, I'd been to Houston already, I'd been to Nashville. Had a publishing deal.

FD: And how old were you then, like twenty?

SE: Twenty. And I knew all about Bob Dylan by then, chapter and verse. I knew the Beatles. I knew that there was this relationship. The epiphany about the relationship between Dylan and the Beatles came later. And I think it's important—that rock and roll becomes an art form at the moment when John Lennon wants to be Bob Dylan and Bob Dylan, just as importantly, wants to be John Lennon. 'Cause Bob was born to raise the level of lyrics in modern songwriting. He was a literary animal. He was put here to do that. And Lennon wanted to do it, but I think that he, he had all kinds of chances. He was in art school. There are people who'll write me all sorts of hate mail for saying this, but . . . and I'm not saying that he wasn't an artist, he was. But it was work for him. He had to push himself. The musical talent came very naturally, but I don't think he had the discipline that Bob Dylan had. Bob Dylan drove everybody nuts, listening to every record that they had. And when he figured out that the kind of pop singer that was going to be the next big thing—I do think this was his motivation, at least to impress the girls with turtlenecks he was running into by the time he was college age and got to New York—was folk music. He figured out that that was becoming a big thing. So, he drove everybody nuts, he got a hold of those records, and he hung out at the fucking Folklore Center listening to the entire fucking Harry Smith collection. He knows every single song in it. I've heard him talk about so many of them, there's no doubt in my mind that Bob knows every single song in it.

FD: And the Child Ballads, from there . . .

SE: Absolutely. Without a doubt. Because all that stuff was available. Izzy had all that stuff. And he talks about it in *Chronicles*. Bob gives Izzy props about that, about providing that for everybody. Bob just did more with it. Other people got the idea that they could write their own songs. You know, Tom Paxton started writing songs around the same time that Bob did. The idea that, Oh, we don't have to just sing these hundred-year-old songs, we can start with the form and make our own folk music. That's what they did, you know.

FD: So, making their own folk music, listening to Harry Smith, and you're interested in Dylan and you're interested in literature, how does all that come together, do you think?

SE: At San Miguel de Allende, in 1980, I mean, I'm already doing it. Just like, what I discovered from my iambic pentameter exercises was, oh yeah, I'm already writing in iambic pentameter, I just didn't know it.

FD: So can you describe your iambic pentameter exercise?

SE: Yeah, I basically, wanted to write something in iambic pentameter because I was on this Shakespeare jag, and I finally got it, I finally realized that you're not supposed to get it when you read them, that's not what it's for. And I saw enough Shakespeare between films and on stage, over a period of ten years that I started to get it, and I wanted to do that. And oh, also, *Deadwood* happened. And *Deadwood* was huge.

FD: I remember you showed it to me and Will when we were first together—

SE: I freaked the fuck out. I'm just watching the whole thing—I'm one episode away from finishing the whole series again, 'cause the movie came out. And I met David Milch, and I'm not very often in awe of people, but him I was.

FD: So you saw that, you're into Shakespeare, and you're experimenting.

SE: I decided to write this song, a spoken word piece called "Warrior." The idea was a chorus, like one of these things that Shakespeare did to set the stage. But I sort of made it [differently]; in "Warrior" the character was War. You know, whatever the entity is that's called Mars in one culture and Ares in another culture or Boogla Boogla in a different culture, it doesn't make any difference. It's War as an entity, you know, a god is another thing to call that, but it's just basically War as an entity. That's really all making up the gods was, it's poetry. It is poetry. Writing scripture is poetry. It exists for a reason. So, the idea was War conspiring against the lessers, us. And one inspiration for it was somebody who was very into Shakespeare and into Robert Frost, and translations of French poets—rather than Beat poets: Townes van Zandt. His influences were different from Bob's, they were way more conventional. And I did *The World of Carl Sandburg* in high school, which is, Carl Sandburg was the other big folk song collector besides the Lomaxes. It's based on his folk song collection, *The American Songbag*, and a bunch of his poetry, and I got really into that stuff. And I had just reached this point where I was going to try and do this iambic pentameter thing. I took the chorus, the prologue of Act I of *Henry V*, the "O, for a muse of fire," one of the most beautiful things ever written, and I laid it out on—I divided it into three sort of logical places to stop the narrative—

FD: You wrote it out?

SE: Well, on a computer—I did everything on a computer. I took it and downloaded it off the internet, I copied it, pasted it into a document, and then I divided it to put instrumental sections into it and arbitrary verses, because it's really one verse. It's almost one thought. So, it's just, think when we say "horses" that you see them. He actually says that. He's setting up the audience and he's mainly trying to impress on the audience that you're in the play. It's that fucking wall coming down, it's the fourth wall coming down. He takes it down right at that point. He needs a crowd, he needs a crowd for Henry V to make this big speech to, later in the play, and he's really setting that up at the beginning of the play. So I just divided it up.

I was in a play called *The Exonerated* in New York before this, as a guest, an actor, but wasn't really acting. I was reading it off of a page. It was about death row exonerees, and Bruce Kronenberg was one of the professional actors that was sort of the anchor, actors at either end of this line of people, some were reading, but there were two actors, or four actors actually that were off-book that sort of propelled the whole thing and kept it going. I met Bruce doing that. He was a big music fan and, by that time, he had kind of become part of my family. He was single. He spent Thanksgiving and Christmas with me in Tennessee. You know, it was the summer that I moved, I ended up moving to New York the next summer, but I was in the process, I was spending a lot of time in New York. And Bruce was there hanging out when we made the record, 'cause I just invited him down to hang out. And I showed him what I wanted him to do. I said, "I want you to read this so we can cut a track and then I'm going to write my lyrics." And I already had ideas about it, about where I wanted it to go, but I had him read that chorus, the whole thing. And then, I let everybody go, and I went into the house, they had this house up there, Old Hickory. And I sat down, and in about three and a half or four hours I divided, I doubled-spaced it all, the three verses, on a page. And I wrote in between so I could match it iamb by iamb, you know just visually. And then I finished it, we recorded it, and I remember you saying, you know, you were listening to it and you said, "This is familiar," so I said, "Well, it's in iambic pentameter." And you said, "Oh, that's why it's so beautiful," and I've never forgotten that.

FD: Aw, that means a lot to me.

SE: Somebody told me that they read something somebody wrote about "Warrior," like a negative comment about that song—saying that it was like a grade-school English exercise, and it was. But it was probably someone who had never read in iambic pentameter in their lives. And you know, I was doing it all along. I realized that a lot of the blues, a lot of other stuff, is all iambic pentameter, when it gets right down to it. Sometimes it's not exact—sometimes the lyrics themselves perform the correct pentameter, but the combination of the lyrics and the instrumental stuff doesn't. Because blues has so much call and response stuff, where somebody sings something and the instrumental part finishes the phrase. It's a really common thing in the blues, and a lot of it is back in iambic pentameter.

FD: Right, and I remember you saying when you came to the National Humanities Center that it was something about a heartbeat.

SE: Yeah, it's like [makes thumping sound]. That's an iamb. An iamb's not a beat, it's a beat and the space after the beat. It's just like in haiku. If we're taught to write haiku in this culture, the best we can understand it is based on English, which is this big, square, clunky Germanic language. And, Japanese is not that. And, it's, there's . . . Japanese phonetic divisions and they're more like iambs, it's like the accent's in the opposite place. . . . A syllable is one fucking Germanic clapping on the one beat. You know? Iambs are [makes pounding sound]; it's a heartbeat.

FD: So, how do you think you got from reading Shakespeare or going to those Shakespeare plays after you're sober, reading all the Shakespeare that you read, to deciding that that needs to be in a song?

SE: I just wanted to do it and songs are what I do, it's a spoken word piece. It didn't have to be a song, it's just, I wasn't going to get to do it and get paid for it unless it was a song. I had already written a play by this time.

FD: But were you feeling some sort of desire to connect with what Shakespeare was doing?

SE: Absolutely, I wanted to try to understand it.

FD: In a feeling sort of way, experientially.

SE: They call these things that artists do "disciplines" for a reason. And, you know, it's hard, you have to work really hard at it because no one tells you when to punch the clock. I used to think, for a while there I thought, well I made it—when I was my thirties—because I finally got good enough. But I wrote "Tom Ames' Prayer" when I was nineteen years old and "Ben McCulloch" when I was twenty. We're doing the "Mercenary Song" on this tour, which I wrote when I was nineteen years old. Those are really good songs and I'm proud of them. I wrote a lot of shit that I don't repeat but that's mostly being distracted by trying to find a way to write something that Nashville would like rather than just writing the way that I wanted to. I think I wasted a lot of time trying to please other people. And when I finally decided to write myself an album, I wrote *Guitar Town*.

FD: Do you think that folk music is connected to what Shakespeare was doing?

SE: Yeah, because it was entertainment for the masses. I don't believe that the glovemaker's son from Stratford without an education could have done it; I think education is valuable. Bob didn't have zero education; he's super fucking smart, and he had a year of college, I think, maybe two, by the time he showed up in New York. He was largely an auto-didact, though, not a lot of formal education the way we value it. You know yourself there's this thing about education; I regret my lack of education more than anything else, and that's saying something because I've done some fucked up shit. But I also think there's a track in academia for artists and it's one of those deals. Poets have to be fucking teachers in order to survive, there's no fucking way to survive otherwise.

FD: Bruce Springsteen on Broadway . . .

SE: I saw it, it was incredible, and when you go and see it live, it's theater . . .

FD: Beautiful spoken word in that . . .

SE: It's his book, you realize that right, straight from his book. . . . And he can write.

FD: He says at one point in the performance, you can't do this if you don't feel like running away from school—like this is not for you. What do you think about that?

SE: I believe that. He's like me in that he always knew what he wanted to be, that's what me and him have in common. He's like, Bob Dylan had been in my job, but Bruce Springsteen's probably had more direct effect on me, me watching someone especially from afar. Because I knew Townes Van Zandt when I was seventeen years old, and I knew Guy Clark when I was nineteen. I met Neil Young when I was twenty years old; I met a lot of people. Springsteen though, number one, he is the greatest performer that rock 'n' roll ever produced, probably. And I think that includes Mick Jagger; I think that includes maybe James Brown—Springsteen is his equal if you want to consider James Brown to be part of rock 'n' roll rather than R&B. And I think you can do both, I think he transcends that. Bruce Springsteen is the best communicator I ever saw in rock 'n' roll. Of course he's working post-70s, after Bowie had sort of turned it into theater and put that wall back up, you know, which is great. And it *is* art, but it's a different thing. That was the revelation for me. *Guitar Town* happened when I went to see *Born in the USA*. Given I'm a Springsteen fan from record one, but when I went to see *Born in the USA*, I'd already had a record deal and failed, I'd been in Nashville for thirteen years, and a friend of minc—just to keep me from killing myself—invited me to go with him, journalist Bob Warner, to go see Springsteen and *Born in the USA*. I think it's early '86 by the time that tour gets to Murfreesboro, and I went and I knew the record chapter and verse. But seeing it live, and he comes out and he opens with "Born in the USA," and it suddenly dawned on me, go home and write an album. And I wrote "Guitar Town" the next day—I wrote it to open the record. It was such a singular purpose thing to me, I was shocked when they wanted it to be a single, I saw it as there was no chorus, there's no anything, I had it hammered into me that I had to have choruses and I didn't have them. And you know the most successful songs I've had are "Guitar Town," "Copperhead Road," and the "Galway Girl" [actually in the streaming age, that one streams far more than "Guitar Town" and "Copperhead" together worldwide] and none of those three songs have choruses. I have nothing against choruses and I'm really proud of the ones I've written, but they're not a necessity. They have a structure, they do have a refrain, they repeat the title at the end of every verse. That's what they do.

FD: That's great, that's awesome. So, can you talk about, is what you do making literature? Do you give a shit if that what it's called?

SE: I do! Well, there was a conversation I had that—I was in San Miguel de Allende. I went originally with my, the first time I went was in '75, and I went because my wife, my first wife's sister was teaching there, and she was ending this teaching job that she had had for two years, and she was moving back to Houston. She had a car that she bought in Mexico and she wanted to keep it and bring it back to the States. So her father basically paid to fly me and Sandy down so they would have a guy in the car for two pretty girls to drive back from San Miguel de Allende, which is northwest of Mexico City in the mountains, so it's farther than Mexico City actually, 'cause you gotta go to Mexico City to head north. Or at least to the perimeter. And I went down there and stayed for a couple of weeks. It was a place I'd always heard about, 'cause it's where Neal Cassady died.

FD: I was going to say, this is starting to sound a little bit like *On the Road*.

SE: Yeah, it was an American artist colony. I was in Nashville, I had a publishing deal by that time. I knew some American guys that played down there. There was a guy named John Muir, no relation to the naturalist, but he was a NASA engineer. He quit because he warned them that the pure oxygen atmosphere wasn't going to work, and when the Apollo 1 fire happened he quit. And he went to Santa Fe, New Mexico, and opened up a Volkswagen repair shop because he thought Volkswagens were engineering genius. And every hippie in the world drove one of those things. Muir wrote a book called *How to Keep Your Volkswagen Alive: A Guide for the Complete Idiot*, which every hippie that drove a VW had. And literally he tested it by getting his wife, who was very nonmechanical—I knew her, she passed away just a few years ago—and his stepson, who was eight or nine, to follow the instructions that he wrote and rebuild a fucking Volkswagen engine. He published it himself, started the whole self-publishing thing. It had underground comics-looking illustrations, and it had, you know—all hippies had this book in the '70s. And the guy that worked on everybody's Volkswagens in Nashville, a guy named Bobby Walker. He did everything from that book, that's where he learned to do it all from.

FD: Right.

SE: The point is, this guy was really smart, and he was kind of the head hippie. And he started . . . summering in San Miguel, and he lived in Santa Fe part of the year. They had houses in both places. And he became the center of the sort of expat hippie community in San Miguel. So everybody wanted to hang out at his house. His neighbor was Eric von Schmidt, who was the folk singer—he was also a painter, you know, who was painting *Custer's Last Stand*, because his father had painted the *Custer's Last Stand* that we grew up with and he had fucked it up historically and Eric was down there correcting it when I went down there and met him. And Clifford Irving was there, who was the guy who wrote the fake Howard Hughes biography, and he got trapped down there by the devaluation and he lived there from, from then on, because he couldn't go anyplace else. He changed all his money into pesos, and the peso went from, you know, 8 to 1,600 in a period of about two years, so he was fucked. Anyway, quite a crew down there.

And two things happened: One was, I was talking to a guy named David Miller, who was a painter, saying "Man, I wish I had finished school so I could write something besides songs." Because there were other people down there that wrote novels. And he goes, "Man, what you do now is way, way, way, way more viable as literature than anything anybody can put on a page because you write literature that people can consume when they're driving in their car." And that was when the light went on, and I realized, oh, that's what Bob did. You know, that's what's different. That's what changed, and that's when I became cognizant of it. And also, John Muir told me one day that I needed to get the fuck out of there. I started going down there off and on and I ended up kind of moving there in the late seventies when I was in between publishing deals, and Muir finally told me that I needed to get the hell out of San Miguel or I was never going to. It was a place to come to when you'd made it, not a place to come if you still had something to do . . . I was drinking—I have no idea what San Miguel looks like after dark 'cause I drank a liter of tequila pretty much every night. So that was solid advice, and I bailed out.

FD: Amazing. So that's when it dawned on you, that what you're doing is literature. Could you maybe talk about Dylan's win of Nobel Prize in Literature?

SE: I mean, do I think he deserved it? Absolutely.

FD: Why not?

SE: Well, I've heard people argue against it. The one musician I heard argue against it was a bass player . . . it was a guy in Woodstock, and he just railed about it to everybody that'd listen. I wouldn't listen. . . . You remember the deal with me and Guralnick. Guralnick believes that Bob Dylan is overrated. And he believes that because he thinks Robert Johnson is the same thing that Bob Dylan is. But with Robert Johnson, it is about the songs. It is about the lyrics, [yes]. But it is about the lyrics and the music together—the *songs*. There were guitar players that were every bit as good as he was. Skip James was as good as he was. Son House was as good as he was. You know, Son House started the "crossroads legend." It's traceable to one fucking interview. He said "All I know is, he went off somewhere, and that motherfucker couldn't play nothing and he came back and he played better than everybody." And he was the first one to speculate; he said, "I heard that he sold his soul to the devil." And that's where the crossroads thing starts. It's not a legend; it's a lie that Skip James told, you know, 'cause he was jealous.

It's that thing of—I like to juxtapose, to make the argument for my case, which is that Bob Dylan is something that's extremely special, and that's, take Robert Johnson and take, who else, we could take Cole Porter, for sure. That's two people that were writing songs way above the level of anybody else around them. Nobody else was really writing songs, they were just repeating the same stuff, as far as the other blues guys. Every song that the modern electric blues in Chicago is based on is a Robert Johnson song or something based on a Robert Johnson song. It's that big a deal. Cole Porter was born into money, educated, probably was expected to write something more than pop songs, but he liked to write pop songs. And he liked to be in New York, and he was gay, and probably no place else that he could possibly have lived the way that he lived except in the theater world, and even then he needed a beard to survive it. So, you know, what Cole Porter was doing was slumming. Robert Johnson was going all out, but he was doing what absolutely came natural to him. The literary component of Cole Porter's stuff, which, if you look at it, it's so much better written than most of his contemporaries. Irving Berlin's the closest. He was technically that good, but I don't think Irving Berlin's stuff has anywhere near the heart that Cole Porter's stuff does. He's not giving up enough of himself. He's not taking his ego out of the way.

I wrote a song once for Meatloaf, and sent it to him, 'cause I was asked to, and I sent it to him, and he sent it back. It's called "The Shadowland." We recorded it later, I recorded it because it's a good song—I think Will played on it—and there's a line that just says, it says, "Well I ain't as handsome as I was back then." And he wouldn't sing that line out of ego. I think Cole Porter would do that, whereas I don't think Irving Berlin would. I don't think he could be that kind of really genuinely self-deprecating in what he does, but it came naturally to Cole Porter, it came naturally to Robert Johnson, it came naturally to Bob Dylan, but he decided, the difference is Dylan decided that oh, I've read all this stuff and I can put these things all together. He did it on purpose, I really truly believe that. I don't think Bob's ever done anything by accident in his life, because Bob Dylan knows he's Bob Dylan. I'm guessing but I trust my guess. I am a betting man, and I would bet on it.

FD: Yeah, and so making it literary on purpose, in other words, bringing his literary sensibilities into popular music, that's what you're saying.

SE: I think he did it because it made his songs better than everybody else's, and he could apply those things. I don't know whether he realized he was going to change everything at first, but I think he realized once it happened. Bruce Springsteen knows he's Bruce Springsteen, Bob Dylan knows he's Bob Dylan, and he always has.

FD: And the prize, so for you, it's just a no-brainer. Of course he deserves it, because he's producing literature.

SE: Yeah, for me it's just, what I do, what I teach in my courses, songwriting is literature. Because I think it did become literature at the moment that Bob raised it to that level, once and for all. There may have been attempts at it before, and probably thousands of years ago songwriting was as much literature as anything else.

13

Sir Patrick Rocks!

Dragging Ancient Ballads into the Twentieth Century, and What That Can Do to Fragile Young Minds

By Richard Thompson

We didn't want to sing it. Something by Buddy Holly would have been more up our street. But there was really no choice. We stood in a semicircle in the music room at Hargrave Park Junior Mixed School, and sang the old ballad "Barbara Allen," and our attention was at least partially engaged—especially the bit where the flowers grow out of their graves and twine together. It was a safe choice from the school's point of view, because there was no sex in it, and no violence (they died of broken hearts)—the Victorians had seen to that. God bless the British education system anyway, for giving us some taste of our own folk music.

If you go back far enough in British history, the music of the underclass, usually referred to as folk music, is not too far beneath the surface. Perhaps because the classes intermingled to some extent, the toffs, the aristos, would hear the maid or the ploughboy singing songs learned in the verbal tradition, and hear dance music played by the village band, and indeed import it into the great hall. The music of the lower classes would have been known, enjoyed, and probably looked down upon as being unsophisticated. The more subversive songs remained hidden, of course. The more scholarly music of the upper classes might move in the other direction; songs and tunes would filter down, and sometimes end up in fragmentary or simplified versions, as folk songs, twenty or a hundred years later. Occasionally, someone thought this Folk Music beautiful or important enough to be written down, like Wynkyn de Worde's collection of Robin Hood ballads, circa 1495, and Bishop Percy's *Reliques of Ancient English Poetry* in 1765. Gradually though, court music became increasingly pan-European, and increasingly divorced from humbler forms, so that folk music became a thing less obvious, there to be "discovered."

In time, other factors emerged that may have given collecting a different impetus. The Industrial Revolution changed the way that society functioned and redistributed the population away from the farms and into the cities. Some saw this as endangering the old rural ways of life and traditions, and song collecting became seen as something more akin to preservation. Another factor was nationalism. It was important to wave the flag musically, whether to prop up the unification of England, Scotland, and Wales, or to emphasize Britishness under a succession of monarchs who were Dutch, Scottish, German—and occasionally English. To this end, British classical and popular composers would borrow their airs from the folk tradition, cynically or with love. Today, when we see a scene of the rolling hills of England on TV, it is no surprise to hear a traditional tune like "Lovely Joan," as arranged by Vaughan Williams, mirroring the sentiments.

By the time of the great Victorian collectors, there was no doubt that the matter was acute. Cecil Sharp, Lucy Broadwood, George Butterworth, and their fellow enthusiasts and academics were on a mission to collect everything sung, played, or danced by the working classes before sooty industrial Britain with its dark, satanic mills swallowed it all up. Cecil Sharp House was founded in 1932 as a place to sing, dance, and generally preserve the old ways, with the aid of an excellent library and cylinder and disc field recordings.

The next significant revival was sparked in the early 1950s. After the disruption of war, a uniquely British phenomenon seemed to come out of nowhere. A New Orleans jazz revivalist, Chris Barber, would allow his banjo player, Lonnie Donegan, to play during the interval at his live shows. Lonnie would switch to guitar, and with washboard and bass accompaniment, play songs by Leadbelly, Arthur Crudup, Woody Guthrie, and other blues and folk artists they had learned off (difficult to import) records. Lonnie's spots became more popular than the main entertainment. Lonnie went in the studio and recorded some of these iconic American songs (but unknown to the British audience), and had a string of massive hits. Suddenly skiffle, as it was known, was everywhere, and everybody wanted to be in a skiffle group, which wasn't too hard—all you needed was a guitar or three, a washboard, and a bass made from a washtub or tea chest. Many British bands who flourished in the sixties cut their early teeth in skiffle groups, from the Beatles on down.

Parallel to this was the opening of folk clubs, giving amateur musicians a place to play and to share their enthusiasm, and significant in all this was the founding of the Ballads and Blues Club in London in 1953. This was started by Ewan McColl and A. L. Lloyd, the two most important figures in the British traditional music revival. The music you would hear at the club was from a huge range of cultures, and sung in many languages, reflecting the sense of international brotherhood and socialism that the folk world existed in at the time. Gradually the skiffle took a back seat, guidelines for performance were drawn up, and Ewan's way of singing a ballad became somewhat dogmatically the norm, and appropriately for someone who came from the theatre, his delivery was always laced with drama. Ewan insisted on singing sitting back to front on a chair, with a hand cupped over his ear. Many followed suit. Other clubs sprang up, and by the middle of the sixties, there may have been upward of three hundred clubs in Britain—a healthy folk revival, and a platform for many wonderful performers like Martin Carthy, the Watersons, Davy Graham, Shirley Collins, and Bert Jansch.

Where does my old band Fairport Convention fit into all this? That's part of the next revival. Fairport were a group of North London suburban teenagers (mostly), with a love of a wide range of music. We formed in 1966, and would mold our style to pursue the available work; if there was a spot at the local blues club, we'd be a blues band; a group needed to headline the folk club? We'd be all-acoustic. Mostly we were an electric guitar-driven band, with a great fondness for lyrics, and we would do covers of Phil Ochs, obscure Dylan, Joni Mitchell (before she released her own records), Leonard Cohen, etc., before we got our act together and started writing our own songs. We turned pro in 1967, and were accepted by the incredibly tolerant (or just stoned) audiences of the underground, and plied our trade up and down the trunk roads of Britain. We talked a lot about direction, and musical content, and we were always consciously trying to be different from other groups.

Two things then happened in reasonably quick succession. The Band put out *Music from Big Pink*. This album was a perfect blend of American roots music, that went totally against the grain of hippie culture. We were stunned, awed, and asked ourselves just exactly what were we doing, being from North London, being middle-class intellectuals, trying to ape American styles, when we could never be as good as The Band? We planned to do something a little more homegrown in the future. Our singer, Sandy Denny, had come into Fairport in 1968, and brought with her her repertoire, which included many traditional English, Irish, and Scottish songs, and we had recorded a few on our previous two albums. We were performing British folk songs alongside our usual repertoire of Dylan and Joni and, by now, our own compositions, but we were aiming somewhere more radical.

The second thing that happened was a motorway accident that killed our drummer, Martin. This was a devastating event for the group, and almost the end of us, musically. For weeks afterward, we were numb with the shock and the disbelief that this could happen to young people with their whole lives ahead of them. When we resolved to carry on, it was with the intention of not going back to older material, but to go forward and experiment with taking the songs and tunes of the British tradition and playing them in a rock music context. We thought that if we could blend the tradition with the lingua franca of the times, rock, we could create a new kind of popular music that would have immediacy and resonance for the people of Britain, and would also be something that we could play with authenticity and satisfaction, and we wouldn't have to be second-best to Otis Redding, or Muddy Waters, or indeed The Band.

We spent the summer of 1969 holed up in the Hampshire countryside. Dave Swarbrick had joined the band, a leading figure on the folk scene, who had spent the last couple of years in a superb duo with Martin Carthy, and he brought considerable knowledge with him. Traditional songs would be suggested, and versions considered. When you are dealing with material that may be four hundred years old, there are fascinating forks in the road. A song may have an historical origin, but such is the folk process that a singer removed only a generation may prefer to change a line or two to make it "sing" better, and in doing so, alter the facts. Lines may be misheard; verses forgotten, so gaps appear in the narrative; and as a song spreads out around the country, different dialects may take over and change lines to make more sense for different vowel sounds and local word use. So we would compile a version of a song, consulting perhaps Francis James Child's *Ballads of the British Isles*, or the library at Cecil Sharp House; we were also fortunate to have at the end of the phone singers and collectors like Cyril Tawney and A. L. Lloyd, who might chip in with their own opinions. A great shorthand example of the folk process is Fairport's version of the ballad "Matty Groves." We were on the phone to Bert (A. L. Lloyd), and he was reciting a version of it to us. We misheard Lord Arnold as Lord Darnell, and went with that for a good few years!

One of the things that excited us about some of the bigger ballads was the power of the language, and the idea of coupling that with the power of the rock band. "Matty Groves" isn't a bad example of that:

Then Lord Arnold he jumped up
And loudly he did bawl
He struck his wife right through the heart
And pinned her against the wall

Immediate and powerful stuff. Lord Arnold's wit wasn't lacking either:

A grave, a grave, Lord Arnold cried
To put these lovers in
But bury my lady at the top
For she was of noble kin

Such is the quality of some folk songs, that the question is frequently asked—who wrote them? Ben Jonson used to say about the "Ballad of Chevy Chase" that he had rather have been the author of it than of all his works. Sir Philip Sydney, in his "Defence of Poetry," said "I never heard the old song of Percy and Douglas that I found not my heart more moved than with a trumpet":

The dint it was both sad and sair
That he on Montgomerye set;
The swan-feathers that his arrow bare
With his heart-blood they were wet.

Of course, some of them have been sung and altered and honed to sharpness by generations of singers, but there has to be an original version back there, languishing in obscurity. The answers may lie in a number of sources. It is not beyond possibility that many songs originated with talented ploughmen, shopkeepers, milkmaids, soldiers, or sailors, who had a good understanding of the song form, perhaps by being singers themselves. Some songs, we know, were "improved" by the likes of Robert Burns or Baroness Nairn; it is logical to suppose that the local schoolteacher or vicar with an interest in music might also have intervened to "clean up" a local song. We know many of the printed or "broadside" ballads were written by professionals, and oral versions would then diverge from there. More recently it is possible to trace the authorship, or semi-authorship, of songs in the folk repertoire that are often considered traditional, but were clearly the work of known writers adding to and extending the tradition:

"Wild Mountain Thyme" by Francis McPeake—words and music probably based on older sources

"Mingulay Boat Song" by Sir Hugh Robertson—to an older Gaelic melody

"She Moved Through the Fair" by Paidric Colum—adding verses to an existing song

In all three of these examples, it is the work of the most recent hand that has crystallized the song into something that others relate to and take joy in singing.

One of the songs that Fairport tackled in that summer of 1969 was "Sir Patrick Spens." This has to be one of the most anthologized of ballads. I studied it at school, in a book of English poetry, nestled somewhere between "Piers Plowman" and "The Faerie Queene." To the compiler's credit, he had used a Scots dialect version, without cleaning it up too much. The first verse may be familiar:

The King sits in Dunfermline toun,
Drinkin the blude-reid wine
'O whaur will a get a skeely skipper
Tae sail this new ship o mine?

Sir Patrick Spens himself is a shadowy figure . . . if he existed at all, he is largely lost to history. There is grave site on Papa Stronsay in the Orkney Islands, which has been known since time immemorial as Sir Patrick Spens's burial place—this on an island where the ballad is not sung. Spens could be a corruption of Vans; Sir Patrick Vans was a Scottish ambassador who accompanied James VI when he set out during foul weather in October 1589 to bring home his bride, Anne of Denmark, but they were driven back to the coast of Norway by storms. It may also refer to a daughter of Alexander III, who was married to Eric, King of Norway, in 1281. The courtiers who accompanied the new queen to Norway in August of that year were drowned on the return voyage. The song might also refer to Margaret of Norway, shipwrecked off the Scottish coast in 1290. But then, in true ballad tradition, it could be part conflation of several events, and a small dose of fiction, all to make something entertaining to sing.

Unlike other poems in an anthology, which once written tend to be preserved in aspic, a ballad of the antiquity of Sir Pat tends to morph in various directions, from rewritings, mistakes, and preferences in the oral transmission, to the extent that it is difficult to discern the original. The first written version we know of is in Percy's *Reliques*, but the dates of historical events that may have been the source of the ballad suggest it may be centuries older.

Fairport, for reasons I cannot remember now, chose to use the tune from another ballad, "Hugh the Graeme," for "Sir Patrick Spens." It scans a little differently, but has the advantage of a chorus, and a fanfare-like verse, which fits the electric interpretation well.

Were we self-conscious about singing such an anthologized song that rubbed shoulders with great literature? We probably didn't think about it that much. Though we all would have known the song from school, it wasn't that far away in style or content from other ballads we were considering, many of which had, in varying degrees, the virtues of good poetry and good songwriting. Some of those virtues might be:

- Economy of language: A good ballad doesn't mess around with nonessentials. If it does, those are the verses that tend to get trimmed down over the years.
- Colorful description: The language frequently appeals to the senses. The king drinks his "blood-red" wine, the horse is a "milk-white" steed, hair is like "the strands of corn."
- Shifting viewpoints: There is often a shift of narrator, usually without any warning, no "he said," "she said." For the most part, this is comprehensible.

- Shifting chronology: There can be leaps in time with no explanation. Again, the ballad rarely seems to suffer. This can be the result of verses missing, but usually it all seems to hang together.

In the singing is the understanding. Once you sing a traditional song, and you feel the resonance of history, of the story itself, and the reverberation of the singers down the years who have loved and sung the song, something happens to you, and you are altered. You become a link in a chain, and you feel all those other singers throughout the centuries, but you are not intimidated, because the song matters more than anyone who ever sang it. A good singer of traditional music will restate the title of the song at the end of the performance, quietly and modestly, to emphasize that fact. This is why some people devote their lives to these songs, why people will spend fifty years touring the folk clubs of Britain, singing, researching, finding the perfect version of a ballad from hundreds of years ago. It gets to you . . . and when you sing it, you see what it does to other people. I don't think our audience ever questioned the lyrical content of the songs we sang. They seemed to accept that these stories were there to be told, stories of incest and people being carried away by the faeries, and ancient battles, and adulterous lords and ladies, even vampires—and of course, love. Before TV, before most people had access to newspapers, way before the internet, this was how the news was carried. What was extraordinary was that from 1969 to the present day, audiences would allow themselves to be entertained in the same way people had always been entertained. They willingly would sit there for five or ten minutes, and listen to a story unfolding, defying notions of shrunken attention spans. For what may only be a cult audience, these songs are deeply loved and respected.

Fairport's style from 1969 onward was popular up to a point. I think the rocked-up traditional music idea was always marginalized by the public, who were used to being cynical about their own culture. This has been described as a kind of post-imperial malaise, a discomfort with the role of Britain in the past, and a disbelief that the culture can have any real worth in the present. Hence the love of all musical styles from the United States, and the belittling of such things as Morris dancing. ("I'll try anything once," said Sir Thomas Beecham, "except incest and Morris dancing.") Even a commercially successful band like Steeleye Span, who had real UK hit singles, were treated almost like a novelty act. It couldn't be "real" music—that came from America, or was played and sung in an American accent by British interpreters. Steeleye were lumped in with comedy songs by TV personalities, or perhaps a soundtrack to a beer commercial.

Personally, I'm still there—still writing songs in a style heavily derived from the tradition, still singing the occasional ballad. Ask me for a favorite, and I'll probably choose a song with whiskers, something that's been knocked around for a couple of hundred years, a song that's had the corners rubbed off. That's where I still go to learn about melody, to learn about a lyric.

Here's my version of "Sir Patrick Spens," close to Fairport's version, which I think is a good anglicized take on a wonderful story. Aberdour is probably more accurate than Aberdeen, but I think the latter sings better. That's the folk process for you.

The King sits in Dunfermline Town
Drinking of the blood-red wine
O where can I get me a skeely skipper
To sail this mighty boat of mine?

Then up there spoke a bonny boy
Sitting at the King's right knee
"Sir Patrick Spens is the very best seaman
That ever sailed upon the sea."

The King has written a broad letter
And sealed it up with his own right hand
Sending word unto Sir Patrick
To come to him at his command.

"To Norway, to Norway,
To Norway over the foam,
The King's daughter in Norway
'Tis you must bring her home."

The first line that Sir Patrick read
A loud, loud laugh laughed he,
The next line that Sir Patrick read
A tear blinded his eye.

"An enemy then this must be
Who told a lie concerning me
For I was never a very good seaman
Nor ever did intend to be."

"Last night I saw the new moon
With the old moon in her arm
And that is the sign since we were born
That means there'll be a deadly storm."

They had not sailed upon the deep
A day, a day but barely three
When loud and boisterous blew the wind
And loud and stormy grew the sea.

Then up there came a mermaiden
A comb and glass all in her hand
Saying, "Here's to you, my merry young men
For you'll not see dry land again."

Long may my lady stand
With a lantern in her hand
Before she sees my bonny ship
Come sailing homeward to dry land.

Forty miles off Aberdeen
The water's fifty fathoms deep
There lies good Sir Patrick Spens
With the lords of Scotland at his feet.

14

Two Blue Suedes

By Laura Cantrell

It isn't lost on me that one of Dylan's first choices as an artist was to claim a literary name, after Dylan Thomas, whose "Do Not Go Gentle into That Good Night" was surely some sort of talisman, as Dylan raced headlong into the raising of his own lights. Whether Dylan's lyrics were moored by a plaintive solo strum or a bloody roar of noise, he preceded other literary songwriters of the rock era, the bones of his poetry cloaked in rhythm, melody, harmony. It is funny, though, thinking of Dylan as a Nobel Laureate for Literature, not because Dylan's work doesn't merit the highest honor, but funny to call his work literature. Call me a doubting Thomas, but I wonder what such a prize really accomplishes, other than to allow that literary academy to claim the considerable power of Dylan's music as its own. I am skeptical of this academic enthusiasm, no matter how well-earned by Dylan and well-intentioned on behalf of the Nobel committee.

I'm contemplating the subject tonight from the hotel bar of the Guesthouse at Graceland, on Elvis Presley Boulevard and next to Graceland itself, Elvis's beloved home, final resting place, and tourist mecca, as fitting a place to think about American art as any, especially rock and roll and literature. Full disclosure: I'm two "Blue Suedes" (tequila, blue curacao, and some grapefruit juice thrown in for maximum twang) into this meditation and the hotel bar isn't an unpleasant place, a band of cute twentysomethings playing note-perfect Beatles, Chuck Berry, and Carl Perkins covers for an internationally and racially diverse crowd of hotel guests. It's a neat illustration of the state of theme-park rock and roll. For me, a Tennessean at heart, I'm thinking beyond the hotel bar and the refrains of "Honey Don't," out to the deep, humid, cicada-filled evening descending on Elvis Presley Boulevard, the hotel's half-built wedding chapel standing in the gathering dusk at just a respectful distance from Graceland's southern grandeur, while traffic races past adjacent businesses like AutoZone, Checkers, and a Shell station whose fluorescent lights illuminate the wear on the roadway's brown asphalt. This place, with its air conditioned, consumerist comforts surrounded by flagging strip malls, cheap motels, liquor stores, and tourist trinket shops is, as Memphians would say, "American AF."

If you pointed yourself in any direction from Memphis and walked, you'd traverse a huge swath of the history of American music: due south is the Mississippi Delta, birthplace of the blues; five hundred miles north you'll find "Sweet Home Chicago," as many a migrant laborer and musician did in the early twentieth century, electrifying and professionalizing their blues along the way; head east back across Tennessee to the Appalachians and Carolinas, land of the Crooked Road and the "mountain minor," fertile ground for old-time country, folk, and bluegrass musicians both Black and white; and west, of course, might have been the most heroic of the journeys available to American musicians, past Arkansas and Texas, across the plains and the deserts, west of the Great Divide, where Woodie Guthrie, Dizzy Gillespie and Charlie Parker, Janis Joplin, and countless others would play up and down the West Coast, fashioning their music into something electric and modern along the way. Whether traveling by wagon train or Route 66, you'd encounter Native American, African, and European elements of music getting acquainted on that journey.

You wouldn't have very far to go from Memphis to find the hamlet where my father was raised, in rural west Tennessee, a small agricultural community off the highway between Paris and Jackson, a place hardly more than an intersection if you were driving through it, but in its heyday comprised a post office and bank, a Baptist church and Church of Christ, flourmill, sawmill, and school. From this working-class community, my father was proud to recite the scrap of Shakespeare his tenth-grade English teacher made him memorize in high school. Though survival in that place in the early twentieth century required manual labor, the residents were not without "culture," and my father kept that memory fresh as he'd recall the words "shall I compare thee to a summer's day . . ." More interesting to me, hanging around my grandmother's house as a kid, was the proximity of their home to one of the wellsprings in early rock and roll. From the 78s of Vernon Dalhart and Jimmie Rodgers in her record box, to his family's love of *The Grand Ole Opry* and *Your Hit Parade*, to my aunt's list of all the things she'd do if she ever got to meet Elvis ("an autograph, a picture, a kiss . . .") it seemed exciting that my family had borne witness in real time to an explosion of popular music that was still reverberating in the present.

OK, literature. Let's just take as a given that writers' real work is to build narrative—framing stories, histories, persuasive arguments. I remember a quote from Hemingway, after reading another writer's work that he admired, describing his own ability as that of "a carpenter with words . . . that could maybe build an okay pigpen." Those are the writer's tools of trade—words, to describe ideas, facts, experience, feeling. Depending on the type of literature, a writer may use very many or very few—the words, and maybe the page or space they occupy, are the material.

I've heard admirers of a certain type of songwriting call the music "literature," and likewise have heard the term "poet" applied to musicians from Chuck Berry to Tom Waits. Hank Williams was called "the Hillbilly Shakespeare"; Merle Haggard earned the variant "the Poet of the Common People," while Tom T. Hall was called simply "the Storyteller." In my college days, as I was studying English at Columbia University and working at its campus radio station, WKCR, I was bemused to see an album by Eddy Arnold (whose early career moniker was the elegant "Tennessee Ploughboy") titled *And Thereby Hangs a Tale*, a brief quote from Shakespeare's *As You Like It*. But when I hear someone compare a songwriter's work to literature, I take it as an emphatic admiration for the lyrics. And there are certainly songwriters who intentionally lean into lyric composition, ably conjuring character, setting, action, emotion. Of his classic tune from 1968, "Mr. Bojangles," Jerry Jeff Walker has said, "I wanted to play with the internal rhymes—'I knew a *man*, Boj*an*gles *and* he *danced* a bit,'" a classic poetic technique from the writer's toolkit applied to song lyrics.

Dylan is the epitome of the singer-songwriter in the rock and roll era, and his blending of the darkness and mystery of folk and blues song traditions into the rhythms and electricity of rock and roll, along with his ability to write critically about the culture of the times, showed everyone from the Beatles to Dion to Sam Cooke a higher form of lyrical accomplishment. The times really were "a-changin'" and how people wrote songs changed post–Dylan's influence. What had seemed liberatingly nonsensical in early rock and roll, like the "wop bop a lu bop a lop bam boom" of Little Richard's "Tutti Frutti," would seem quaint next to the lyrical gamesmanship of a "Subterranean Homesick Blues" or "Positively 4th Street." Leap another few years forward, with artists like Joni Mitchell, Bill Withers, Kris Kristofferson, Gil Scott-Heron, Leonard Cohen, the McGarrigle Sisters, Dolly Parton, John Prine, Randy Newman . . . or think of these titles: "Sunday Morning Coming Down," "Coat of Many Colors," "Paradise," "Car Wheels on a Gravel Road," each a great example of songs with elegant, poetic writing.

But in any of these songs, it is the lyrics in combination with the music that gives them life, makes them feel like dreams, transport to worlds you can enter and explore. In his memoir, *Chronicles: Volume One*, Dylan himself says, "a song is like a dream, and you try to make it come true. They're like strange countries you have to enter." And while creating that environment does involve getting out Hemingway's carpentry tools, the voyage to the strange country of a song relies on much more than the words; in fact, whether or not a song can really carry your attention to its particular world begins with the music, the pull of the rhythm, the quality of the melody, and the color of harmony and instrumentation. Imagine you're building an "okay pigpen" that can also fly, or float, or both.

Another question tugs at the mind here on Elvis Presley Boulevard: How do we define rock and roll? In Dylan's own words, from the notes to the *Biograph* compilation album, released in 1985, "ain't Bessie Smith rock and roll?" Some of my favorite writers on the subject, like Peter Guralnick, Robert Gordon, and Ned Sublette, recognized the disparate but related communities who gave us New Orleans's early jazz, Mississippi's Deep Blues, New York's Tin Pan Alley, Appalachia's old-time music, and so many other building blocks in the DNA of rock and roll.

Early twentieth-century writers like Carl Sandburg, Langston Hughes, and Zora Neale Hurston recognized the art in blues lyric and form and collected examples of Southern folk music as an exploration of the many varieties of American culture, and used this knowledge to inform their literary style and output. But it seems to me that while American writers were creating great works such as *The Sound and the Fury*, "The Negro Speaks of Rivers," *The Grapes of Wrath*, or *Their Eyes Were Watching God*, something arguably more immediate and powerful had already begun within the music culture of America, even in the "pre-rock" era, as all those strains of regional music from African, European, Native American, Afro-Cuban, and Eastern strains had traveled this country freely for a century or more, on foot, horseback, and rail, electrified via the wireless, eventually dancing and drinking from jukebox to jukebox. This abundance of music steeped itself up in different places, creating different versions of a great expression, and it is rock and roll itself, and all the subgenres that combined to make it, that is the engine, the "high art" of our culture, the great miracle that somehow transcends the pain and limitations of our history, that reflected, and still does, the real potential of this place.

I was eager to meditate on these themes in college, a southern transplant to a northern school, and perhaps from a distance, trying to make sense of my own experience and that of my family, of the Southern culture that seemed both mysteriously rich and pained. While studying literature as an undergrad and learning more about music out of my own interest, primarily at WKCR and with music-minded friends, I had great hope for a course, "High and Low Modernism," a comparison of the "high" and "low" arts of the 1920s, specifically paralleling the literature of F. Scott Fitzgerald and Ernest Hemingway and others with the "low" modernism of popular blues and jazz music. Louis Armstrong was on the syllabus, along with some of the female singers of the classic blues and popular entertainers like Sophie Tucker. I was dismayed, however, to find that our focus on Louis Armstrong in a classroom setting would only be on the lyrics of a few of his songs. I had already hung around jazz historian and WKCR disc jockey Phil Schaap enough to know that to contemplate Louis, to truly experience Pops' art, you had to *hear him blow*. You had to *feel* his playing and singing, his flow as he played with lyrics and phrasing, his ease and mastery over the rhythm of the song, no matter what its lyrics might be (another twist: Louis Armstrong wasn't a lyricist). You *had* to contemplate Louis Armstrong as a musician. Any other consideration of his stature or image, no matter how flatteringly framed in academic argument, missed his true importance. Sitting in a lecture hall a short way from Harlem while a very circumscribed version of Louis Armstrong was utilized for an academic argument about high and low art, with Armstrong being relegated to the "low" pile, became plainly ridiculous to me. Whatever the professor's intention, I couldn't separate from the fallacy of comparing Louis Armstrong lyrics to F. Scott Fitzgerald's prose; they weren't on the same spectrum. And Louis Armstrong didn't need the favor of highbrow contemplation in a classroom, didn't need to be assigned to be understood. His music was widely available, and even though he had been dead for over fifteen years at the time of this class, his art seemed to be very much alive, perhaps more free and influential than the work of his literary companions on the syllabus of "High and Low Modernism," Columbia College, circa 1988.

Enter Wynton Marsalis: I had occasion once to sit at a dinner table with the great jazz musician and scholar, who was playing a concert that evening with Willie Nelson. Realizing how rare it was to have access to a musician of his talent and knowledge, I tentatively asked a few questions about what it was like for Marsalis to play non-jazz repertoire. It was a difficult exchange; somehow the subject veered to singers like Bing Crosby and Elvis Presley. Marsalis had none too high an opinion of either and wasn't impressed by those (me) who'd brought them to mind. We plodded along politely, but none too easy. The mood was somehow saved when I remarked how hard it was to find a drummer in New York who could play a classic Texas 4/4 shuffle. "That's RIGHT," Marsalis said (I finally exhaled), and continued on to detail his preferences for a drummer who could play it like they were from Louisiana, with a particular emphasis on the right sides of the 2 and 4 and the space between the beats just so. "That's where the emotion of the music is, in between those beats, and each place plays their own version," Marsalis said with such authority that he laid the conversation peacefully to rest just in time for us to tuck into our dinner before it got cold.

On a similar note, also in *Chronicles: Volume One*, Dylan describes an interaction he remembers with blues guitarist Lonnie Johnson—no less a fine communicator than Dylan himself—who showed Dylan a technique meant to deepen the musicality of his self-accompaniment. Dylan returns to this advice in the late 1980s when he's considering going on tour after a hiatus and is anxious about the dull prospect of singing his songs from twenty-five years earlier the same way, night after night. Johnson's technical formulation gives him a method to mix it up:

> The scheme works in a cyclical way. Because you're thinking in odd numbers instead of even numbers, you're playing with a different value system . . . things

> that strengthen a performance automatically begin to happen and make it memorable for the ages. . . . In a diatonic scale there are eight notes, in a pentatonic scale there are five. If you're using the first scale, and you hit the 2, 5, and 7 to the phrase and then repeat it, a melody forms. Or you can use 2 three times. Or you can use 4 once and 7 twice. It's infinite what you can do, and each time would create a different melody. The possibilities are endless. A song executes itself on several fronts and you can ignore musical customs. All you need is a drummer and a bass player . . .

Follow that? Even the most studied musician might have to read this passage twice or thrice, but that mystery underscores my point. Even Dylan, *especially* Dylan, knew his art did not reside in words. The words were just the frame of his pigpen; the rest of the mystery of his music would be contained in the playing, what would become for him an almost unbroken haul of noisemaking that has extended from the late 1980s to the present.

In the last twenty years, Dylan has continued to release albums, a volume of memoir, and several books of his artwork. His later albums and songwriting have been parsed by scholars and amateur sleuths alike—the songs of *Time Out of Mind*, *Love and Theft*, *Modern Times*, and *Tempest*, to name a few, have had every phrase traced to its inspiration in previous song or verse. Academic careers have been made analyzing Dylan's repeated return to the "old, weird America" that inspired his most gripping work of the 1960s and of the last twenty years. For me personally, I enjoy most when I recognize a scrap in the crazy quilt of Dylan's music making, a reminder that Dylan's brilliance has included his own version of the "folk process"—the adaptation of previous words, rhythms, riffs, or parts of melody that gave us rock and roll in the first place.

Johnnie and Jack and the Tennessee Mountain Boys were energetic purveyors of a spirited hybrid of hillbilly music, featuring the "close harmony" of a brother-style duet, an able instrumental combo with searing fiddle and guitar, and a loose repertoire built on a core of sacred and sentimental songs, rhumbas, boogies, and proto-rockabilly. The band was a blend of two Tennessee families, that of Johnnie Wright, who sang baritone and played guitar (and whose young wife Muriel would join the group for their early morning radio shows), and that of Jack Anglin, the high tenor singer, married to Johnnie's sister, Louise. Jack's brother, Jim Anglin, rounded out the group, not as a performer but as a songwriter with aspirations to be a published author, described by one historian as a "frustrated Hemingway," who also published a few short stories under a pseudonym for the *New Yorker* and the *Atlantic Monthly*. Also a country boy scuffling to get paid before shipping off to World War II, Jim Anglin sold several songs to Roy Acuff (and others) who recorded and published them under his own name as he was founding one of country music's most successful publishing companies, Acuff-Rose. Jim Anglin had a way with a mournful lyric, penning "Lonely Mound of Clay," "Unloved and Unclaimed," "Searching for a Soldier's Grave," and the affecting "What About You," written about the breakup of his first marriage upon his return from service. A gulf of disillusionment sits beneath the song's lilting melody, while the lyrics make a compact indictment of a false lover. Despite having many songs recorded by artists as diverse as Bill Monroe, Kitty Wells (née Muriel Deason, wife of Johnnie Wright), Waylon Jennings, and Dr. Hook, Jim Anglin worked as a lineman for the Nashville Electric Service for many years, and along with his band is now obscure to fans and even most historians of country music.

Dylan, however, has not forgotten, and references Johnnie and Jack in at least three songs—phrases from Jim Anglin's post-divorce ballad turn up in both "Tryin' to Get to Heaven" from *Time Out of Mind* and "Pay in Blood" from *Tempest*, including the song's potent final declaration, "my conscience is clear, what about you?" Equally striking, Johnnie and Jack's 1961 spoof of Beat culture, "Uncle John's Bongos," becomes the rhythmic mooring for "Tweedle Dum and Tweedle Dee" from *Love and Theft*, the recognizable drum and bass arrangement from the first tune interpreted with an undercurrent of foreboding before the song's action begins. I can only imagine that the intensity of Johnnie and Jack's high spirits and equally high lonesome spoke to Dylan as something he could use. For a group that was influential in its day but is now mostly forgotten by the public and keepers of country music history, this fleeting reuse in Dylan's work may be their highest honor. The Nobel Laureate of Literature drew from the working-class musicians hustling for a hit, "frustrated Hemingway" and all.

You could proclaim it right here on Elvis Presley Boulevard: Dylan might be the American artist most akin to Shakespeare, most likely centuries from now to be widely quoted. But the epic span of his songs float and fly with the music that animates them, traveling furthest on those melodies and rhythms Dylan chose. And if you see him in concert, with the elements he creates in real time, grasping for the feel of the moment, defying expectation, daring an audience to breathe in and out, he conjures the strange world of a song to actual, immediate life. Footlights are required, a bit of paint and powder helps, the band like a troupe of traveling minstrels and jesters ready to "make show." But Dylan and his musicians couldn't tread those boards in a vacuum; their world is built from all the canny, lowly, rough and rowdy stuff that made rock and roll.

I would invert the presumption of that old college class and the Nobel committee: the academics haven't yet caught up with Louis Armstrong's high art, and Dylan's as well—virtuosic, complex, and accessible, and much like Shakespeare's plays, built to continue traveling.

As the "Blue Suede" of the evening deepens, I'm reminded of the words of a different kind of artist, much concerned with the topics we've enjoyed this evening: Nick Tosches, who exalted in "the accelerating theft and flow of all this between Black and white, rural and metropolitan, field and stage—it has been a glorious wreck . . . that nameless black-hulled ship of Ulysses, that long black train, that Terraplane, that mystery train, that Rocket '88, that Buick 6—same journey, same miracle, same end and endlessness." Dylan is now somewhere far away from the Guesthouse at Graceland, where the image of Elvis is ever a smiling, gorgeous prisoner, in constant loop on the hotel's cable TV system, reminding you to celebrate your own rock and roll moment by the night or with special weekend rates.

PART IV

Don't Let Anyone Write Your Story

Musings on Rock as Literature

15

When We All Get to Heaven

By Randall Kenan

New York City.

Ed Phelps was walking north up Seventh Avenue. He'd just come along Fiftieth Street from seeing Rockefeller Center—just the way he remembered it, all spit-shined and brass-bright, the great big golden statue above the skating rink where they shot the *Today* show—and he wandered up the avenue, with no particular direction in mind. This was all after having splurged on a ten-dollar pastrami sandwich at the Carnegie Deli. His buddy Dr. Streeter had told him he would have to get one, and had relayed this information to Ed Phelps the way teenagers speak of sex or the way grandmothers speak of grandchildren. After having attacked the monstrous mound of spicy meat, Ed Phelps understood the good doctor's worship of said sandwich. And now he too would hold it in high esteem—it was indeed more than the sum of meat and bread and mustard and sour pickles.

He had left the deli happy, and continued in his delight as he walked about. Happy to be back in the metropolis after thirty years—was it thirty years? Had it been that long? Since he came back from Korea? He reckoned it to be true.

Ed stopped at a grocery stand where they displayed a fine selection of tomatoes, oranges, asparagus, apples of three—no, four—varieties, greens of all color and manner, and juices. And gladiolas and carnations—pink, red, white, yellow—and roses and a tall tower of water bottles, sweating and looking so very inviting on a hot summer day, the moisture drip, drip, dripping and condensing upon the bottles white like frost. The idea of actually paying for something that came free out of the tap bothered Ed, but he was sorely tempted to buy a bottle. He did not, ultimately, succumb.

As Ed stood and took in all the fare, this young fellow, who appeared to be Mexican, eyed Ed steadily. Ed smiled at the man. Of course Ed didn't know if the man was Mexican or not. But the man said not a word, nor did he blink. Ed continued to make miration at the fruits and vegetables and flowers, surprised to find such a fresh bounty available in the middle of New York. Lickety-split, right there on the street. He noticed the prices and shook his head. *Well, I reckon they damn well better be the finest apples in creation!*

Ed walked away, saying "Afternoon" to the Mexican fellow, who, again, did not blink.

But Ed was feeling good. Ed was feeling fine. Smack-dab in the middle of the rough-and-tumble of New York City, and no one paid him any more attention than they did to anybody else, and he was feeling safe and he was watching the people—so many people, stepping fast, on the move.

Ed and his wife, Isaline, were in town for the National Baptist Convention, being held at that very moment in the Javits Convention Center way, way over on Eleventh Avenue. Isaline was the delegate representing not only First Baptist Church of Tims Creek, but her district of North Carolina. Ed was just tagging along. He was a trustee of the church, but not a deacon; Isaline was the mover and the doer of the family. She liked to call herself a people person. Ed thought it a wonder that she found the patience and the energy after all the time she spent fixing hair. She had just added a fifth chair to her beauty parlor, and putting in six days a week was the norm for her nowadays. But she said it made her happy to be doing and doing, and he believed her, and he had no intention of getting in her way, even when, from time to time, she took a bad mood and set to fussing about all she had to do, knowing she wasn't going to stop and just wanted him to rub her feet and acknowledge how much work she did, day in and day out, and tell her that she worked too darn hard and needed to slow down, knowing, of course, that slowing down was her last intention. Besides, every now and again being her husband took him places—for free—places like New York City, where he hadn't been in thirty? . . . Twenty-nine? . . .

The noise worked like a tonic. He didn't remember the noise. Cars. Trucks. Horses and buggies. Jackhammers. Horns. Shouts. Rumblings coming up from under the ground. Mysterious hisses. Cranes in the sky. Barking dogs. Folk hollering. Crying babies. Horns and more horns.

He saw a woman dressed like the first lady step over a bum without even hesitating. He saw a man in a fine-looking business suit and fine shoes throwing up in the gutter, right there in the middle of the street. A man walked up to Ed and handed him a pink slip of paper. You look like you could use the downtime," the dark-skinned man said under his mirror shades, giving Ed a schoolboy grin. On the card was the outline of a woman with bodacious proportions, front and back, and the legend read—in pink—New York's Most Sophisticated Pussy. Ed dropped this in the next trash can he saw, embarrassed at the prospect that somebody might have seen him handling it.

But Ed's spirits were still high, and he looked all about him, and most people—white, brown, yellow—were just stepping. He liked that. He liked to see the haste and the fast movements, people on their way somewhere. Where were they going? Lord knows, but they were aiming to get there. In a hurry.

And Ed was feeling good. He was stepping. He was happy and dandy and fine.

Plumbing was Ed's trade and he had done well. After he came back from overseas at twenty-seven, he settled on pipes. His daddy had said, *Folk always gone need somebody to fix they pipes.* He got a job working for Old Man Yancey Carter for a while, who was a white fellow, but a fair fellow. He next took a job down at Camp Lejeune. When he found out that the government would pay for courses, he took classes in plumbing at Owen Cross Community College in the seventies, and, by and by, he was working for himself. Today he had three people working for him, and he had no complaints. No sir. Put two girls through college. Was prepared to put a boy through, too, but Edmund wound up going to the Air Force Academy, which made Ed proud.

Ed walked up Seventh Avenue to Central Park South and strolled over to Columbus Circle, where he beheld the statue at the entrance to the park, a monument to the *Maine*—he had seen that on the Discovery Channel—all doused in pigeon doo-doo, but that didn't stop the young folk from sitting all around its base. He stood for a spell watching the scruffy teenagers on their skates—the kinds that look like ice skates with wheels—and it made him smile. He watched one woman for a particularly long while—she must have been Puerto Rican with her light caramel skin and long jet-black hair and a body that brought to mind a fawn—her movements were a thing of beauty to Ed Phelps, and he didn't want to look away, but he didn't want to stare either, so he walked on.

Feeling fine.

Ed Phelps was two years shy of his sixtieth birthday, and he could say in all honesty that he had no notion of retiring. Ed's own daddy had worked—out in the hot fields—till he was eighty-eight, and Ed planned to go at least that long. Besides, he was in good health. He'd given up the cigarettes now on ten years. Isaline watched his diet like a hawk. Doctor said his cholesterol was low. And his heart was as strong as a buffalo's.

Ed thought about walking up into the park, to see that bridge over that pond that's in every other movie about New York, along with the Sheep Meadow, and that pond where little toy children play with little toy boats, but he looked at the time and figured he should begin to make his way back to the convention center. The day before, he had sat around with Isaline, attended the opening ceremony and a few panels but today Isaline was in meetings, and Ed really didn't want to just sit around. He didn't feel like going back to his hotel either—the were staying at the Milford Plaza—so he continued walking.

He wore that day the suit Isaline had bought him for his fifty-fifth birthday—and it still fit—along with a red tie his son Edmund had given him for Christmas. And though it seemed most men these days didn't bother with hats, he fancied his black wide-brim and kept it on his head.

At Fifty-Third Street, for no particular reason, Ed decided to turn west again. He was feeling fine. Adventuresome even. Enjoying his walk. Enjoying the way the air in New York smelled, all full of car exhaust, cooking food, sewer gas, garbage, and perfume.

Ahead of him—about midblock—he saw a large group of young people, mostly white folk, gathering. Why, he did not know. Part of him knew he should go across the street, but—feeling adventuresome as he did—he kept on toward the group to investigate.

Boys and girls mostly they were, dressed casually in their T-shirts and jeans. He did, however, notice a lot of the T-shirts bore the same likeness of a man with spiky hair and the word "Billy" and something else he couldn't quite decipher, but Ed Phelps had no idea who or what he was, and decided right away that he didn't care. This was fun. This was a lark. In a few days he'd be back in Tims Creek snaking out septic lines.

As he waded through the throng—which he now saw was only about twenty or thirty people—and saw they were waiting for somebody, obviously, to show, probably coming out of that door there, he set his mind—"Excuse me, please. 'Scuse me. Pardon me"—to getting through to the other side of the crowd.

A white stretch limousine pulled up at that moment (a Lincoln, Ed Phelps took note), and the crowd of which Ed was now plumb in the middle began to buzz like a hive of hornets. A door flung open and two leggy white women dressed—barely—in one-piece black outfits that left not one thing to the imagination except the color of their pubic hair, emerged from the car. Following them was a much shorter man—the one with the hair standing straight up in the air, all blond like hoarfrost and needle-looking, like a porcupine, or like a man who had stuck his finger into a light socket and saw God all at the same time.

The man chewed gum and had a sneer about his face, and quickly slipped on a pair of dark shades. He certainly didn't dress like a man who rides around in limousines. He wore a black leather jacket over a T-shirt that was shredded, showing his pale underbelly, and his pants were like vinyl—but Ed quickly thought better and figured they had to be leather, and next reckoned that those pants had to be mighty hot on a day like today, even if you were riding around in the back of a limousine. And though the man did not in the least look happy to see this score and more of eager young people, they certainly were—without a doubt—happy to see him—"Billy! Billy!"

The doors to the building swung wide and three gorilla-sized men rushed out to push the crowd back, creating a path between this Billy man and the door. It just so happened that Ed Phelps stood at that path, just like the adoring fans. Ed couldn't remember the last time he had felt so aware of his own presence, and so embarrassed to be somewhere. Though he had to admit it was a little exciting. Something to report on when he got back home.

As the Billy man and the four legs attached to two women walked through the path the three men had created, the crowd grew louder, reaching out with posters of this Billy and compact discs and albums and little books and pens.

At this point, almost by design, Ed and Billy were standing face-to-face—it was a mere flash of a second, a moment in time, before one of the human oxen came to push Ed Phelps to the side and sweep Billy into the brick building.

Billy snatched off his sunglasses, stuck his arms up and out wide, and hollered: "Deacon!" This ejaculation caused nearly everyone to pause—the two long-legged women, the three grizzly-bear security men, a quantity of the nearby crowd—and Ed Phelps. Before Ed could say—what?—Billy made a kingly motion to the Three Muscle-teers, and everyone—Billy, the women, and Ed—were swept into the back of the building.

Oh hell, Ed thought, *what am I going to do now?*

The hallway itself was dim and dingy and narrow, and Ed had no choice but to follow along with the pack, as he was in their midst. Directly they came to a larger room. The door was open and several people, some in suits and some in nice dresses, lolled about, but perked up when Billy walked through the door. The back wall was one long mirror about a long table full of bottles and jars and brushes and tubes. Goose-egg lightbulbs ran all along the top.

"Francesca!" Billy said to a woman dressed all in black. He kissed her on both her cheeks and gave her a third peck as if for good measure.

She said, "Billy," once, and kissed at his cheek—not touching it—only once. She did not smile. Her eyes had a fish-like flatness that made Ed Phelps uneasy.

"This," Billy said, and made an extravagant flourish with his hand, "this is the Deacon." He had an accent like one of those Beatles, or some of those British people on those PBS shows Isaline liked to watch sometimes, and not the rich and fancy kind, more like the kind who drove trucks and worked in butcher shops. And at that very moment it was quite clear to Ed Phelps that Billy was winking at him, his back turned to the Francesca lady. To be sure, this Billy fella was up to something and wanted Ed to be in on it. But the question was: Was he up to good or to no good? Ed Phelps would just have to hang out to find out.

"Francesca Eberhardt here, Deacon, is my A & R person. She's an executive with my label. She gives things the ups and the downs, the green lights, the red lights, the yellow lights, the black lights—d'you know what I mean?—I mean she's a real, real, real powerful bitch. And my fate is in her hands, innit?"

Francesca said not a word. She simply stared at Billy with her rattlesnake eyes. She was dressed in a black dress that could have been spray-painted on her swamp-weed frame. Her long, inky hair was pulled back, making her face look even more gaunt and pale against all that black.

"You see, Francesca here has a BA in economics from Stanford, an MBA from Harvard—was it Harvard, love? Yes, Harvard—and a PhD from the London School of Economics, but, funny thing—she don't know nothing about no music. It's a riot, innit?"

"Billy," Francesca finally said, her voice a bit warmer than Ed Phelps would have expected, but chilly nonetheless. "If this is about your contract, I assure you—"

"Me contract? Me contract? Fuck the bloody contract."

Francesca pointed a long and well-sculptured finger at Billy: "Look, my friend, I can put up with a lot of your crap, but there will be no fucking of any contracts. Don't you fuck with me. You belong to me now. Capiche?"

This brief lecture seemed to achieve the desired effect upon everyone in the room, all of whom were looking at their feet, to windows, to doors, away from eyes—all, that is, except for Billy.

"Belong? Did you say belong? I mean how insensitive can you be?" Billy thrust his hands toward Ed. "I mean, really—*belong?* We call that bad form where I'm from, missy."

It came upon Ed that he would be expected to hold forth on this development, and the idea sat with him not at all well, and he began to look for a way out of this prickly situation.

"I bet you don't even know the Deacon's music, do you, Francesca?"

"Well," she said, "to be honest, I—"

"Well, of course you don't. I mean, how old are you? Sixteen? Miss Stanford, Miss Harvard MBA, Miss I-actually-prefer-Mahler—Jesus Christ! Can you fucking believe she actually said that to me?"

"Mussorgsky, actually. I said, Mussorgsky, not Mahler."

Billy began to close in on Francesca, and in turn wagged his finger at her: "The Deacon is a legend, young lady. The Deacon and His Hounds of Hell. From Hell. They were fantastic—I saw them in Berlin in 1972 . . ."

After turning to one of his long-legged assistants ("Give us a fag, eh, darling?") and lighting up, he launched into a long, detailed story about how Ed/the Deacon had grown up on a plantation in Mississippi, and had run away to Memphis at the age of twelve, and how he had run into a great big chicken at the same crossroads as had Robert Johnson ("You do know who Robert Johnson is, don't you, darling? Yeah, I thought you might not"), and how he got a recording contract with Sam Phillips and then Chess Records—and Ed Phelps couldn't keep up with the story, but found it so very compelling that he wanted to hear this man's music until it hit him—making him laugh—that he was, indeed, this very man. Lord, this boy could tell a good lie. Ed more than halfway admired that.

His cigarette almost done, Billy took a long draft followed by a long pause. His eyes seemed even darker and more impish. Francesca let out a big sigh and looked at her watch. Billy walked over to a corner, smoke flowing like fog from his nostrils, and picked up a case and put it on a table. He undid the latch and the top gave a slight creak open. A guitar. Of course. Just wood and wire. Billy ran a finger over it and looked directly at Ed Phelps. Ed Phelps beheld the guitar and he beheld Billy. He wanted to shake his head, *No*, but something about the entire situation tickled him, and he grinned despite himself. Billy himself grinned right back at him. It might have looked as if the two of them were drunk.

"Deacon," he said, with a rather studied deference: "Would you be so kind as to play for us?"

Oh, hell. Ed Phelps wondered how things had come to this particular pass.

At that moment, between them, something odd and familiar occurred: two boys who together and without words recognize and acknowledge the Dangerous Thing, and, being like-minded, imagine assaying said Thing, and with each passing moment feel the Thing exert greater gravitational force upon the two, each to each, and along with the weight comes glee, anticipation, heat, so much so that the Dangerous Thing becomes the Irresistible Thing, the Inevitable Thing.

Ed Phelps picked up the guitar and began to strum. As he tuned the instrument, a look of quietness and acute observation overtook Billy's face, very like a cat.

The tuning did not take too terribly long, and, truth to tell, though Ed Phelps had not picked up a guitar in over fifteen years, and had probably forgotten more than he had ever known, as he strummed and hummed to himself, doorways in the back of his mind began to slowly open, then more and more, one by one, two by two, four by four, and he remembered his grandfather and how he played and how he taught Ed to play, and he remembered playing on the back porch with Mr. Moses Rascoe, who drove a truck, but who was so good he played sometimes for money, and like a silverfish under a sink, a song jumped up into Ed Phelps's head and he commenced to sing and play:

You get a line and I'll get a pole, honey.
You get a line and I'll get a pole, babe.
You get a line and I'll get a pole,
We'll go fishin' in the crawdad hole.
Honey, baby mine.

Ed Phelps looked all about and Billy's face was no longer catlike, but all Christmas, and all the young people in the room were beaming and tapping their feet—with the logical exception of Francesca, who looked as if she might bite him at any second.

He remembered a verse that Mr. Moses had taught him:

What did the catfish say to the eel, honey?
What did the catfish say to the eel, babe?
What did the catfish say to the eel?
The more you wiggle, mama, the better I feel,
Honey, baby mine.

Ed Phelps put an end to the song with a sweet ping and run that brought back blueberry-pie memories. Billy rose, and was full of whoops and hollers and hot praise, and his friends and folk were clapping, and Billy set in straightaway figuring how he could get Ed up onstage with him.

"Oh, hell no," Francesca said.

"Seriously, it'll be a riot," Billy said.

"Well," Ed said, "I have to meet the wife in a little bit anyway."

"Oh," Billy said, "she won't mind. We can invite her. It'll be a riot."

"I. I would mind, Billy." Francesca was now standing in front of Billy, towering over him, upon her face the expression of the schoolteacher who has finally reached her limit: "He can stay. He can watch the show. He can even bring little Mrs. Deacon and his hellhounds for all I care. But he is not going up on that stage with you, bubba. You dig? Fuck not with me, kiddo. Now—I believe you have a show to do, and I promised you'd be on time. For a change." Francesca walked out the door.

As soon as Francesca left the room, Billy embraced Ed Phelps, kissed him on the cheek, and said, "Thank you, mate. You're a real trouper." He introduced Ed to his two assistants, saying they would take care of all his needs and that he'd see him after the show.

Ed did not realize that all this time he was in a theater called the Ritz, and he was ushered up into a VIP box to overlook the standing crowd and the stage. One of Billy's assistants led him to a phone where he left a message for Isaline, that he wouldn't be able to join her for *Les Misérables* but he was all right and he'd see her after the show.

After a long, long time, the lights went down and the music finally began. Ed Phelps was at once excited and deflated. He was happy to be here, happy to be a VIP, but he did not particularly care for the music, which made him a little sad. It was silly music, it was loud music, it was all catch phrases and easy beats, stuff he heard on the radio, and he figured he might have heard some of this music on the radio in the past, but, to tell the truth, it all kinda sounded the same these days. But the young people seemed to enjoy the music, and they seemed to enjoy Billy, and this made him happy.

Billy himself came off as a rough boy, a rude boy, a loud boy, a dirty boy, a tough boy. All of which made Ed Phelps laugh. He wondered how Billy would have done in the navy. There were some mighty tough men there, and a lot of them were even smaller than Billy, and they did not wear leather.

During the intermission, Francesca came up to him and shook his hand. She did not have a smile on her face, but she did seem more pleasant. "You never played guitar professionally a day in your life, did you?"

"Ah, well, no, ma'am. You are correct."

"He thinks I'm an idiot, but you don't get to be senior executive vice president at thirty for not knowing music. I know music."

"Yes, ma'am."

After the concert, he found his way back to the greenroom, and to the assistants. He wanted to thank Billy, but didn't want to take up any more of his time. So he asked the assistants to thank Billy for him, and he donned his hat and headed for the door, on his way back to the Milford Plaza and to Isaline.

Just as he reached the outside door, he heard Billy calling, his boots tapping against the floor.

"Deacon, my friend, a bunch of us are going down to Bobby De Niro's new place. Would you please by my guest? You'll love it. It'll be a riot!"

Ed Phelps thought on it, thought about what he would say to Billy and these young people, thought about the senior executive vice president and music he didn't respect.

"Thank you kindly. And you have been awful kind. But I need to get back with my wife. She may think I'm laying dead in a gutter somewhere."

"All right, my friend. I can dig it. At least let me drop you off. Where are you staying?"

Just Billy and Ed in the back seat, and as soon as they sat down Billy launched into a long discussion of his career and the music business these days, and how he was once on top, and then the bitch hit him, sent him in a spiral, how you always need to look out for the bitch because the bitch is jealous . . . and Ed was beginning to have a difficult time following him, and couldn't figure if the bitch was the music industry, a woman, or just life, and he didn't really care. The leather seats were deep and plush, and he couldn't help but admire the scenery as the large car glided through the streets of Manhattan, and his mind wandered as Billy carried on . . .

The men, the women, the girls, the boys, all well lit in the nighttime, but accompanied now by long shadows, the bikes weaving in and out of traffic, the hot dog carts, the ambulances and flashing police cars, the subway entrances issuing forth human after human like ants from a mound, the streetlamps and the blinking colored lights, above stores and offices, the giant words crawling across buildings that told the world news, and the giant head twenty stories high or more, saying, obviously, something of grand importance, but at the same time nothing nowhere could be as important as being there right there, right then in all that color and size and flash . . .

By and by, the car came to a stop, and the driver got out and opened the door for Ed. He turned to Billy and said, "Can I ask you something?"

"Shoot."

"How did you know I could play a little guitar?"

"I didn't, mate. I had this feeling though. Call it me intuition. I figured if you couldn't you'd just tell me to fuck off, or something like that, innit? Just having a laugh."

They shared a chuckle. As he was getting out Billy asked his name.

"Ed. Ed Phelps of Tims Creek, York County, North Carolina."

"Ed." Billy stuck out his hand and shook Ed's. "Very pleased to make your acquaintance, Ed Phelps of North Carolina."

The walk to his hotel room took a while, the hall of the Milford Plaza being long and skinny and harshly bright.

When he got to the room he found Isaline in the tub—he called to her, and opened the bathroom door, and saw nothing but mist and was hit in the face by a wall of heat so thick and by the scent of pomegranate and strawberry and God-knows-what, all of which quickly took his breath away—

"Close that door, man! Don't you let out my heat!"

I will never understand, he thought, *why this woman insists on turning her nightly bath into a sauna*, but left her to her devices, glad to finally be home. He'd tell her all about his day when she got out, which could be in thirty minutes, which could be an hour.

He put on his pajamas—the fancy silk paisley pair Edmund had given him for Christmas—much too fancy for his tastes and much, much too fancy to wear every day, but they seemed appropriate for this trip. He got into bed and waited for Isaline. The TV was on, the sound cut down, playing some Lifetime TV drama she was forever watching. Ed took hold of the remote and commenced to flip through the channels, hoping to find the Hitler Channel on Discovery.

Something caught his eye and Ed Phelps paused and there he was. He looked tiny there on the screen and much younger than he had just a while ago, and so very white, all that white hair against such glowing white skin. He looked downright sick and pitiful. He looked like he needed to go home to his mama and get something good to eat.

He was singing one of his songs he had sung earlier that very evening, the son about dancing with himself, and Ed Phelps still couldn't make heads or tails of it, and figured it meant something dirty, but just didn't care to know, nor did he care for the beat, which was monotonous and straightforward and boring—and oh my Lord . . .

In the music video—which made even less sense than the song—all these white folk who were supposed to be zombies or homeless people or such, in either event scary-looking, he supposed—though they couldn't have scared a baby goldfish even if they tried hard—were climbing up this tall, tall, tall skyscraper to get at Billy, who was singing about masturbation or whatever up on the roof of his building. There are puppets and all kind of random foolishness thrown in . . . and at the very end, Billy grabs ahold of some electrode-looking thing and becomes electricity and shoots bolts of lightning at the pretty zombies and they all fall down to earth, form the supertall building, and Billy continues to go on about how he wants to dance with himself, and Ed Phelps is left to wonder about so many things. And the day makes more sense and the day makes less sense, and he is happy to be in bed, and have it all to think about, all to tell about, to Isaline, to Dr. Streeter, and he must remember to tell Isaline about the pastrami sandwich at the Carnegie Deli . . .

The day weighed down upon him, but the day was feather-soft, the day was sweating bottles of water, the day was loud like cigars and smelled of truck horns, the day was a golden giant flying among the skyscrapers delivering fire to a beautiful Latina—*Oye mama! Oye mama-sa!*—hot day, long day, sweet day, music day, and the day turned to a guitar and the guitar strings turned to worms and the worms turned into cucumbers and the cucumbers turned into his mother's fingers, and she gave them to him peeled white with salt and pepper and a little vinegar, and the taste was childhood, and the taste was still new, and the sun was high in the sky, and it was 1946 and he was fourteen, and he was in the tobacco field, and deep in the lugs, and the day was hot, but he was happy—BACCOOO! BACCOOO! AIN'T NO BACCO IN HEAVEN I KNOW!—and he heard his grandfather's voice, and his grandfather was singing, and he heard his grandfather's voice and his grandfather was singing.

16

English as a Second Language

By Warren Zanes

A wop bop a loo bop a wop bam boom!
—Penniman/LaBostrie, "Tutti Frutti"

How that bump made us jump!
—Dr. Seuss, *The Cat in the Hat*

While working on Tom Petty's biography, I talked to Petty at length about school. He hated it. Useless stuff. There was, however, one class he found almost tolerable. English. He liked the stories. But not all of them. He found the Dick and Jane books to be little more than fantasies of children and parents living in some impossible dimension, beyond conflict and wrinkled shirts. "I remember them well," he told me. "That was how we all learned to read: *See Dick run. See Jane run. See Dick jump. See Jane jump.*" He elaborated: "Pure bullshit."

Oh, father.
See funny Dick.
Dick can play.
Oh, Mother.
Oh, Father.
Jane can play.
Sally can play.

Long after Petty was out of the main building and off school grounds, focused instead on carrying Fender amps in and out of motor vehicles, the Dick and Jane primers were still common fare in American schools. The critics of those primers were many, not just guys in Florida rock and roll bands. But those critics stumbled in their efforts to remove the books from the classrooms. And, as a result of the predominance of those volumes, English, as a discipline taught in American schools, had little to do with the language of youth. Dick and Jane's words, like their personalities and the events of their lives, were stiff, wooden, unnatural, repetitive in all the wrong ways. Reading Dick and Jane was like getting a slow beating with language. Young Americans were all but *forced* to find and learn their English elsewhere. The English of the Dick and Jane classroom was, at best, a second language.

Rock and roll offered one alternative. *Shake, Rattle, and Roll.* It gave young people a language of plasticity and invention, a language that could be broken and rebuilt in the course of a song. It had ambiguity, allowed for a nonsense that made sense. It had repetition that felt good. Rock and roll was a language disruption, refusing the rules and instead celebrating the possibility of linguistic misconduct, baby talk, street talk, stupidity, the unschooled. For its young audience, this was a *new* language, and one that in some way—*and so different from Dick and Jane*—reflected the world in which they lived. It had no closure, where Dick and Jane was a sealed can of meaning.

In the second half of the 1950s, however, it wasn't only in rock and roll culture where language disruptions were taking place, where people were looking for a more effective and affecting language. Simultaneous with the emergence of early rock and roll and consistent with its emancipatory effects, in children's literature there were changes going down that were themselves part of a postwar language shakeup, changes that very directly targeted Dick and Jane's pristine world. What is lost over time, however, is the *connectedness* of these seemingly discreet disruptions. History is a process of organizing things that weren't organized, of bringing order. But the fifties had a special *dis*order that we hear as a kind of freshness in the best of its rock and roll, that we see on the pages of the decade's new children's literature. It's a disorder that's both euphoric and, if sometimes less obviously, anxious, born of a time in which uncertainty gave art a reason to throw off something new. Rock and roll and children's literature, children's literature and rock and roll, children's literature and bombs, bombs and rock and roll.

Published on May 24, 1954, John Hersey's *Life* magazine article "Why Do Students Bog Down on the First R?" opened with a few examples drawn from Dick and Jane, the first from a story entitled "See It Go":

> "Look," said Dick.
> "See it go.
> See it go up."
>
> Jane said, "Oh Look!
> See it go. See it go up."
>
> "Up, up," said Sally.
> "Go up, up, up."

As Hersey makes plain, when it came to exposing the problems of Dick and Jane as classroom material, the best approach was to let the kids talk. Dick, Jane, and Sally reveal themselves to be bloodless, the flattest of flat characters. To that end, Hersey offers those few examples of their "adventures," without adding his own commentary, after which he comes in with his argument: *this must end*. Or something along those lines. It was the same general conclusion at which Tom Petty arrived.

The article was published just a few months before Elvis Presley's first Sun Records single, when rock and roll, slurring its way to the top, was about to rip the girdle off America. But what's worth considering, even more than Hersey's article of 1954 and the upheaval about to take place that would put young people at the center of American cultural struggles, is the writer's *New Yorker* essay from eight years earlier, "Hiroshima," the longest piece published in that magazine to date, taking up the majority of an issue. In that article, Hersey describes the aftermath of the Hiroshima bombing, relaying the experiences of select survivors. Through their descriptions of the bombing, the survivors give *New Yorker* readers a feeling for how Japanese everyday life was, very suddenly, turned into its own kind of nonsense, if only because there could be no sense made of life in Hiroshima after the bombing. After the atomic bomb, a new language was needed, though it could only be described using words from the old language.

> At exactly fifteen minutes past eight in the morning, on August 6, 1945, Japanese time, at the moment when the atomic bomb flashed above Hiroshima, Miss Toshika Sasaki, a clerk in the personnel department of the East Asian Tin Works, had just sat down at her place in the plant office and was turning her head to speak to the girl at the next desk.

Hersey's interviewees convey the almost incomprehensible manner in which they saw their mundane lives erupt with a radical violence. The writer ends his piece with the words of ten-year-old Toshio Nakamura:

> The day before the bomb I went for a swim. In the morning, I was eating peanuts. I saw a light. I was knocked to little sister's sleeping place. When we were saved, I could only see as far as the tram. My mother and I started to pack our things. The neighbors were walking around burning and bleeding.

The point here is to consider the effect of those survivor accounts on Hersey and how, a few years after the fact, they might have informed his view of children's literature. One can certainly imagine that the faces of those atomic bomb survivors stayed in Hersey's mind. And one can also imagine that in the years immediately following that celebrated *New Yorker* piece, back home in Connecticut, working on issues relating to education and early reading, Hersey may still have been seeing those survivors, even when the topic was a literacy crisis among American youth. Though the trauma of Hiroshima was not his—he sat beside it. So, for someone who had spent time with Hiroshima's trauma victims, was the great offense of Dick and Jane perhaps more than just a matter of stale, ineffective classroom materials that failed to engage young people? Did the awful truth of Dick and Jane, for one in Hersey's position, relate as much to the way their inane exploits exposed the tragic denial that was at the center of American life? Did Dick and Jane give away a nation's dirty secret, that the ultimate American privilege is *unknowingness*?

From this angle, those schoolbooks into which Hersey was looking might have appeared tools used to construct the denial that allowed American people to look past the horrors wrought by their nation. Isn't it really only a superpower that can tell tales like Dick and Jane's, so chillingly removed from the truths of the world beyond their nation's borders? In "Hiroshima," Toshio Nakamura's descriptions, initially tilting toward the mundane world of Dick and Jane—". . . I went for a swim. In the morning, I was eating peanuts."—shatter into disconnected images, that "burning and bleeding" of neighbors in the street. In Hiroshima there can be no Dick and Jane. Dick and Jane are, in this light, an obscene privilege that, for Hersey, needed to end. For Hersey, the seemingly disconnected—the atomic bomb and Dick and Jane—were indeed connected. And he called for a language disruption.

Like Adorno's much-quoted phrase, "There can be no poetry after Auschwitz," Hersey's experience suggests that one can't simultaneously be aware of Hiroshima's bombing and also tolerate Dick and Jane. After Hiroshima, a different art, a different language is needed. Hersey, feeling the aftereffects of one of the modern world's great tragedies, reveals some of his cultural-political disposition in that later *Life* article that is not about bombs but is about American literacy and Dick and Jane's role in its undoing:

> There is, besides, a possibility that not happiness but its very opposite may result from the creation of an image of life, or a pretense of that image, that does not correspond at all with reality. Stories of happy play, helping others, cheerful good-hearted neighbors, and so on, describe things that are desirable, but they do not exactly offer a slice of life. A small child who through accident or parents' carelessness one afternoon watches on television not *Howdy Doody* but a documentary moving picture about unspeakable degradations in a Nazi prison camp goes to school the next day and is given reading readiness, but perhaps not life readiness, in an antiseptic little sugarbook showing how Tom and Betty have fun at home and school.

In the year following Hersey's *Life* article, not only was Chuck Berry's "Maybellene" released on Chess Records but the first big attack aimed at Dick and Jane from within the education community came with the publication of Rudolf Flesch's *Why Johnny Can't Read*. If "Maybellene" is celebrated for its impact on popular music, most of that impact is measured in relation to what happened after 1955. "Maybellene" *became* important. But 1955's big recordings were "The Ballad of Davy Crockett," the McGuire Sisters' "Sincerely," "Mister Sandman" by the Chordettes, Mitch Miller's version of "The

Yellow Rose of Texas." "Maybellene" didn't compete with those "sugarbooks." And so it was for Flesch's volume—its impact is best measured from a historical distance.

In Flesch's book, the Dick and Jane primers are described—in a remarkable sentence—as "those horrible, stupid, emasculated, pointless, tasteless little readers, the stuff and guff about Dick and Jane or Alice and Jerry visiting the farm and having birthday parties and seeing animals in the zoo and going through dozens and dozens of totally unexciting middle-class, middle-income, middle-I.Q. children's activities that offer opportunities for reading 'Look, look' or 'Yes, yes' or 'Come, come' or 'See the funny, funny animal.'"[1] The counter-approach that Flesch would promote was called "phonics." Phonics was only a method, however, and the books that came of it would range in style and content. Just like rock and roll was a "method" that would yield recordings as different as "Maybellene" and Bill Haley's "Rock Around the Clock."

What phonics did not do was dictate what the content of a book should be. So, while John Hersey faulted Dick and Jane for presenting a world that did not "correspond with reality," this doesn't mean that what he and other critics such as Flesch were calling for was a children's literature capturing the world's troubles in a realistic manner. Put another way, picture books presenting the devastation of Hiroshima were not what Hersey was after. "This is not to advocate," he wrote, "a pre-primer of horrors." In fact, in one of the most celebrated instances of a children's book that *did* represent the interests of those seeking to remove Dick and Jane from the schools, the book was hardly bound by the codes of realism or related to the devastations of the modern era. It was titled *The Cat in the Hat*. It was the "Maybellene" of its own world.

Theodor Geisel met William Spaulding when both men were among the enlisted during World War II. Spaulding went on to become the head of the education division at Houghton Mifflin, commissioning Geisel, by that time writing under the name Dr. Seuss, to write the book that would become *The Cat in the Hat*. Both men were aware of and affected by John Hersey's article in *Life*, as they were by *Why Johnny Can't Read*. As Spaulding would later say, "[*The Cat in the Hat*] is the book I'm proudest of because it had something to do with the death of Dick and Jane primers." A strange, unexpected book, *The Cat in the Hat*, as much *Mad Magazine* or *The Catcher*

1. Rudolf Flesch, *Why Johnny Can't Read* (New York: HarperCollins, 1955), 6–7.

in the Rye or "Tutti Frutti," is an artifact of the disruptions and challenges to language and thought that came at midcentury. Seuss's book was as rock and roll as anything coming out of Memphis or New Orleans.

"Too wet to go out, and too cold to play ball. So we sat in the house and did nothing at all." So *The Cat in the Hat* begins, with two children doing nothing, lost in postwar leisure time. One of the children is named Sally, not coincidentally sharing a name with Dick and Jane's youngest sister. The other child, a boy, goes unnamed. The near obsessive repetition of names that marks the Dick and Jane primers is pointedly rejected as the main character goes nameless. Similarly, the beneficent parents who appeared in those earlier primers, smiling with their support and always understanding, are banished from the scene. In *The Cat in the Hat*, the father gets no mention at all, while the mother has left the house, entering the picture only at the story's end, as a figure of some anxiety, shown only from the knees down. For the remainder of the book, Sally and her brother are alone in the family house, not doing nothing, in fact, but watching as the domestic space is thrown into a state of chaos by the Cat and his two henchmen, Thing One and Thing Two. A three-piece act. It was the era of the small combo. The lingering voice of "reason," the fish, is hardly effective at all. Like some malfunctioning superego, the fish attempts to reinstate the law . . . but no one gives a shit.

Among the directives given Dr. Seuss with the commissioning of *The Cat in the Hat* were the following: "Write me a story that first-graders can't put down!," William Spaulding told him, going on to tell Seuss that, no matter the book's length, the author could not draw on more than 225 vocabulary words, all of which would be selected from a predetermined list of 348 possible words provided by the editor. As Seuss would later insist, the book's content emerged from the first rhyme he came upon, *cat/hat*. Rhyme and rhythm. Rock and roll. The story, a secondary feature, would have to follow from there. *Green Eggs and Ham* of 1960 took vocabulary limits one step further, purportedly the result of a bet proposed by Random House publisher Bennett Cerf that Seuss could not write a book using only fifty different words. It was another victory for feeling, the groove of the thing, over content. Beatrix Potter, of *Peter Rabbit* fame, using six words and foregoing a sense of rhythm, praised Seuss for the, "natural truthful simplicity of the untruthfulness."

There were, however, several books published under Seuss's name before the writer-illustrator was celebrated as a visionary and innovator. *The Cat in the Hat* got positive reviews among those who felt Dick and Jane belonged to the past, such as Ellen Lewis Buell, who praised the book in the *New York Times Book Review*. But there were others, like Rita Roth, who initially felt that Dr. Seuss, "like comic books, provided a frivolity that was not appropriate for school." Roth later proved a convert, and Seuss eventually achieved the kind of status reserved for individuals like Walt Disney and Jim Henson. But Seuss's first advocates had their work cut out for them in their efforts to bring Seuss into the world, and certainly into the world of early learning. Dick and Jane would not go gentle into that good night, only to be replaced by what many saw as, yes, nonsense. Mitch Miller showed a similar reluctance in 1955.

To save their man, Seuss's supporters felt the need to lift Seuss from a lowlier station—he was being lumped in with comic books, for God's sake!—through a kind of high art rescue mission. And this is where Seuss was forcibly removed from rock and roll. He was a *poet*. His rhyme schemes had a sophistication that couldn't be stumbled upon by mistake. He was trained! He was driven by explicit intentions and could reel off iambic pentameter when the situation called for it! He was a modernist, practicing a kind of minimalism related as much to work housed in the Museum of Modern Art as that in the children's section of the New York Public Library! These legitimators of Seuss went as far in one direction as his detractors went in the other.

Among those detractors were individuals who felt Seuss's writing tilted toward American slang, rock and roll's language, not English. Still others viewed Seuss's background in advertising as suspect. And, oddly enough, some sensed a disturbing regionalism in Seuss. These latter critics located that regionalism in some of Seuss's neologisms, words such as "snerl" and "thars." In an effort to address this, Philip Nel agrees that, first, "*Snerl* sounds like *snarl* as it might be pronounced by a person from central Appalachia (Eastern Kentucky)," and, second, "People from the Ozarks might pronounce *theirs* as *thars*," and, third, here citing sociolinguist Thomas E. Murray, that such words do "connote a sort of rural, lower-class, uneducated speaker." But, Nel counters, "Seuss's willingness to experiment with words—even if that means breaking the rules—is one reason that his books are so fun to read." Nel himself engages in that "high art rescue mission," that celebration of Seuss for his artistic experimentation in order to differentiate him from, in this case, the hillbillies. Artists, it seems, *intend* to break the rules, they experiment with form. Hillbillies don't know the rules in the first place. Seuss had intention. Elvis Presley? Just feeling. And, lest we forget, Seuss went to Dartmouth.

The rescue of Seuss was a thing of categories, of installing Seuss in one place rather than another. *Where do we put this new thing? What is it?* If there are historical junctures at which category confusion triggers greater anxiety than at others, Seuss was in one of them. It became a matter of pulling Seuss away from commerce in the form of the world of advertising, the lowbrow in the form of comic books, the "uneducated" in the form of the southerner. And by most measures, the rescue was successful. Unfortunately. *The Cat in the Hat* could not be rock and roll. That made too many uncomfortable. It seems Seuss's language disruptions had to be removed from Little Richard's.

Seuss's privileging of rhyme and rhythm over story, his willingness to let the content be determined by the feel, put him close to the rock and roll music (much of it still classified as R&B) that was being born just as his Cat was coming to life. But folks like Big Joe Turner, Fats Domino, and Presley, they often worked in a world removed from the kind of artistic *intention* that Seuss's advocates imposed on Seuss in order to elevate him. "I found my thrill / on Blueberry Hill." "A wop bop a loo bop a wop bam boom!" It could've been Seuss. And it couldn't have. But it could have. The stories of Little Richard spontaneously coming up with "Tutti Frutti" while on break during an unproductive recording session, or Elvis Presley cutting "That's All Right (Mama)" because Sam Phillips heard him playing the song during yet another lackluster session's break—these are the moments of spontaneity, moments removed from intention in the sense Seuss's advocates used it. But it was the very kind of spontaneity embodied in that moment when an author named Seuss looked for the first rhyme he could find, *cat/hat*, and wrote a story from there.

What history loses when everything is forced into neat categories in the name of reducing cultural anxiety, when the hillbillies are separated from the Dartmouth grads, is substantial. Of course, there is no *outside* of categories, which is just another way of saying there is no outside of language. We need those categories to convey meaning. But there is the possibility of interrogating them, testing them for their strength, of offering historical reappraisals that are, sometimes, capable of a reordering of things. And the reason to attempt this "reordering" may not be to bring *The Cat in the Hat* closer to "Tutti Frutti." No, it may be that the reason to attempt such a reordering is to bring "Tutti Frutti" closer to "Hiroshima." The Cat is just the connective tissue.

But what one bumps up against, time and time again, is this matter of *intention*. We have no record of Little Richard saying that "Tutti Frutti" was his response to the atomic bomb, that he believed the world needed new music because it was no longer the same world. He didn't say that language had to be disrupted after Hiroshima's historical trauma and "Tutti Frutti" was going to be a part of the disruption. The received story is that Richard was at the Dew Drop Inn in New Orleans, stuck a couple falsies up his shirt, and let loose with the song. And everyone liked it for the next sixty years or so. But nothing about an intended disruption to language. We know that later Sputnik would scare Little Richard back to the church, at least as the myth has it (and not permanently). But that story resonates more as a personal crisis of faith, not as much a musical response to a changing world. Without *intention* as the operative category, it's not as easy to make the case that these hillbillies and southern Black artists of the 1950s were cultural revolutionaries whose work is connected to the events in the wider world. Their disruptions to language were certainly as impactful, lasting, and crucial as Dr. Seuss's, but rock and roll doesn't have as many John Herseys to help us see that rock and roll's disruptions to language were indeed connected to, well, shit out there.

Todd Gitlin's claim that there would be no sixties without the fifties is, I think, as profound as it is obvious. And I believe it's a viewpoint that still gets too little consideration. His claim holds true in part because of the way the disruptions to language that gave the fifties its rhythms, whether rock and roll's or Dr. Seuss's or Allen Ginsberg's, created a before-and-after effect that opened up certain freedoms that would come to define the sixties. Freedoms of both the body and the mind. The fifties were the decade when rhythm was made primary. Reason took a back seat to *feel*. Intention? That's what you use when you drop atomic bombs. A new language, a next-generation language, was needed and delivered. *The Cat in the Hat*, in its own, tells the story of a new youth culture's emergence and the related disconnect young people would feel in relation to the parent generation. Told through rhythms. Driven by rhyme.

The Cat, American con man at the door, enters the house selling his idea of fun, releasing trouble in the form of Thing One and Thing Two. Pure disruption. The ineffective fish, clownish in his failed masculinity and efforts to be the man-of-the-house, can do nothing to bring about domestic stability. The children don't really say it, but they're interested in the Cat. Something is happening for them, finally, and on a day when it seemed nothing would. But this disruption isn't just a matter of the kids' rooms getting messy. The Cat fucks with adult stuff. That gown. That rake. That cake. It's like a bomb's gone off. The Cat is, of course, gone by the time mother returns. The story leaves off thus:

> Should we tell her about it?
> Now, what SHOULD we do?
> Well . . .
> What would YOU do
> If your mother asked you?

No resolution. No moral. Reason does not rule here. Instead, the boy turns to the reader, asking what that reader would do in the face of such a quandary. Does one speak of something so new as the Cat to a *mother*? Or is it better that the mother doesn't know about that which she wouldn't understand anyway? After all, she belongs to another world, speaks another language, and both are over. Handed a finite selection of words, starting with the first rhyme he could find, Seuss—perhaps not even intending it—let everyone know what was coming, as the generations would lose one another in the rubble.

In writing Tom Petty's biography, the most challenging period to grapple with was that in which Petty's first marriage ended. The personal changes in his life affected everything at the time, from parenting to work to friendship to inner dialogue. It was like a bomb had gone off in his world. Petty spoke of it all very openly, and on numerous occasions, but there was a sense as we talked that no matter the time that had passed, he was still processing it all. "I probably spent a month not getting out of bed, just waking up and going, 'Oh, fuck.' Lying there . . . The only thing that stopped the pain was drugs." The album he made in the midst of that upheaval, *Echo*, he spoke of with little warmth. Understandably. To his ears, *Echo* brought back a hard time. The only strange part is just how good the record is.

Rick Rubin describes the *Echo* sessions: "He was in his head more, less open, wearing shades all the time. Just, like, *separate*." Rubin didn't know a lot about what was going on in Petty's personal life. That wasn't their relationship. But he knew his artist was in a darkness. Whatever Petty was going through, artistic strategies that made good sense during the time the two men made *Wildflowers* no longer made the same sense. There was a breakdown in meaning for Petty. In discussing it with me, he spoke about heroin use publicly for the first time. "I'd never come up against anything that was bigger than me, something that I couldn't control. But [heroin] starts running your life. It went for a while before Dana and my family got involved. And *Echo* came in the middle of that mess. I'm lucky I came through. Not everyone does."

What Rubin did is remarkable in many ways. The job of a record producer is not straightforward. There are those who are musicians, those who are not. Some producers do their job well just by helping the artist pick the best songs for a collection. But a good producer is either the right producer for an artist, or knows how to become the right producer. When the client is a star, however, it takes a very self-assured individual to go through this *becoming* process, finding out what an artist needs from them. Had Rubin failed in this regard, he wouldn't have been the first man to lose his focus around a rock and roll star. But he didn't fail. He went to Barnes and Noble and purchased magnetic poetry sets.

Taking all of the words out of those magnetic poetry sets, Rubin went through them, removing the prepositions and other small words. What was left he spread across Petty's metal music stand in the recording studio. Rubin describes the scene: "Then, when Tom had songs without words, just chord changes and melodies, he'd randomly look at words and make up sentences. I could show you specific lines he wrote that were words from the poetry set. It was remarkable and beautiful. He could draw on this pool of information to create stories."

Rubin rightly saw that a man was in the middle of some wreckage and a language disruption was needed, a language disruption that could help the artist work amidst the other disruptions. Like William Spaulding to Dr. Seuss, Rubin created for Petty a situation in which a frame, a limiting mechanism, allowed new pictures to be drawn, new stories to be told. The worlds of rock and roll and the children's literature again looked like one another. And in all that activity were clues about the world beyond. But history wouldn't remember it that way.

17

Cosmic Ray

How Ray Charles's "I Got a Woman" Transformed the Music of Ray Charles, Allowed Him to Keep His Band, and Created a Musical and Social Revolution

By Peter Guralnick

"Music is not just my life, it's my total existence. I'm deadly serious, man. I'm not just trying to feed you words."

Nervous, intense, compulsively polysyllabic, Atlantic Records' recently installed vice president and minority owner Jerry Wexler could sense the excitement in the voice at the other end of the line. It was not unusual for him and his new partner, thirty-one-year-old Atlantic Records founder Ahmet Ertegun, to receive calls from their recording artists from the road. Usually it was the result of some kind of foul-up, as often as not they were looking for money, but this call from Ray Charles in November of 1954 was different. He was going to be playing the Royal Peacock in Atlanta in a few days, Ray announced in that curious half-stammer in which words spilled over one another to convey energy, certitude, deference, and cool reserve. He still had that same little seven-piece outfit he had put together a few months earlier as a road band for Atlantic's premier star, Ruth Brown—but he had changed the personnel around a little, he told Wexler. The sound was better, tighter, and they had worked up some new original material. He wanted Jerry and Ahmet to come down to Atlanta. He was ready to record.

There was no hesitation on Wexler's or Ertegun's part. Ertegun, a sardonic practical joker who had first been exposed to the deep roots of African American culture as the son of the wartime Turkish ambassador to the United States, had started Atlantic in 1947 on a shoestring with veteran record man Herb Abramson out of their mutual passion for the music. He had purchased Ray's contract from the Swing Time label in California five years later without even meeting his new artist or seeing him in person. Twenty-five hundred dollars was not easy to come by in those days, but such was his belief in the dimensions of Ray's talent, he was so "knocked out by the style, vocal delivery, and piano playing" of this twenty-one-year-old blind, Black blues singer whose popularity so far had derived primarily from nuanced interpretations of the sophisticated stylings of Nat "King" Cole and Charles Brown, that he had no doubt he could make hit records with him. "I was willing," he told Ray Charles biographer David Ritz, "to bet on his future."

So far, though, that bet hadn't really paid off. Atlantic had released half a dozen singles from four sessions to date, with just one of them, a novelty tune called "It Should've Been Me," released earlier that year, making any real dent in the charts. More tellingly, Ahmet's direct attempts to move Ray away from the politely stylized approach with which he had up to this point made his mark could not be said to have fully succeeded. They had in fact met with only faint approval from Ray, who, as pleased as he was with his recent progress ("All I wanted was to play music. Good music"), was not particularly "ecstatic" about his present situation either. He had started out imitating Brown and Nat King Cole both because he was drawn to their music and because they were popular. "If you could take a popular song and sound like the cat doing it, then that would help you get work. Shit, I needed work, man!" But now he wanted to get work on the basis of his own sound, with the kind of music he heard in his head, every kind of music from Chopin to Hank Williams, from the Original Five Blind Boys of Mississippi to Artie Shaw and Benny Goodman, with "each music," he said, "[having] a different effect." He just wasn't sure where, or how, to find it.

Ahmet and his original partner, Herb Abramson, had tried to help him. Initially they recorded Ray in New York, using, Ahmet said, "the formula we had used so successfully with artists like Big Joe Turner": a house band made up of the best New York studio musicians, with A&R chores assigned to veteran Black songwriter and arranger Jesse Stone, who had been involved in nearly every one of Atlantic's hits to date. But Stone and Ray had clashed ("I respected Jesse Stone," Ray told David Ritz, "but I also respected myself"), and no one was fully satisfied, not even when Ray was given more leeway at the second New York session in the spring of 1953, exuberantly driving the boogie-woogie pastiche that Ahmet had written for him, "Mess Around," and throwing himself into the part of a slick, jive-talking jitterbug on the slower, but just as emphatically rhythm-driven, "It Should've Been Me."

Then, a few months later, he found himself in New Orleans—"I never lived there," he told me in response to any attempt on my part to make something more of it. "I spent some *time* there. Let's not get the two confused. I got *stranded* there is the best way to put it. Meaning, I got there, and I didn't have any money, and the people there took me in."

It was a situation that he absolutely hated. He had lost his sight at the age of six, but his mother had taught him that there was nothing he could not do; she refused to allow him to consider himself "handicapped"; she insisted fiercely that he always assert his independence. He was educated at the Florida School for the Deaf and Blind in St. Augustine, but he had been on his own since his mother's death when he was fifteen and had made his way in the world as a professional musician ever since. He had had a hit record on Swing Time at eighteen, then gone on the road with blues singer Lowell Fulson for two years, where he soon became the leader of Fulson's nine-piece band. He prided himself justifiably on his resourcefulness and intelligence—but here he was stuck in New Orleans in the summer of 1953, just *scuffling*. He was twenty-two years old, a heroin addict almost from the time he entered the music business, a musician with a certain measure of success but clearly not strong enough to carry a band to play his music or support himself as a single. He was, in short, dependent on the kindness of strangers.

Sometimes you can do things, and it'll be too soon. The people ain't ready for it. It can be all kinds of things, but if it's good, that's the main thing. At least you won't have to be embarrassed.

Whatever the circumstances of his arrival, New Orleans proved a fortuitous landing place. He moved into Foster's Hotel on Lasalle ("The guy let me stay there sometimes [when] I couldn't pay, and he didn't throw me out on the street"), got bookings at local clubs while playing gigs occasionally out of town, in Slidell and Thibodaux, and every day, with neither a cane, a seeing-eye dog, nor the assistance of anyone else, negotiated the four-block journey from Foster's to local club owner Frank Painia's Dew Drop Inn for a lunch of red beans and rice. Asked how he could find his way in life so confidently and precisely, he told a fellow musician it was easy. "I do just like a bat. You notice I wear hard-heeled shoes? I listen to the echo from my heels, and that way I know where there's a wall. When I hear a space, that's the open door."

In August of 1953 Ahmet and his new partner (Jerry Wexler, a one-time journalist and fellow jazz and R&B enthusiast, had joined Atlantic after Herb Abramson was drafted just two months earlier) went down to New Orleans for a Tommy Ridgley session that represented the thirty-six-year-old Wexler's first foray into the field. As Wexler described it in his autobiography, this was the first of many such trips, in which they would hit town after a rocky flight and Ahmet, who had either slept through the turbulence or kept "his head buried in Kant's *Critique of Pure Reason* or the latest issue of *Cash Box*, [would] be ready to roll [and] I'd be ready to crash. . . . The next thing I knew it was morning and Ahmet was just getting in, brimming over with tales of . . . existential happenings." Given Ray's current residence and his obvious need for work, Ahmet got in touch with him to play on the session, at whose conclusion Ray cut a couple of blues with the all-star New Orleans band that Ahmet had assembled for the occasion.

The first, "Feelin' Sad," was a song written and originally recorded by a twenty-seven-year-old New Orleans–based bluesman who went by the name of Guitar Slim and whom Ray had met through Dew Drop proprietor (and Slim's manager and landlord) Frank Painia. Slim, whose real name was Eddie Jones, frequently dressed in a fire-engine-red suit, used a two-to- three-hundred-foot-long guitar cord that permitted him to stroll out the door of the Dew Drop and entertain passersby on the street, and occasionally dyed his hair blue—but the eight-bar blues that Ray chose to record didn't really stand out from the traditional blues material with which Ray had always worked, except for the churchy, exhortatory feel that Slim had imparted to it.

Ray brought some of the same fiery passion to his performance, wailing the words with an almost tearful break in his voice, calling out to the musicians—and presumably his listeners—to "Pray with me, boys, pray with me," and concluding with a hummed chorus that burst into a rough-edged gospel shout, with a bed of horns standing in for the amen corner. Even the second song, "I Wonder Who," a much more conventional composite blues, carried with it some of those same hints—though they were only hints—of the gospel pyrotechnics that Ray so admired in singers like Archie Brownlee of the Five Blind Boys of Mississippi. It was a slow, almost doleful blues, enlivened only by the passion in Ray's voice, and while Jerry and Ahmet were both glad to see Ray abandoning some of his stylistic refinements, neither felt they had made any real progress toward establishing a new direction in Ray's music, a new voice of his own.

Ray certainly didn't take it as any great turning point—he would have been the first to admit that at this point he was still just feeling his way. At the same time he recognized that if he ever expected to get anywhere, he'd *better find* his way pretty damn quick. He wasn't all that sure how he felt about the new man either. He had always taken Ahmet's wry enthusiasm—for him *and* the music—at face value. With his dry nasal voice, his sharp wit and parrying intelligence, above all the unmistakable respect and belief he had shown in Ray from the start ("[He] never, ever said to me I couldn't record a piece of music. That kind of tells you."), Ahmet could never be deflected from the ironic assurance of his outlook or the certitude of his goals. Wexler on the other hand seemed edgy, almost jittery in his need to show who was in charge. At one point when Ray was playing behind Tommy Ridgley, Wexler told him, "Don't play like Ray Charles, you're backup." Which might have been the first and last straw if Ray had been dealing with anyone else, but he could see that Jerry was the same with Ahmet and Cosimo Matassa, the recording studio owner and engineer, both of whom seemed to just laugh it off as part of the makeup of a man who clearly was passionate about what he was doing but just wasn't cool.

He remained in New Orleans for the next few months, taking gigs as far away as Baton Rouge but generally returning to the Foster Hotel on the same night, even if it meant getting home not long before the break of day. He played blackjack, using Braille-marked cards, with fellow musicians ("Best blackjack player I ever saw," said one), maintained his drug connection, but kept to himself a good deal of the time, sometimes listening to his spiritual records and gospel music on the radio all day long, "the best singers I ever heard in my life [with] voices that could shake down your house and smash all the furniture in it. Jesus, could they wail!"

Gradually he put together a group of like-minded musicians, fellow eclectics to play and jam with on a semiregular basis. "Feelin' Sad," his fourth Atlantic release, came out in September and did nothing. Then in October of 1953 he was approached by Frank Painia to play on a Guitar Slim session, Slim's first for the West Coast label Specialty. Painia asked him, would he mind listening to some of the songs that Slim wanted to do, maybe he could write some arrangements. "See, everybody knew I could write," Ray said. And everybody knew Slim's utter lack of organization. That was how Ray Charles became leader, arranger, and taskmaster for a series of stark, Guitar Slim–composed compositions whose riveting centerpiece was a number called "The Things That I Used to Do."

"The Things That I Used to Do," Eddie Jones claimed, had been presented to him by the devil in a dream and was a fiery, gospel-laced number with little sense of form until Ray got hold of it. It was not, Ray insisted, an easy task. "I liked Guitar Slim, he was a nice man, but he was not among the musicians that I socialized with. Believe me, we worked our ass off for that session. We started in the morning and worked well into the night, and once we got through it, I said, 'Okay, I'm glad to be part of it.' But my music had absolutely nothing to do with what we did with Guitar Slim."

There was more to it, though, despite the emphatic disclaimer. The unrestrained way that Slim attacked the material, the loose, spontaneous feel that he brought to the session, above all the sheer, uninhibited preacher-like power of his voice must have struck some kind of common chord, for all of Ray's vehement denials. And—something he denied even more vehemently, to the end of his life—the way that Guitar Slim *attacked* his songs surely must have had some kind of liberating effect. There was, it seemed, something almost inevitable in the feelings that it would come to unleash in his own music, feelings that up till now he had experienced only in his passion for gospel music. And the gargantuan success of Slim's record in the early days of 1954 (it went to number one on the R&B charts in January, remaining there off and on for fourteen weeks and becoming one of the biggest-selling blues records of all time) must surely have left its mark, too.

Ray continued to rehearse and play with some of the musicians who had provided the nucleus for the Guitar Slim session, and when Ahmet and Jerry Wexler came back to town for a Big Joe Turner session on December 3, 1953, he was ready to record. They couldn't get the use of Cosimo's studio the next day, so they went to radio station WDSU, where Ray opened with an exuberant falsetto whoop in his takeoff on a traditional blues composition, "Don't You Know." This was no knee-jerk approach to the blues, though, interspersed as it was with his own preacherly gruffness and churchy squeals, while the band followed right along without prompting from Ahmet or Jerry. It was, clearly, a very different kind of session, with even the more somber traditional blues that followed expressing itself with that weeping, wailing sound that had first manifested itself on Slim's "Feelin' Sad" at the last New Orleans session. It was, as Jerry Wexler would come to realize afterward, "a landmark session . . . because it had: Ray Charles originals, Ray Charles arrangements, a Ray Charles band. . . . Ahmet and I had nothing to do with the preparation, and all we could do was see to it that the radio technician didn't erase the good takes during the playbacks."

Ray moved his home base to Texas and went back on the road as a single at $75 a week early in the new year. "It Should've Been Me," the novelty song from the second New York session, hit the charts at the beginning of April 1954, rising as high as number five, while Guitar Slim's "The Things That I Used to Do" remained at number one. Which was all very well, but the musical exigencies of life on the road as a single were becoming more and more unendurable for Ray. He played a gig in Philadelphia, and "the band was so bad," he told *New Yorker* writer Whitney Balliett, "I just went back to my hotel and cried":

> I was going crazy, man. I was losing my fucking head. Because, you know, you go into a town, and the guy says he got the musicians, and the musicians weren't shit. And if you're a very fussy person like me—and, I mean, I'm fussy even about good musicians—well, I just couldn't take it.

That was the final impetus for putting his own band together. "I pestered the Shaw [booking agency] to death," he told Balliett, "and they loaned me the money to buy a station wagon, and I had enough money to make a down payment on a car for myself. I went down to Dallas and put a band together out of people I had heard one place or another." But the booking agency, Ray told me, said he still wasn't strong enough to be booked on his own. "Which they were right. They said, 'In order for you to work, we gonna put your band with Ruth Brown.' I said okay, and we worked four or five dates with her. In fact, we only did four, because the second date we missed. That first date we drove all day doing a hundred-and-some-odd miles an hour, from Dallas to El Paso, it's amazing we didn't burn [the engines] up, because they both were new cars. The next job was in Louisiana, all the way back from where we just came from and then some. Drove our ass off, and we were late and we missed it. We got there at eleven o'clock at night, and the people canceled the job on us. Now you talk about *sick*—we was SICK." Then they worked a few dates in Mississippi and Florida, "and that was it. Ruth Brown left and went in [one] direction, and we went in another."

There was no question of the direction that he had set for himself. With the band, he wrote in his autobiography, *Brother Ray*, he was able at last to become himself. "I opened up the floodgates, let myself do things I hadn't done before. . . . If I was inventing something new, I wasn't aware of it. In my mind, I was just bringing out more of me." His immediate problem, though, in the fall of 1954 was to figure out a way to sustain the band. And for that, there was no question, he needed a hit.

He appointed trumpeter Renald Richard, whom he had originally met in New Orleans, musical director for an extra five dollars a week, then paid him an additional five dollars to write out the charts according to Ray's dictation as they drove along in his brand-new '54 DeSoto. "Ray dictated fast," Richard told Charles biographer Michael Lydon. "And he didn't work out the chart in the concert key, the chords as he played them on the piano. No, he'd give me the parts transposed . . . do one instrument, on to the next, and I'm writing and writing!" They listened to the radio, too. "Ray loved blues singers like Big Joe Turner," Renald Richard told Lydon, "but most of all he loved gospel singers. He used to talk all the time about Archie Brownlee, the lead singer with the Five Blind Boys of Mississippi, how much he liked him. Then he started to sound like him, turning his notes, playing with them to work the audience into a frenzy."

They were out on tour in early October. They had just played South Bend and were on their way to Nashville, with the radio tuned to whatever gospel music they could pick up as the stations faded in and out in the middle of the night. All of a sudden a song called "It Must Be Jesus" by the Southern Tones came on the air. It was a simple midtempo variation on the old spiritual, "There's a Man Going Around Taking Names," with the kind of tremolo guitar accompaniment that had come into fashion lately in a music that had up till now been sung mostly a cappella. The tenor singer took the lead on a pair of verses which began at the high end of his range, with the first line ("There's a man going around taking names") repeated in a slightly higher register and the third ("You know, he took my mother's name") rising yet again to the point where the singer's voice broke intentionally, the same way that Ray broke his voice in a kind of "yodel" on "Feelin' Sad" or "Don't You Know."

Almost without thinking about it, Ray and Renald Richard started singing along, but where the Southern Tones started out their second verse ("There's a man giving sight to the blind"), Ray and Renald broke into a secular verse ("I got a woman / Way across town / Who's good to me") with Ray's voice echoing exactly the Southern Tones' lead singer's intense intro and resolution. Then, after the second verse, the gospel number broke into a kind of syncopated patter between the tenor and the bass singer, the kind of give-and-take that the Golden Gate Quartet used for novelty effect but which in the contemporary gospel mode could be drawn out in live performance, building in tension until at last it was resolved by returning to the verse. Ray and his band director broke themselves up on this part as they substituted secular and profane variations on the spiritual message ("He's my rock / He's my mighty power") along the lines of "She gives me money / When I'm in need." Ordinarily that would have been the end of it, just a bit of late-night foolishness, but there was something about the song, and their lighthearted extemporization, that got to Ray in a way he couldn't quite put his finger on, and, rather than explore it himself, he asked Renald if he thought he could formally write out a song that was structured around their improvisation. "I said, 'Hell, yes,' and the next morning, ten o'clock, I was in his room with [it]. I didn't really write it all that night. I stuck in the bridge from another song I had written years back."

Ray sketched out an arrangement and started singing the new song, "I Got a Woman," in the show almost immediately. Renald Richard left shortly thereafter, largely over the way drugs seemed to be taking over the band, but the song continued to get a stronger and stronger response. Ray worked up a couple of other originals, along with "Greenbacks," a novelty number that Renald had contributed to the band's book, until he felt like he was ready for a full-scale session. That was when he called up Atlantic Records and announced to Jerry Wexler that he was coming to Atlanta and was ready to record. It was the first time he had called a session on his own, and he may have seemed more confident than he was. After all, he was not about to reveal his insecurities to just anyone, least of all someone like Ahmet Ertegun, who had treated him with so much respect and consideration. But if he wanted to keep the band together—and that was just about like saying if he wanted to keep on breathing—he needed a fucking hit.

Ahmet and Jerry met him at his hotel, just a few doors down from the club, the Royal Peacock, on "Sweet Auburn" Avenue, the hub of Black life in

Atlanta. It was a street humming with life, there were dozens of independent Black businesses of greater and lesser repute, clubs, bars, beauty shops, and shoe-shine stands, all packed together up and down the street, with the Peacock, along with Martin Luther King Sr.'s Ebenezer Baptist Church less than half a mile away, one of the twin centers of that life. The club was owned and operated by sixty-four-year-old Carrie Cunningham, an imposing woman of considerable entrepreneurial imagination and ambition (she owned the hotel, also called the Royal, in which Ray was staying), who had originally come to town as a circus rider after leaving her home in Fitzgerald, Georgia, in her teens with the Silas Green from New Orleans traveling show. She had opened the club in 1949 as a means of keeping her errant musician son at home, and it had almost immediately become a way station for every musician of any repute who passed through Atlanta, from Duke Ellington to Big Maybelle. True to its name, it was resplendent with hand-painted images of peacocks and flamboyant color combinations that seemed to come to Miss Cunningham in visions that she had her regally attired staff carry out.

Ahmet and Jerry didn't have time to notice the decor, Ray was in too much of a hurry. They could barely keep up with him as he practically ran down the street, and when they entered the club he already had his seven-piece band set up onstage, two trumpets, two saxes, bass, drums, with a local pickup on guitar, all just sitting there as if waiting for their cue. Ray took his place at the piano and counted off, and the sound of the new song filled the room, a sound for which Ahmet and Jerry were totally unprepared.

It opened with a long, drawn-out, unaccompanied "Wellllll . . ." from Ray, with the band falling in solidly behind him three words into the first line. Ray's voice was altogether commanding but controlled as he sang the words that he and Renald Richard had fooled around with, but he was bearing down in a way that, while it was a recognizable elaboration on everything he had done before, was also something new. And when he got to the part where his voice ascended, with the horns ascending behind him, his voice rose to a kind of controlled climax.

The second verse drove just a little bit harder until, when he reached his highest natural pitch, it rose to a falsetto that was not so much an imitation as a tribute to Archie Brownlee's all-out attack, ending in a kind of discreet groan that signaled a honking solo from Donald Wilkerson on tenor sax. Then Ray took it back, delivering the syncopated recitatif that substituted for a bridge, with his own discreet version of the preacher's trick of a sharp expelling of breath, a pronounced huffing and chuffing that served to mark a kind of ecstatic release. Whereupon it was back to the first verse, his voice commandingly roughened, until he took it out with a tag that announced, "Don't you know she's all right? She's all right, she's all right."

Ahmet and Jerry sat there for a moment, stunned—but they knew right away. Ray ran through his three other new songs, and there was no question about it. Everything was ready, the band was fully rehearsed—it was as if, Ahmet said, he was simply announcing, to himself as much as to them, "This is what I'm going to do." "It was such a departure," Wexler said. "The band was his voice." All that was left was to set up a session.

This turned out to be easier said than done. There was no recording studio in Atlanta readily at hand (the recent regional success of Elvis Presley's first Sun record had not yet set off the explosion of local recording facilities that would soon follow in the mid-South), so they turned to their old friend Zenas "Daddy" Sears, a white New Jerseyan who had moved to Atlanta just before the Second World War, then took to the airwaves upon his return from the service, where he had acquired a love for gospel music and rhythm and blues while operating a little fifty-watt radio station in the hills of India for the mostly Black troops who were stationed there. Just eight months earlier he had moved to a brand-new station, WAOK, dedicated exclusively to Black programming, which before long he would come to own. It would have been logical to use the new radio studio, but WAOK had a full programming schedule, and eventually Zenas set up the session at WGST at Georgia Tech, his old station, the only catch being that they would have to break every hour for the news. There was some talk of Zenas bringing in a female singer he had worked with, Zilla Mays, to underscore the gospel sound, but nothing came of it. Jerry meanwhile tried to prep the less-than-enthusiastic radio engineer on the uniqueness of what they were about to do, but he quickly gave up on the idea when he realized that however earnestly he cued him for a sax solo that was coming up, all he got for his efforts was a quizzical shrug after the solo was past.

Ray kicked off with "Blackjack," an impassioned minor-key blues he had been working on while out on tour with T-Bone Walker, the consummate guitar stylist of the age. (B.B. King was one of his many disciples, as was, evidently, Wesley Jackson, the local guitarist on the session.) "T and I were up all night at a boarding house in Hattiesburg, Mississippi, playing blackjack," Ray told the coauthor of his autobiography, David Ritz. "I'm winning big, over $2,000. T is down to his last 80 bucks . . . and just as he hits 16 with a 5, the Christian lady who owns the house sees him taking my money and starts yelling, 'How dare you take advantage of this poor blind man?' She was so irate she wouldn't let T touch my bread. Afterwards T told me, 'That shit's so funny you oughta write a song about it.' Well, I did." A song that ended with the horns coming in only on the last two drawn-out notes for an ironically sober Amen.

Jerry and Ahmet were no less impressed than they had been the day before. The arrangement was perfectly calibrated to the new rough-edged sound of Ray's vocals. But "I Got a Woman" was what they were waiting for—that was the reason for the session—and from the deliberate, almost stately pace of the count-off, and the elegantly elongated "Welllllll" that would soon become the musical catchphrase of a generation, their expectations were not just confirmed but exceeded. The guitar had by now dropped out—if it was present at all for the rest of the session, it was strictly as another element in the percussive mix. "Ray had every note that was to be played by every musician in his mind," said Ahmet, who had recorded some of the signature sounds of the past decade. "It was a real lesson to me to see an artist of his stature at work. You could lead him a little bit, but you really had to let him take over. For the first time, we heard something that didn't have to be messed around with, it was all there."

Even Ray, as determined a non-determinist as I have ever met ("My thing, man, has always been to do what I do, that's all," was about as much as you were ever going to get from him in the way of causative explanation), recognized the significance of the occasion. This was the moment, he said, that "I started being me." From this point on, whatever vicissitudes life might have in store for a blind heroin addict living by his wits in an indifferent world (a tendentious formulation with which Ray, who before long would quite rightly come to be called "The Genius" by his record company, would contumaciously disagree), there was no turning back. "The minute I gave up trying to sound like [someone else] and said, 'Okay, be yourself,' that was all I knew. I couldn't be nothing else but that."

18

Ain't It Always Stephen Stills

By Lorrie Moore

Several years ago an academic colleague and I embarked on what we called a "Stills-off": we would listen to our record collections and narrow the musician Stephen Stills's oeuvre down to its top five songs. Then we'd see whose list was better. I assumed our choices would overlap, and that high among them would be "4+20," whose piercing Appalachian melancholy seems to belong more to the ages than to the moody twenty-four-year-old who wrote it, as well as "Find the Cost of Freedom" with its sea shanty cry of grief and endurance. We would both surely include his Buffalo Springfield resistance anthem "For What It's Worth," with Stills's calm, urgent baritone and rhythmic stops; originally released to protest a Los Angeles curfew—its composition probably began earlier when Stills was still nineteen—it has endured long past its original occasion. According to Tim Rice, it is "one of the best songs ever written with just two chords." (Rice is a lyricist: the song has more than two chords.)

But my colleague and I could not stay away from Stills's rocking guitar solos—"Crossroads," for instance, or "Ain't It Always," pieces that got Stills labeled "Guitar God" on YouTube. Then there is "The Love Gangster," from his double album, *Manassas*, on which Bill Wyman of the Rolling Stones plays bass. Wyman wanted at the time to leave the Stones and join Stills's band; the instruments on *Manassas* are all in the hands of virtuosos. Stills has put out recordings in which, like Prince, he has played all the instruments and sung all the parts. ("Do for the Others," a song from his first solo album, is aptly named.) But *Manassas* did not require that.

And so our lists began to burst at the seams and soon the Stills-off seemed an increasingly stupid exercise. Stills, now seventy-two, has often been named one of the top rock guitarists of all time and is the only musician to have recorded with both Jimi Hendrix and Eric Clapton on the same album—his first solo LP (1970). His work has sprung from every stripe of American music—blues, folk, rock, "songs with roots," as he has put it; he was "Americana" and "singer-songwriter" before those terms were used. And although as a child he began as a drummer and tap dancer, the only percussion one is likely to hear from him now might be when he knocks rhythmically against an acoustic guitar. Once, on a 2006 tour that was being filmed, he tripped over some electrical cords and fell to the stage with a certain percussive flair. "We've got more lights than we're used to," he said. "We usually don't care if they can see us because we're old." A year after my misbegotten Stills-off I attended a sold-out concert in Nashville by the Long Players, a tribute band that performs one single album from start to finish at each of its concerts. This time they had chosen *Déjà Vu* (witty!), which is the first and best (and for a long while was the only) album by Crosby, Stills, Nash & Young. (Ampersand and no Oxford comma for Young: when he needs to get out of a band he flees quickly.) No sooner had the Long Players begun with Stills's "Carry On" than the capacity crowd was standing—this cannot always be counted on with members of the AARP—and singing along at the top of their lungs. Jubilant, revelatory, the evening was more than a geezer-pleaser: it was baby boomer church, late-middle-aged ecstasy, a generation stating that it had not just yet entirely surrendered to the next. I started to suspect that no American demographic had so thoroughly memorized an album—not even one by the Beatles or Bob Dylan or Joni Mitchell—as this generation of baby boomers had *déjà vu.*

The summer after that concert, on a porch in New England, I found myself among several dinner guests sitting about postprandially in the July night. Suddenly a guitar appeared, and just as suddenly we were all singing Stills's "Helplessly Hoping." Though we did not know one another that well, working from brain muscle memory we knew the song so automatically that harmony was possible. There was no Beatles or Dylan song we could have sung as successfully. I began to marvel, yet again, at how much, for a particular generation, the songs of Stephen Stills were marinated into our minds, our spines, our bones.

Now it was March 2017, and a friend and I were waiting for Stills to step onto the stage of Nashville's legendary Ryman Auditorium with the Allman-esque Kenny Wayne Shepherd and an old hipster keyboardist, Barry Goldberg. The three of them have been playing together, in a blues-rock ensemble called the Rides, since 2013. (Stills once said that Crosby, Stills, and Nash called themselves by their names not just so they could be free to come and go but because "all the animals were taken.") The Rides, which Stills has called "the blues band of my dreams," got its name from Shepherd's and Stills's shared love of cars. ("We're not Prius people," Stills has said.) That he continues to play gigs at his age is evidence of his stubborn professionalism; from the time he was a teenager—from the early Au Go-Go Singers to Buffalo Springfield to Manassas—he was the one to organize his bands.

The Ryman audience was again primarily made up of the generation that came of age during the 1960s—a sea of snowy hair. Stills himself was twenty-two during the summer of love. Because of prodigies like him, whose careers were enabled by the radio—especially ones in cars—almost every kind of music remains emotionally available to an audience this age, except perhaps hip-hop (though Stills has even done some crossover with Spike Lee and Public Enemy for the film *He Got Game*).

Stills may be hobbled by arthritis—backstage he bumps fists rather than shakes hands with fans; he has carpal tunnel and residual pain from a long-ago broken hand, which affects his playing—and he is nearly deaf, but his performance life has continued. Drugs and alcohol may have dented him somewhat, forming a kind of carapace over the youthful sensitivity and cockiness one often saw in the face of the young Stills. Some might infer by looking at the spry James Taylor or Mick Jagger that heroin is less hard on the body than cocaine and booze, which perhaps tear down the infrastructure. ("Stills doesn't know how to do drugs properly," Keith Richards once said.) But one has to hand it to a rock veteran who still wants to get on stage and make music even when his youthful beauty and once-tender, husky baritone have dimmed. It shows allegiance to the craft, to the life, to the music. It risks a derisive sort of criticism as well as an assault on nostalgia.

The Rides' Nashville concert comes on the heels of a "definitive biography" of Stills by the British author David Roberts. Titled *Change Partners*, after one of Stills's own songs, the book is an act of hurried, sloppy, aggregated love. Ignore the typos—mistakes such as "sewed" for "sowed"; "daubed" for "dubbed"—and don't go looking for any psychological depth. Roberts has collected most of his data from widely available interviews. A speedy checklist of girlfriends—Judy Collins, Rita Coolidge, Joan Baez, Susan Saint James—plus wives and children will largely have to do for an account of Stills's personal life. The lovely "Rock and Roll Woman" is declared in passing to be a valentine to Grace Slick.

Roberts is far more interested in constructing a chronicle—flow charts would have been helpful—of the constantly shifting permutations and reunions that formed Stills's music-making through the decades, and that early on gave us the sublime Crosby, Stills, and Nash (and sometimes Young), cobbled from the Byrds, the Hollies, and Buffalo Springfield. The "beautiful Celtic keen of Graham's and David's cat's purr, and my cement mixer" was how Stills characterized band members' voices. Stills needed Young's guitar-playing to help ignite his own, and sometimes there was electric sparring between them onstage. They all performed like jazz musicians—conversational, improvised—and no two live versions of their songs are the same.

To those looking on, it seemed Nash had the organizational skills; Crosby had the intuition; Stills had the musical chops and the brilliant songwriting; Neil Young—like a comet zooming in and out of orbit—had the poetry and mystique and artistic searching but seldom joined the choirboy harmonies at which the other three excelled. "Neil wants to be Tony Orlando and we're Dawn," joked Stills in the 2008 documentary *CSNY Déjà Vu*. Young had planned the 2006 concert tour as a war protest and decorated the stage with yellow ribbons. Stills seemed afraid it was political kitsch but he went along.

Though born in Texas of midwestern parents, Stills was primarily a Florida boy, having spent his adolescence in Tampa and St. Petersburg, as well as Louisiana and Costa Rica. He speaks Spanish; his father was a building contractor whose peripatetic business often followed the military. Home life mirrored that of many postwar families ("What do we do, given life? We move around," wrote Stills in a 1972 song). Stills went to five different high schools. Skilled at several instruments, he played in high school ensembles, including marching bands, and he has since donated money to the University of Florida marching band. He spent a brief period in a military academy and clearly believes such bands are where many musicians get their start.

Florida has always been an interesting hub of musical styles—a farrago of Appalachian, country, gospel, blues, Latino (Caribbean and Cuban émigré), and Seminole traditions. In jazz the great bass player Jaco Pastorius is often thought to be an embodiment of the region's unique sound, guitar notes bending in a tropical otherworldly fusion. (Hip-hop too has its own south Florida subgenre.) In rock there was Jim Morrison, the Allman Brothers, and Lynyrd Skynyrd, who named themselves after their Jacksonville high school gym teacher. Ray Charles made his early reputation in Florida, as did Tom Petty.

Stills brought a distinctive combination of country, folk, Latin, blues, and rock to every band he was in. One can already hear these influences converging in "Suite: Judy Blue Eyes" (1969), a folk-rock love song written about Judy Collins, whose rousing coda has a strong Latin flavor, due to Stills's overlaid vocal track. CSN performed it at Woodstock. Stills wrote songs of great variety of style and mood and composed quickly but unconventionally, often pulling together tracks he had recorded earlier in his studio before he knew where they might land—the equivalent of a writer's notebook or a chef's pantry. Stills liked to cook, both literally and figuratively, for his bands. "Carry On" was written in eight hours.

Again, one may circle back to wonder—skeptically, impertinently—what causes Stills to keep playing into his advanced years? One reason may simply be that he is bringing an entire generation along with him. Neil Young allegedly once played a new and unpopular album in its entirety before a British audience, to much grumbling from the ticket holders who wanted to hear something familiar. When he announced toward the close, "Now we're going to play something you've heard before," the crowd cheered in relief. And then Young played again the first song he had played that evening. Young has worked at some price, and eccentrically, not to become a human jukebox.

Of course, it is a paying job to tour, and Stills has incurred the expenses of a celebrity who grew up without much. Jimi Hendrix, when asked about the problem of singing the blues once one has made so much money from doing so, noted the hardship of musicians' making money (they are then harnessed by recording companies to make more). Hendrix was overworked and deeply ambivalent: "Actually, the more money you make the more blues you can sing," he told Dick Cavett. Stills himself wandered into fame's trappings: cars, drugs, horses, country houses (one in England purchased from Ringo Starr), seven children both in and out of wedlock, fine wines, ex-wives. (His first wife, the singer Véronique Sanson, was the daughter of celebrated French Resistance fighters; "My French never got over the hump, you know?" he said of that divorce, and one imagines that "Marianne" was written about her.) David Crosby, on the other hand, who drifted toward addiction and eventually solitary confinement in a Texas penitentiary, was Hollywood royalty, the privileged son of Floyd Crosby, the renowned cinematographer of *High Noon.*

Sometimes the desire to make music fuses nicely with the need to make a living. Stills was always focused and driven, although these qualities are usually attributed to his intermittent and more sober partner, Graham Nash (we could drink a case of Nash and still be on our feet). *Change Partners* chronicles Stills's doggedness, his durability, his formation and re-formation of bands, beginning (after some pavement-pounding in Greenwich Village) in Los Angeles in 1966 when he assembled Buffalo Springfield (named after a steamroller that was repaving streets), which included Richie Furay, Bruce Palmer, and Neil Young, who had just driven down from Canada in his legendary hearse, ostensibly to locate the actual "77 Sunset Strip." Tom Petty described Stills's guitar-playing at that time as "fluid and bluesy" and Young's as "fuzzy and angry." For decades after, Crosby, Stills, Nash, and Young kept reemerging in various configurations, though each member was determined to do his own solo records. Hence producer Ahmet Ertegun's title for their first live album, *4 Way Street.*

Backstage at the Ryman this spring, before the show, Stills sits at a table and signs merchandise. When it's my turn in line, I hand him a fan letter and he sticks it respectfully and unopened in the inner pocket of his black sport jacket. (That women's jackets don't have these intimate pockets is a sorrow to me, though a boon to the handbag industry.) He is wearing thick, clear-framed glasses, has a silvering goatee, and his hair shines with a light caramel hue, a reminder of his blond youthful beauty. In the Roberts book women speak repeatedly of Stills's handsomeness and his shyness. People were drawn to him. Black musicians on the road and elsewhere often found Stills the member of CSNY with whom they could most connect, and Roberts seems to attribute this to Stills's southern, country-boy roots. Hendrix wanted Stills to join his band and was seeking him out to do so shortly before he died.

For a stretch Stills was also the only one in the band who could vote—Crosby had felonies, Nash was English, Young Canadian. He has long been engaged by politics, especially midterm elections, and while active in presidential campaigns from JFK onward (in the fall of 2016 he wrote a protest song against Trump), he has also made appearances on behalf of local congressmen across the country, urging Americans to think about our government's legislative branch. He began doing this with some success during the Nixon administration, helping to create Tip O'Neill's House of Representatives, and we should expect similar efforts in 2018. In 2000 Stills was part of the Democratic Credentials Committee from Florida during the Democratic National Convention and in previous years served as a delegate.

Perhaps because I work at a university, after taking my letter, Stills mentions to me that he recently received an honorary doctorate from McGill. Because he has been a working musician since he was a teenager and never went to college, he is visibly proud and amused by this. He says he is going to do a project with the neurologist Daniel Levitin, the author of *This Is Your Brain on Music.* I don't mention the Roberts book, which makes no reference to this and is probably not a book Stills has even read, though there is a handy index for skimming. Stills signs our CDs, and we thank him and moved on. There is a line forming of fans hoping to have their photos taken with him, and out of a fear of carnivals and cameras my friend and I do not get in it. My head is full of Stills's songs, one of which from decades ago includes these words: "Help me . . . / My life is a miserable comedy / Of strangers posing as friends" ("Love Story").

Stills tolerates the backstage meet-'n-greet/merch-perch rather well, although there is little revel in his demeanor—how could there be? He's a trouper, a player, a generous musician with his audience and his bandmates. But he is not an award-winning actor. In interviews he tends toward quiet diplomacy, restraint, a dry quip. His signature costumes on stage and album covers have been football jerseys, military jackets, and ponchos.

Resilience then is the theme. Stills is one of the last remaining rock-and-roll geniuses from a time when rock music was the soundtrack to an antiwar movement—"For What It's Worth," "Woodstock," "Ohio" (about the 1970 Kent State shootings)—back when the global counterculture was on the left rather than the right. Roberts's book makes this inexactly clear. Stills has been on the scene from the start, forming Buffalo Springfield when Jimi Hendrix was being booked as the opening act for the Monkees on tour. He has seemingly played with everyone—from Bill Withers to George Harrison. He was the first person to be inducted into the Rock and Roll Hall of Fame twice in one night, for his work in Buffalo Springfield and Crosby, Stills & Nash. "What a wonderfully strange and beautiful cast of characters life has handed to me," he said in his acceptance speech.

On the Ryman stage Stills cuts loose with the young, strapping Kenny Shepherd. Stills often steps back, in a paternal fashion, to let the Shreveport-born Shepherd do his Delta blues thing, long blond hair flying. Spotlights move around the stage searchingly. Stills lets Barry Goldberg, the seventy-four-year-old keyboardist, play his best-known song, "I've Got to Use My Imagination" (a 1974 hit for Gladys Knight and the Pips). Congenitally deaf in one ear and now partially deaf in the other, Stills is brave to attempt his own "Bluebird," with its difficult singing, and on its high notes his voice becomes a bit of a bray. "I've always sung flat," he has said smilingly into cameras, and this embrace of time's wear and tear feels spiritually strong and unself-pitying. Soon he unbegrudgingly performs what has become something of an albatross for him, his hit single "Love the One You're With." The human jukebox aspect of a concert is difficult to avoid.

He shakes out his hands to rid them of pain. Colorful, freshly tuned guitars are brought in at regular intervals. At one point he takes off his jacket and flings it across the stage. "Oh, well," I say to my friend. "There goes my letter." The band closes with Neil Young's "Rockin' in the Free World." (It is a custom of Stills's concerts to include one song by Young.) Shepherd remains a gifted, impeccable, shiny part of it all. But Stills is the one we love. He's the one we're with.

PART V

Losses and Erasures

19

Black Cowboys and Jimi Hendrix

An Interview with Dom Flemons

By Florence Dore

Florence Dore: It's been just a joy to delve into your work. I thought I would start off by just telling you a little bit about where I'm coming from, and then I would love to ask you some questions about your albums, *Black Cowboys* and *Prospect Hill*.

Dom Flemons: That's great with me!

FD: Rockin'! Oh wait! First I have to tell you something very funny . . .

DF: Oh, yes!

FD: My husband used to be for fifteen, sixteen years Steve Earle's drummer.

DF: Ah!

FD: And he knew I was going to be interviewing you and last night he said, "You know, I have a video of him doing 'Hey Joe' by Jimi Hendrix, and do you want to see it?' And so he showed it to me, and it was great.

DF: [laughter]

FD: It was a soundcheck at some festival that you guys were at together. He had gone to see you.

DF: Yeah, that was that when the Chocolate Drops opened up for Steve. And yeah I used to do that one just to mess around . . . of course it was a little tongue in cheek.

FD: Well, I really enjoyed that you put the guitar behind your head like Jimi Hendrix and I thought it was really cool in the context of what I was going to ask you about today. Because I don't know any Black musicians in any kind of popular music—rock, hip-hop, folk genre—or whatever who don't think of Jimi Hendrix as paradigmatic in their musical journeys. So, actually could I start there, and ask you how did you come into playing neo-traditional music? What came first: Jimi Hendrix or folk music?

DF: Well, technically . . . folk music and Jimi Hendrix came in somewhat at the same time for me, which was interesting. You know when I started to play music, my first instrument was the drums and I played in high school. I played all of the auxiliary percussion as well as the marching bass drum in the marching band so . . .

FD: Oh, wow.

DF: The idea of polyrhythms were always of interest to me and around the time I was I guess sixteen, the big Quincy Jones history of rock 'n' roll documentary came out on public television.

FD: Right.

DF: And so they had that wonderful episode called "Plugging In" that began with the 1960s New York folk revival and ran all the way into the Monterrey Pop Festival. So, the line between Dylan to Hendrix was a direct one for me. And that episode, you know they . . . after it came out in the public library they had them on VHS and . . . you know . . . so I'm thirty-eight . . . so when I was doing this this was like 1997, 1998, 1999, so this was a little bit before the big digital revolution, so the internet was present. You could learn some songs from the internet, but for the most part you had to either get a songbook, figure it out on your own, or possibly needed another musician who knew the song and could show you something so that you're . . . you're learning your own version, so there wasn't like YouTube lessons like you would have now. And so, you know . . . the first time I started to see Louis Jordan, and Chuck Berry, and Jimi Hendrix . . . Muddy Waters . . . any of these real heavy guitar players . . . I wanted that power when I played, but I also didn't want to be burdened down by these electric guitars because I was also someone who was interested in performance poetry and spoken performance art and I did slam poetry for many years. And the acoustic guitar was a perfect avenue in which to be able to move freely . . . while still giving out a message.

FD: That's really . . . that's beautiful. I'll just ask you this because you brought it up. The line from Dylan to Hendrix and the acoustic guitar and I notice on your . . . in much of your work you venture into spoken word and you move between spoken word poetry and folk song quite fluidly. It reminded me actually a little bit of Patti Smith in that way—

DF: Yeah!

FD: —when I was listening to it. So this is such an over-asked question but it sounds to me like you wouldn't have any issue at all or confusion at all about Bob Dylan winning the Nobel Prize.

DF: Oh no, no confusion at all. I thought it was . . . I thought it was long overdue and I felt like it was . . . it was elevating poetry within popular song in a way that I think was necessary, especially because on top of Dylan being a great songwriter, his songs get covered quite often all the way up until, you know like "Wagon Wheel" you know or . . . "Knockin' on Heaven's Door" . . .

FD: Of course.

DF: Or "Blowin' in the Wind." Any number of songs that, even now in the twenty-first century, they're still proving to be just as relevant if not more so than ever before. I always think of "Only a Pawn in Their Game" has continued to be more and more relevant to me over the years.

FD: Yes, in the Black Lives Matter moment, the Medgar Evers tribute.

DF: Yeah.

FD: It sounds like you're saying that certainly folk song could or even should be understood as literature.

DF: Absolutely, yeah, and especially in the case . . . especially that specific era of people like Dylan and Eric Anderson and all of the singer-songwriters. I mean they really put their literal heart and souls into how they wrote songs. I think they elevated the literary game in terms of what you could talk about. Of course, Dylan has been able to take it to such a high level. I have a BA in English, so I also went to school for English and I finished it out and so the poetry of all the classics are also written within Dylan's poetry as well, so even the allusions to mythical characters from either real life as poetry or folkloric icons or archetypes are all a part of it. So that's something that I've always thought about when I've been writing my music as well. So I kind of went in different stages where . . . first I was just interested in early rock 'n' roll and then as I got into the folk revival, I was fortunate enough to get a bootleg copy of Murray Lerner's film "Festival," and I guess around 2001 or '02 I found a copy. And that really catapulted into a full, um . . . research mode for me into the folk revival and what it meant outside of just Dylan or the Paul Butterfield Blues Band but into Brownie McGhee and Sonny Terry and into everything from Doc Watson to John Lee Hooker. I mean once you get into that era it's sort of never-ending. But again, this was before the big digital changeover had happened so I had to find people's LPs and records in junk shops and in record stores, so there was a lot of that time delving in. . . . Then when I went to college . . .

FD: Right, right. Where did you go to college? Did you go to UNC?

DF: I went to Northern Arizona University. And so as I was going there, I would go to the record stores and I would buy LPs in the discount bin, and I found LPs. I found a lot of Joni Mitchell, a lot of Joan Baez's records, Cat Stevens, Van Morrison. You know, a lot of the catalog that . . . at that time all of these artists were still so active that their old records were just common stock everywhere. So, I was able to buy them for two or three dollars. I spent a lot of time sitting and studying those styles, and then when I was in college, the LP collection had the Library of Congress recordings. Folkways. Arhoolie Records. So, by the time I got out of college, I had a lot of music in my mind.

DF: Then, as I was finishing college, I was invited to an event called the Black Banjo Gathering, so by this point . . . so if you can imagine, musically, I start out as just someone who picks up a guitar after having played drums knowing nothing about music, so starting to play guitar and just banging along with Beatles and Bob Dylan . . .

FD: Yeah.

DF: Hendrix. Doo-wop. Fats Domino. Buddy Holly. Any type of . . . anything. And then later on, it turned into . . . you know, uh . . . Dylan and Koerner, Ray, and Glover, or . . . when I was eighteen, I had a chance to see Dave Van Ronk . . .

FD: Oh, you're kidding.

DF: Right before he passed away in 2001. So, at first I was just playing music, but then when I saw Van Ronk in concert, I loved the way that he told stories between his songs and so then I started forming my set to be that. I'd picked up a banjo around 2002. I had heard quite a variety of banjo players in Phoenix at the local folk festivals. And so as I was playing, learning country blues, I found that that fit on the banjo as well, so I developed a way of playing slide banjo, country blues on the banjo, as well as doing bluegrass, some Dixieland and . . . a variety of styles in that way, so I started to develop my own style. Then I got invited to go in this event out in North Carolina.

FD: So that sort of moved you in a folk direction?

DF: Yeah, and then I just decided . . . that was when I followed what I'd seen Dylan and a lot of those guys do. I had nothing holding me down, so I sold everything I owned, jumped in my car, and just drove down I-40 straight to North Carolina and started to work with the original Carolina Chocolate Drops, forming the group.

That was when I started to learn about traditional North Carolina blues and a lot of the traditional music on the ground level, compared to it being an academic research, and sort of doing it my own way or going from what the books were saying. I then got to meet people, learn a little bit more about southern culture by being present, and from there . . . that was when I started to see that my collecting and my advocating for the music was something more than just something that I was doing for fun. I then saw that I could get into the professional world of music as someone that was interpreting and presenting the old-time music in the old-time styles.

FD: Was the *Anthology of American Folk* part of your development as a traditional artist?

DF: Without a doubt. You know, when I was at Northern Arizona University they had a copy of the *Anthology* in the library.

FD: Right.

DF: And I was able to really just dig into that collection, and it just kind of knocked me out because it had such a variety of songs. But then, also the sort of open-ended intuitive art aspect of the writing of the liner notes, as a literature person, also intrigued me. Because the idea of the celestial monochord and all these bigger conceptual thoughts outside of just the literal music. That that really just turned me on to the whole collection as well.

FD: I wonder, can you talk about what you see as the relationship between your interest in literature and your interest in traditional music?

DF: Well, you know my interest in literature was always first and foremost. I've always enjoyed poetry, and so the words and the stories that people tell are always something that have been of interest to me. I also really love spoken word albums as well. I have the Caedmon series of Richard Burton and Carl Sandburg and people like that. I also got a great T. S. Eliot record as well, which is just a beautiful one from the fifties . . . reading "The Love Song of J. Alfred Prufrock," you know?

FD: ". . . the butt-ends of my days and ways." It's a beautiful reading.

DF: Yes! I've always been drawn to literature first when it comes to the way that words are put together. Traditional music is interesting. Literature drives the music, but then there's our styles. And there are forms of music that people use, and a lot of times nowadays, we tend to break them up into geographical, stylistic traits. I became interested past the idea of a singular song—and more interested in looking into a lot of the regional styles. And then I began to study that. You know, Lead Belly was of the first people who really opened me to the idea of the songster. I remember my first album was Lead Belly's last sessions. And I just loved the record because of course he tells all these stories about the songs between. But then there was a personal note to the record as well. Because my grandfather, he actually grew up around thirty miles away from where Lead Belly grew up, and so when I heard Lead Belly speaking, he spoke very similar to my grandfather in a certain type of way that also turned . . . that really brought me into his music even more. So for me there was a personal connection. And I found over time, too, that while I didn't necessarily get into folk music as an African American person to focus on the African American music specifically, it came out of an interest. I found that there was a need for someone to tell some of the stories that are within the history already. And I also found a personal interest as well, 'cause I'm also of African American and Mexican American descent. The idea of people being able to navigate between multiple worlds whether they're social or racial or time and space and place: I found that there was a need to tell some of those stories. So I also found I had a lot of fuel to work with.

FD: You had a personal motivation and historical motivation.

DF: Yeah.

FD: Can you talk about that racial aspect for a moment? You mention your interest in a lot of different forms of music. And so for example, your work spans country-western and hip-hop.

DF: Yes.

FD: And that is not a link that a lot of people make. I wonder if you can talk about the racial mixture that comes into these popular forms that interest you.

DF: Absolutely. Well, one of the things that I've always been interested in from the very beginning are the places where music overlaps with uh . . . with itself. Cross genre lines, you know like . . . I think about people like Hank Williams doing "My Bucket's Got a Hole in It." And having listened to Washboard Sam's version, I can find appreciation for both versions. But I can also tell that Hank is kind of looking over his shoulder, and I can tell that Washboard Sam is looking over his shoulder too. And then I can tell that their contemporaries are also looking over their shoulders when it comes to taking in musical ideas and presenting them in new forms. And that's something that I wanted to on my record *Prospect Hill*, specifically, was to take a couple of old forms and present them in a new way.

So for example, "Have I Stayed Away Too Long?" That's a song that is a part of the country and western field, and it's been performed by a lot of Opry members, but on Arhoolie Records, there's a great album of a group

Blind James Campbell and His Nashville String Band, and they do a rough-hewn and funky version of the song that I fell in love with. So I tried to bring a little bit of their version as well as sort of a little bit of that hard honky-tonk flavor into my arrangement. And then when we recorded it in the studio, the saxophonist ended up putting a nice little sort of Tex-Mex saxophone to overlay on top of it, and it just made for a real mix. Again, Hank Williams is a perfect example because you can hear the mixture of styles—it's not just straight-ahead country music; there's a little jazz; there's a little bit of the blues. And then when the fiddle comes in there, the fiddle's doing a little bit of an extra New Orleans jazz, sort of Dixieland flavor. Even though it's still within the vocabulary of country music as a form. I wanted to do that, so that was how "Have I Stayed Away Too Long?" was set into place.

From the other side, a song like "Grotto Beat" for example, it kind of took on this sort of hip-hop flavor. I took a traditional form from the hill countries of Mississippi—the fife and drum tradition, which includes fife, snare drum, and bass drum. And first we just did it as an instrumental and that felt really great, and that was very much in the style as it originally was played uh . . . on the field recordings that Alan Lomax made. But I decided I wanted to add a little something extra onto it. And one of my collaborators on the session, Guy Davis, he mentioned that it needed a few words too. And so I started to come with these few little chants, and just adding those words on top of it, it turned into this . . . almost like an early Tommy Boy record, sort of rap record from the seventies, which was something that I hadn't necessarily planned for when I started the record. But what an amazing result—the juxtaposition was really something.

FD: And what's interesting about this is that you're not just a historian—you obviously are when you talk to me, you tell me all this history that you know—but your songs have a kind of historical sedimentation in them that draws on that interracial history and that racial overlap. I wonder if we could talk about the fraught history of uses of African American music by rock and rollers. The idea that there's appropriation—theft in addition to love. John Lomax puts his name as coauthor on a lot of those songs he learned from Lead Belly and other Black musicians. I'm also thinking of like Jim Jackson, who was another artist who appeared on that Harry Smith Folkways anthology. And "Kansas City Blues" and "Old Dog Blue" that then got taken up and played by Janis Joplin, the Byrds. I'm just wondering about your sense of the racial politics of that. I mean, Janis Joplin—turns out she was a huge Lead Belly fan, and some of her earliest performances in Threadgill's included Lead Belly songs. And then of course, we have Lead Belly talking about Gene Autry as one of his huge influences, right? So the question I guess I would put to you as a historian in, both senses of the word is: When does the crossing become appropriation?

DF: Well, when I think about . . . when I think about the idea of people reaching over racial lines on music—and by the way, music is like foodways and religion, those tend to have these sort of inroads that are different than other situations. In any case when it comes to people like Janis, and a lot of the interpreters from, let's say, the midsixties on, we're seeing a change in the way that African American culture is being accepted within the United States. I think by '65 you're seeing the remnants of strict segregation, which was a part of the United States, and so I in one way there . . . there's an invisibility in the African American community until that time that relegates them to only Black-only spaces within a segregated world. I think in one way, we see the rise of white blues interpreters come out of an era where the interest in this music is bubbling over so much that people just can't help it anymore. Also, in the post–World War II era, you have the advent of the LP, access to Library of Congress recordings, 45s that begin to come out of Black music, and the advent of rock 'n' roll. I think these things also brought an acceptance that, in Lead Belly's age, I just think was just completely unheard of. And that's one of the hard things for us to be able to understand now. It's sort of the Pat Boone doing "Tutti Frutti" thing. Why does Pat Boone have to do "Tutti Frutti," you know? We know the business at that time; Pat Boone has to sell however many records that he's selling for a mainstream audience, while of course Little Richard is really the definitive writer and performer of the song. That's something that we can't conceive in the twenty-first century, but back then, Little Richard's a little too hot to handle in terms of just having him in, you know, America's living room.

FD: So Pat Boone doing "Tutti Frutti" as distinguished from Janis Joplin or Van Ronk or Dylan doing Blind Lemon Jefferson or something?

DF: You then have Chess Records people starting to push on their own. The blues revival is interesting because it's part of the folk revival. But then—by '66, '67—there were efforts to bring the living blues tradition and the folk revival tradition into one place, which of course brings Buddy Guy in with Bukka White and tries to justify electric blues rock next to traditional blues. So there are a lot of different segments that are coalescing together by 1968, 1970. And it gets a little messy along the way. In 1963 and '64, you can much more easily pick out the different communities.

FD: Right.

DF: Who ends up being famous at the end of the day, who doesn't? How interested are people in that fame? You know, with Atlantic Records, with the Clovers and people like that—they sent their songwriters down south to find the new dance steps and then they made songs off of the dance steps so that it was pop music, of course, in one way. But of course it was also folk—folkloric-based rhythms and sounds. That's also what Ralph Peer also did in the twenties. The experimentation of folk and pop ended up coalescing into something new. But with doing that, Black music began to veer away from the straight-ahead folkloric practitioners, so it continued to be a specialized form. Then even after that, I keep reminding people when I'm in the deeper academic circles that, post-1978, folklore doesn't account for things like hip-hop. And now there's been so much scholarship on hip-hop and folkloric scholarship of African American music of the South. But they haven't connected the two things fully, so there is a gap between those two things, which is part of why I bring in old-time music *and* I allude to hip-hop. I don't really do hip-hop in a straightforward sense, but the notion in my songs that folk music and hip-hop are connected came from holes in the scholarship that I found that needed to be filled.

FD: I guess your most recent record, *Black Cowboys*, was nominated for a Grammy. Congratulations!

DF: Yep, it got the nomination. It was a real great honor to be able to put that project together; all of the elements came together in just the most beautiful way. I started thinking about doing more cowboy music after I had—let's see, I guess it was around 2010 or so, I was driving back to Arizona to visit family, and I found a book called *The Negro Cowboys* near the Painted Desert. It was just at the gift shop and the book talked about how one in four cowboys who helped settle the West were African American cowboys, and it mentioned the story of diversity that goes back to the early Spanish settlers from I guess around the 1500s. The story I wanted to tell emerged as I began to find more stories connected to the Pullman porters, especially through the autobiography of Nat Love. I just wanted to connect this story of movement and migration going all the way from a horse and buggy all the way to the Pullman porters on the train, which technically leads all the way to commuter airplanes and everything like that. But it was the idea that African American culture moves and the work and the jobs have continued to move continuously together—and Black cowboys are a part of this. The idea of Black cowboys—I didn't want to just put on a cowboy hat, which . . . is ironic 'cause then someone did put on a cowboy hat and then made a huge hit out of it. But, nevertheless, being a good folklorist, I . . . I wanted to not just do a cowboy hat album, you know?

FD: Yeah.

DF: But also being from Arizona, I've always been a fan of Marty Robbins's gunfighters and trail songs. *Gunfighter Ballads and Trail Songs* album. So I wanted to have something that had a universal appeal like Marty Robbins, because that's what really makes cowboy music shine the most is when you have this perfect balance between a little bit of . . . a little bit of glitz and glam but the real cowboy music. And people love that. And that's why the cowboy is one of the most iconic characters of the entire American culture.

FD: It seems so important that you reinsert African Americans into that tradition. I take it that some of these original cowboys were based on historical figures who were Black? That's what your research has uncovered?

DF: Absolutely. One of them was a fellow by the name of Bass Reeves, and he was said to be the historical precedent for the Lone Ranger, and so that alone was something that I thought was of interest. So I researched him out and he ended up being just a real interesting person—a just lawman of the West. He brought three thousand people to justice. He had a perfect photographic memory, which helped him catch his perpetrators. There is a very interesting fact about his life on the plantation, where he lived with his mother. He had a master who had lost everything in the war, and he was a bad drunkard. One of the things that he did was that he started to teach Bass how to play cards. One night the master wanted to cheat Bass out of his money. And so he put Bass's collateral, as well as his mother's freedom up for collateral.

FD: Wow.

DF: It was pretty shocking. And Bass found out that the master had been cheating on that round and so he just knocked him out right there on the spot. And then he grabbed one of the horses and took off. After that he lived on the Cherokee Nation for couple of decades. And then as Arkansas was becoming a US jurisdiction, he was then called in to be a deputy US Marshal.

We were talking about literature. When I was writing the lyrics out, I wanted it to be a blues number in the style of Lightnin' Hopkins because that was going to be something I thought would have the most impact. There's actually a fictional story called "The Legend of Bass Reeves" and in it his mother told him that even though he was enslaved, he was as free as he could be when the master wasn't looking. And so that was something that just really just uh . . . struck me right to the heart. I alluded to this in my song.

FD: I was going to ask you about your song, "Steel Pony Blues."

DF: After I read the autobiography of Nat Love, I was drawn to his story of being born into slavery and then becoming a cowboy and then a Pullman porter.

FD: Right.

DF: But then, as I began to speak with my own father about Pullman porters, he began to tell me his stories about when he was an apprentice Pullman porter in Flagstaff, Arizona.

FD: Your father was?

DF: Yeah, so my father grew up in Flagstaff and he was connected to Winslow and Holbrook, Arizona, cause his father, my grandfather, was a preacher in Holbrook, Arizona, which is a real small town two hours north of Phoenix. Holbrook and Winslow were sort of the northern rim of Arizona that connect Route 66 all the way to Los Angeles. These were very small rural towns, and my dad used to be an apprentice porter before he decided to go to college in Phoenix—he was a basketball player. But he started to tell me stories about being a Pullman porter and then he was a skycap for most of my life. So he was telling me the way that that type of work translated over into commuter flights later on. And sort of when he was growing up in the mid- to late sixties, still a strong Pullman porter community in Arizona. To be able to connect cowboys and porters, I just thought it was a beautiful juxtaposition of modernity as well as telling the history of the past. Because you know there are two Wests—there's the literal West, which you can go to today but then there's the imagined West that we've created in American culture that is part of movies, it's a part of stories, books. And to bring Black cowboys into any of that starts to create this very fascinating tapestry.

20

Anatomy of a Canned Heat Hit

"Let's Work Together" by Wilbert Harrison

By John Jeremiah Sullivan

In the open square white cabinet where I used to curl up and look at the covers of my father's albums (he owned twenty max), the one that has stuck is the cover of Canned Heat's self-titled 1967 album. It's an orange-red, at least in memory. They're all sitting around a table, eating random food, and one person is smoking a cigar. Very exciting! But it had effortless vibe. J'adore Canned Heat to this day. Not so much for their music—some of which is great, in the mode of old Blues songs ushered into the electric-hippie era—as for their inspiring vibe. The big hairy guy up front, Bob Hite, in his vest with his wonderful boyish dancing. . . . They called him "The Bear." He seems not so much to have used drugs as been drugs. He is said on one occasion to have done two lines of coke while unconscious.

Then there was "Blind Owl," Alan Wilson. John Fahey gave him that nickname. He was almost totally blind without his thick spectacles, but did not like to wear them onstage. When you see him performing, in old clips, he can't see anything. One time, playing a wedding, he walked off after a set and put his guitar down on top of the cake. His falsetto must be numbered among the weird and lovely artifacts of the 1960s. Partly he was trying, with that voice, to keep alive the Bentonia blues tradition and its high-pitched, eerie vibe (exemplified by Skip James). Wilson had studied blues history with a monkish dedication. When Son House resurfaced in the '60s and was getting ready to perform again, he found himself unable to play a lot of his greatest songs from the thirties (which had never been easy to play). His hands were old. His managers brought in the Blind Owl, who had long before taught himself to play those songs note for note. Wilson had the experience of reteaching one of his gods how to play the god's own music.

Wilson's death came early. He took too many sleeping pills and lay on his back in a sleeping bag behind The Bear's house and died looking up through trees at the stars. He had already tried it twice. He was twenty-seven. Brokenhearted, people said. "I didn't have no faro, not even no place to go." Broken up, too, about the planet. He had always been obsessed with Redwood trees. He collected leaves and soil. "His trip was one of nature," said the Miami news when he died, "and he really wanted people to be aware of how the country is being raped by lack of concern for nature." His funeral back home in Massachusetts was silent. Friends brought forward his instruments on chargers of pine boughs and white birch logs. Two harmonicas and a guitar. The rest of the band did not attend. European tour.

The well-known Canned Heat song "Let's Work Together" was a cover, not an adaptation like their other hits but an actual cover, of a song written sometime around 1960 by Wilbert Harrison, who was born in Charlotte, NC, where he grew up one of TWENTY-THREE CHILDREN, playing a washtub bass. Harrison scored a #1 hit in 1959 with his famous version of "Kansas City," which features a guitar solo that some consider the first fully fledged electric guitar solo. It was played by Wild Jimmy Spruill, of Fayetteville, NC, an unquestioned pioneer on the instrument.

In 1962, Harrison's original 45 of "Let's Stick Together"—as it was called at first—came out and fizzled. Six years later, however, in 1968, Harrison himself reworked the song as "Let's WORK Together," and it charted. That's the version Canned Heat covered. They were, in other words, recording a song, a hit, that had been released barely two years before. Yet when Canned Heat's record came out and the song blew up, critics described the band's "recent success" as having been "written by Wilbert Harrison, another name from the glorious rock past." Another reviewer named, as his "favorite" song on the new Canned Heat album, "Wilbert Harrison's oldie 'Let's Work Together.'"

Sometimes it feels like the strange instantaneousness of the transmogrification by white people of early Black rock 'n' roll songs into "oldies" was part of a complicated process of psychic suppression that went hand in hand with subliminal shame over the ongoing theft of the same music. It was not possible to distance oneself from the evidence in space. But in time? That could be done. In the case of Harrison's song, the phenomenon continued up to 1976, when Bryan Ferry released his version. Ferry had gone all the way back to Harrison's 1962 lyrics ("stick" instead of "work") for the song, which is sort of airless and pointless, on purpose I think. The papers incorrectly reported that he had rewritten the words himself, to honor fiancée Jerry Hall. "Nevertheless," said a critic, "Ferry handles a bunch of oldies in ways that will surprise you."

By that time Wilbert Harrison had become a one-man band. Seriously—he was one of those guys who play the cymbals with their feet and whatnot. Rack harmonica, traps, washboard. (It was how he'd gotten his start, at the Excelsior Club in Charlotte.) There was a carnival quality, maybe, but people said he could still make it shake. He died in Spencer, NC, in 1994.

21

John Prine (The Reluctant Genius)

An Interview with Dave Jacques, Jason Wilber, Fats Kaplin, and Pat McLaughlin

By Florence Dore

Florence Dore: So I wanted to ask you all about a couple of things, if I may. Picking up on a conversation that we had when you played in Durham and my friend, the chef Andrea Reusing, put on that amazing spread for you all . . . how many courses would you say that was?

Fats Kaplin and David Jacques: Many! Pat, I'm sorry you missed it.

Pat McLaughlin: Was there any flat meat at all? [*laughter*]

Jason Wilber: There were all kinds of meat!

FK: . . . but it was not flat!

FD: That meal was a big deal, breaking bread with John Prine. It was the night before the show, and the next night after seeing you play, I think it was you, Fats, started saying "It's so interesting that John's songs all seem to be about something mundane, all these beautiful portraits of everyday life. And then in the middle he plants these flights of fancy."

FK: Yeah.

JW: Sounds exactly like something Fats would say.

FK: I was talking about his writing; everyone talks about John Prine as a great writer. Okay, but *why* is he a great writer? One of the things is his songs can seem to be, even his story songs, very tossed off, like oh, I could do that in five minutes. But then there is almost always in his songs, when it comes to the chorus, or the last verse or whatever, something that takes it out, somewhere else. It reminds me of an abstract impressionist and somebody comes up and goes, "Oh that's just a painting of a circle on a canvas. I could do that." But then you really start looking at it and you realize the depth of it; and in art and music, that's one of the most difficult things to do. It just seems effortless. And it does with John's writing. "Sam Stone" is a good example. It's a story song, but then the chorus is very cryptic—like what does that mean?

FD: Right, that's what you were saying: "Little pitchers have big ears"—what does that have to do with the rest of the story?

FK: Right, is it cryptically this, or is it, sometimes we know, as Jason has said, John'll just say, "Oh, I just like the way that sounds." But I think that's a very self-effacing thing to say—because it's always like perfect. Why is it perfect? That's the art.

JW: Pat could speak to this really well because he's written with John so much. But I think one of the things that was so brilliant about John is, things would come out of him and he wouldn't question them, he'd write them down or say them. And he had really high standards, and it's not like he would keep everything he wrote. But such left-field things would come out of him, and it's not until later, and even for him, that you really might appreciate what it might mean or what's good about it. You know, Pat, when we would be riding in the car and you and John would be talking, sometimes I would be thinking to myself, "This sounds like John and Pat writing a song together." Because you'd just be saying funny stuff to each other, but it would sound like song lyrics to me. And I'd just be curious to hear what your take is, having written with him so much.

PM: You know, I didn't ever put cowriting with John, maybe I'm wrong, but I didn't ever put it in the body of work of John's other writing. Even other songs that I knew were cowrites, like "Long Monday" or something; mine were so personal to me. And I kinda spent the cowriting thing with John trying to figure out what he had done. And I'm not sure I ever really figured it out.

FD: You mean, you were trying to figure out what to learn for yourself as a songwriter?

PM: Yeah. But it's just hard to learn honesty or virtue or something like that. I couldn't ever learn the person or anything like that. So you're still stuck on your own, you know. But I always held his other songs in—I don't want to say higher esteem, but not knowing where they came from made them pretty magical. I do know that in "I Remember Everything," he had a line: "Got no future in my happiness." I thought, I have no idea what that means, but I'm gonna leave that one alone, because he was hanging with that line and I knew he wanted to say that. Somebody hit me up online and asked, "What do you mean by that line?" And I said, "I don't know, I have no idea."

JW: "What does it mean?" is always such a loaded question. It's like the wrong question because it carries with the assumption that the writer is consciously meaning something and knows what that is. At its best that's usually not the case.

FK: That's exactly true because it's the same thing as looking at a painting. Somebody paints something and somebody goes, "What is it? What does it mean?"

JW: That's a painting. It's talking in painting.

PM: I think what was unique for all of us is that we got to be part of the delivery system of the magic of Prine, and that was just a very unique opportunity.

JW: Good way of saying it.

FK: Yeah, very good.

FD: What did that feel like to each of you, to be part of the "delivery system" of John Prine's magic? I think that's a beautiful way to put it.

FK: I've worked with a lot of people, a lot of great people. But with John, every night that you would go out and play with him, even though I've played these songs (and Lord knows [Dave and Jason]have played these songs with him for so much longer), but I'd always say, I'd be playing steel or mandolin or whatever, I'd listen to the song and even though I've heard it dozens of times, I would occasionally forget to come in, like for a solo or something, because I was just listening to him—"oh yeah, that's me!" [*laughter*]. I remember once or twice, I can't remember what song, but I was listening to the song and I was just kinda looking at John, and John turns and kinda looks at me and nods, and I just go, "Oh yeah, right." It never was tiring to listen to those songs, to me. Which is pretty rare, I think.

FD: If I could just ask Dave and Jason . . . I know, Jason, you were like thirteen when you started playing with him? [*laughter*] How old were you two when you started playing with him, and how did you get the gig and what was that like?

DJ: I got the gig because—you guys know Ray Kennedy, right? I played in Ray's band when he was a country star. So I hadn't talked to Ray in a long time, and the next day he runs into Al Bunetta, and Al says, "John's putting a band together and he needs a bass player. Do you have anyone you can recommend?" And Ray says, "Dave Jacques." And my favorite part is that Ray calls me up and leave a message on my answering machine saying:

"I recommended you to Al Bunetta for the John Prine gig. I hope you don't mind."

Then I auditioned for John. Thought it went really well. And then John went to Ireland for like two months, without telling me, and there was one more person that he had promised an audition. So I audition and then he leaves, and then for like six weeks or something like that I'm thinking, I guess I should just . . . I didn't know what to do. And strangely enough, I ran into Doug Lancio, who I didn't even know at the time, I was talking to some people at 12th & Porter about the audition, and Doug goes, "Oh, you got that gig, you're perfect for that gig," and walked away. And I was like, "Who was that guy?" And John comes back and goes, "You had the gig, but I promised somebody else I'd listen to him." So I spent six weeks wondering about it.

But it was great, went in and just started learning the songs . . . And I knew a lot of John songs, but when they sent me his whole catalog, I didn't realize the depth of it. It was mind-blowing for me. So many songs, and so many great songs that I didn't know. Of course, we didn't play that many of them.

One thing I could say about what Pat said earlier about John's songs, some of them being more special, is I noticed the songs we learned, when we put the set together for the Lost Dogs tour, that over the years it seems like—Pat's songs being the exception to the rule—a lot of times the songs that were cowrites I noticed would fall off the list more than songs that weren't. I don't know if there was any reasoning except that, you know, the cream rose to the top. But I did kinda notice it, because there were a lot of Gary Nicholson cowrites from *Lost Dogs*—and great songs, but ones that would kinda fall off, and it was more songs that he wrote. And then eventually, of course John and Pat . . .

PM: You know, we all know what it's like to try a song, to try one out on the audience, and that can sometimes be kind of a weird experience. I don't know if John ever felt that or not; I guess he would've had to. But I don't know.

DJ: Yeah. But it was just like an observation after playing with him a few years, that there are all these songs, and you can't do 'em all, and certain ones would fall off the list. And part of it was because once it was a full band, songs that sounded great with the full band, when it was just a trio didn't work as well, and all those reasons.

PM: I think that by having you and Jason, and the option of going off the list, although he didn't go off the list much, but knowing that if he wanted to, he could and you all would know those songs, was an amazing advantage to him, or gave him breathing room. The list, he adhered to it, but he knew that he could throw something in.

FD: Dave, how long did you play with John?

DJ: Twenty-five years. I got the gig in '95, thinking I would have it for a year. I'd been in Nashville for about five years, so I'd kinda seen how things went, and I thought "this'll last a year, maybe a year and a half." And I thought I was being pretty realistic.

FD: I had the honor to interview John Prine in Akron, I can't remember what year, was it 2002? Dave and Jason were there. And I was hoping to re-create that interview for this book. At the time I interviewed him I just wanted to ask him what to say to my songwriting students in my class. So I didn't really write it down or anything. And I know there's more to this story, and I want to get to you too, Jason, your history too with John. But I said to him, "Okay, talk to me about 'I am an old woman.' You're not an old woman. Talk to me about how you came up with that." And he said, "Well, that's just songwriting."

PM: Oh, it was the "future in my happiness" line. And that "old woman" line, I think about that all the time what a great line that is.

FD: Yeah. "I am an old woman, named after my mother": there's not much there, but it's so much. It's like what you were saying, Fats, about how it looks effortless.

FK: Yeah, it looks tossed off, conversational or something. And a lot of the nugget, it's really all there, it's concentrated.

PM: Yeah, and to me, and these guys all know this game, but I doubt if he was writing to that chorus. I think that "I am an old woman" was the first line of that song, and it's unlikely to me that, I hadn't known him to have a chorus and say, well now we need some verses. I never heard him say anything like that. It would be quite the joyous experience in one's head if he pulled that off—I mean, "I am an old woman" and then he finds that chorus, I mean good Lord.

FD: That's an example of Fats's observation about the mundanity, the mundane, everyday life. And even "Make me a poster of an old rodeo"; what a beautiful line about desire. And then he just goes ahead and says it: "If dreams were thunder and lightning were desire." In that line it's almost both, though, because it's thunder and lightning, but it's so much bigger.

FK: That's one of my favorite Prine moments, actually.

PM: No doubt.

FD: Dave was kind enough to help me get backstage to do that interview, and John was kind enough to agree to it. And then he dedicated "Angel from Montgomery" to me from the stage. That's a memory I'll cherish forever.

So any other thoughts about that song? Because I really like what you were saying, Fats, talking about how you're in the band but you're listening to him and almost forget to come in and do your part. Is it the lyrics or the music or the whole thing? Talking to you now, you sort of sound as much like members the audience, just loving the songs, as members of the band.

FK: It's the lyrics I'm talking about, because the music, I'm up there playing it, but lyrically, I'd be really listening to it, and it just struck me sometimes, like "What is that chorus?" or "I never really thought about it that way."

FD: Do you remember any particular song where that happened?

FK: One is "Sam Stone," because the chorus always struck me as being kind of sideways, or it could mean this or it could mean that. Or one of my favorites is "Lake Marie." After I'd been playing it a while, I looked it up and there were all these people discussing it online about what it is or what it means, things I'd never even thought about, and also kinda ridiculous things. But that's a great example. It's like a talking blues, really, he's telling a story but what is it? Why has that occurred? Suddenly with a gruesome murder, what does it all mean? From the mundane thing of frying sausages to gruesome murder—and it's all put together as a talking blues, basically.

JW: Something that's interesting to me about this is, we can certainly talk about what things mean, and the writer can talk about what things mean, and people can interpret things different ways, and it's totally valid. But I think, even though these are words and it's the English language, it's part of the music, it's music. And I think that what's interesting about it when you look at it in that context, you know, there's that famous Martin Mull thing about "talking about music is like dancing about architecture." And it's so true because, at the end of the day, one of the great things about music is that we don't have to understand it or analyze it to feel a deep appreciation for it and enjoy it. It's music; it's like food or whatever, like that meal [Andrea] cooked for us, it is its own thing. There's nothing to be deconstructed from it. It is fascinating to talk about it, but like "Lake Marie," you can figure out, what are the metaphors, what do these things represent? And that's totally valid, but in the moment, in the experience of the song, what's so meaningful about it is that it works as a song, it works as music. It does what it's supposed to do. Who knows why? I don't think John even knew, necessarily. I just think he was able to recognize when something did work and not to fuck with it.

FD: Like you were saying, Pat, in your experience of cowriting with him you'd find a line and leave it alone.

PM: I don't know if I said it right. But I can't imagine writing "Lake Marie" with him, it's something I just can't really go there mentally. But I think the trick on "Lake Marie" is "whoa-oh-oh"—because it got him out of having to do anything else, and it got to the end of the big chorus. That's just some of the best "whoa-whoa"in' I've ever heard, and it was beautiful. And I've always thought of those "whoa"s as being, are those happy "whoa"s or are those sad "whoa"s? That's the cool thing about John, you don't know.

FD: And Dave, I asked you at the time, when he did that, switching over to the question of live shows with him and what y'all remember about them, I remember asking you, "What's up with that dance at the end of 'Lake Marie'?" I can't remember what you said about the first time you saw it.

DJ: Oh. Well, the first time he did it, he just did it. The first time he put the guitar down and danced around it, it blew my mind. It's one of those things like Fats said you forget to come in, where you almost want to stop playing and go. . . . "Did anybody else just see that?!" It was unbelievable. He put the guitar down and started doing that thing with his hands, the thing that came to my mind . . . was punk . . . was that anyone who thought he was a folk singer . . .

FK: As you said before, Dave, "That's rock and roll, man."

DJ: It was so great when he started doing that. But the first time there was no, like, "I'm gonna put the guitar down and dance around it a little and then leave the stage, you guys just keep playing." But there was—I don't remember when he decided he was gonna leave the stage while we were playing. Because he did that before he did . . .

FD: The dance?

DJ: Well, the dance got better! Like most things, like John's jokes, the great thing about doing it over a long period of time, you could see everything evolve. The jokes were the best for me. To see when he was telling a story, and he got a laugh on a certain line, and then over fifteen years, you could see it. It was really over months, usually, when he'd really land on something. But to see his little stories, and the punch lines and everything, his timing was incredible. But to just watch it evolve, like a comedian. He'd get it perfect, his timing, so he knows where the laugh is and which lines work better. Because he'd switch out lines sometimes on the stories.

FD: Again, what's striking, I've hung around with a lot of bands, and it sounds like your experience is like someone in the audience, in a way.

DJ: All of us, a lot of times when he'd do his solo set, we'd just stay there and listen to John. In twenty-five years I never got sick of just staying on the side of the stage and listening to the solo set.

PM: Hey, you know what was interesting to me, and I don't know if this hit any of y'all, but when he did the first two songs, about two songs in, I would think "Is this going well?" And I would think he doesn't seem happy. And I think he had an amazing amount of confidence that things were eventually going to go really well. And that was so professional to me, that he didn't get bogged down by the reaction of the crowd, or how well the band was playing, what the sound monitors were like, or anything else. He was like a machine up there.

FD: Just let it unfold and have faith.

PM: Yeah. Big time to me.

JW: Yeah, I think one of the amazing things about John is that, and I'm sure it was different from his perspective, but from my perspective, we had world-class songs that, twenty-five years for Dave, twenty-four for me, songs like "Angel" never tarnished, never got less good than it was the first time, which is an unbelievable accomplishment. So we had great, amazing world-class songs; and John, he's one of those outliers as a person. He had such incredible sense of what was good artistically and such an incredible ability to convey it. I mean, you put those two things together, his raw talent and super incredible material, it's really very hard to go wrong. Even our worst shows, and there weren't many, there were a few really bad ones because John was ill, even those were not that bad in the scheme of things.

DJ: Right, there were a few of 'em where it was a struggle. It was a struggle for me just being on stage, but because he was sick. But even then, the audience was always with him. They wanted him to succeed, they wanted it for him.

FD: Wow, a lot of love in those shows.

FK: Oh yeah. Because he's out there really with his heart on his sleeve, going out there doing it. There were a couple shows, like in Colorado with the really high altitude for a couple of shows was really rough, but the audience is going "come on, John, you can do it!" Not that they're saying that, but I'm thinking, okay, John is in this sand trap, *bang*, he knocks it right on the green! I'm going, yeah! It's like you're watching that kind of thing. And at the end, he'd pull it out, and he'd dance off stage.

JW: He always gave 100 percent, he was one of those guys, I never saw him slight the audience or not give it everything.

FK: He did not coast.

JW: He was a very laid-back person, some would even say lazy in some ways. But he knew the few times when he really could not do that, and he would not . . .

FD: He was conserving his energy maybe.

JW: Yeah, right, he was conserving his energy. And he knew where that was important, and that's where he focused and gave it everything.

DJ: He never blew through a song. Even when he was sick, I never saw him just coast through a song. As many times as he sang 'em, he was always really present in the song.

FD: Let me ask you, Jason, about your version of the Dave story. How did you come to the Prine band, and how old were you, and what was that like for you?

JW: I was twenty-six when I started working with John. The year that Dave got the gig, the rest of that band, or a lot of that band—Larry Crane, David Steele, and Ed—they were all people I knew from Indiana. Larry, of course, was John Mellencamp's guitar player. David Steele and I are the same age, we played in a lot of bands together, and we're really good friends. So I was really excited when those guys all started playing with John. I went to see them in Indianapolis . . . at Butler University, and it just blew my mind to see my friend I'd been in a band with, in so many bands with, onstage with John Prine. I met Dave and Phil and everybody that night, after the show.

So, toward the end of that year, David got this offer to go play with Steve Earle. And he had recommended me to John and Al, and I knew Larry and Ed already, too, so they also kinda put in a word for me. And David said, "I gave them your name for this gig, so you might be getting a phone call." But much like Dave's story, that was in October or November, and I didn't hear from Al until like January of the following year or something. So by the time they called, I had just like given up, this is just not going to happen. I never heard anything other than Dave saying, "Hey, I recommended you for the gig." But one night, out of the blue, I remember it so well, I was in my little apartment, I was cooking dinner, six in the evening, probably just before five in Nashville and Al's probably thinking, oh I gotta do one more thing before the end of the day. And so the phone rings and it's Al Bunetta—that's a whole 'nother story just talking to Al Bunetta on the phone for the first time—and basically just asking me if I'd be interested in playing in John's band, and of course I was. And he put John on the phone a few minutes later, at the end of the call, and we just talked for a minute, and then we just hung up. And I just sat in the kitchen, and I was like, wow, did that really just happen?

So for the next month or so, I would come home from work and I would practice the songs and learn the parts. And then a month or so later, we did the audition like a mile from my apartment in Bloomington at the back of this place where they printed T-shirts, just like a warehouse. Some friend of Larry's owned this place. And the whole band was there, and we basically played the whole live show. And John said, "Why don't you go in the other room, so we can talk about it a little bit?" So I did, I went in the other room and waited around for a few minutes, and he said come on back in and he said, "The job's yours if you want it." And of course I do.

And same thing, I had no idea. I remember the five-year mark, the ten-year mark, thinking, wow, I can't believe this has lasted for so long. And then, twenty-four years I played with him. Amazing. I'm fifty-one; he touched four of the decades of my life.

DJ: When Jason had the audition, I'm the only guy living in Nashville, and the audition's up there because most of the guys live up there. So John comes to my house and picks me up. I had been playing in the band not quite a year. He picks me up at the house, and we're driving up to Bloomington. And I get in the car and he says, "I can't believe we live in Nashville and we're driving to

Bloomington to hear a guitar player. This kid better be good." I think part of it for John, and this worked out for Jason, was that John didn't want everybody in Nashville to know he was looking for a guitar player. That's a can of worms right there.

FD: I was wondering if there are moments for you guys, in live shows, particular shows or particular moments in shows playing with John—particular songs, repeatedly, whatever—that you wanted to share stories about.

DJ: I got a question for you, Pat. What was it like for you to play songs you'd written with John onstage with John?

PM: Man, you know I don't really know, I honestly don't know. It wasn't any more amazing than getting to sit in the airport or have dinner or lunch or pick people up at hotels. And as that question was being put forth, I was thinking: the show was the show, but the hang is just a big a part of it to me, the getting through the day sort of thing. It's interesting what slice of the day the show took up. It was just kind of another part of the day. And we've all been amazed when we're sitting backstage and we've just played an hour with him and now we're going to decide we're going to watch him do his solo show. That's a little bit unique, I would say.

That was a great question, because we got to see the faces on those people out there, in different situations more faces in more rows. I do remember people in the audience's reactions, I'm not sure which songs they were, but amazing to get to watch the people. That was a really big part of playing with John for me.

DJ: Yeah, the audiences were incredible.

JW: Yeah, John's were the best audiences. No doubt. I mean, that's why people loved to open for John because the audiences were so fantastic. They loved the music, they loved the words, they listened . . . they were just really high-quality audiences. Which makes sense, because it was John. Off of what Pat said, the amazing thing about John's music that I think people realized when they got to know him personally, was that who he was in his songs was so much who he was in real life. I mean, there was more to him than that, but it was really a reflection of his quirky personality. He had a funny way of looking at the world, talking about it and relating to people, and he was like that all the time. So the John on stage was not very different from the John of the other twenty-two hours of the day. And Dave always says, John could tell you about going down to the corner to buy a paper that morning, and it's going to be a great story.

DJ: Ask me what'd you do this morning? Went and bought the paper. Same question to John, and it'd be an incredible story.

JW: He was a really special person, you know, and he was that way all the time.

FK: When I first joined the band, it had been a very short amount of time, we played somewhere in Alabama, and everybody had their own cars, so Mitchell [Drosin, road manager] goes, "Can you go with John to Memphis? I want somebody to go with John to Memphis." And I go, "Sure I'll drive with John." So we put our stuff in the car, and John goes, "I'll drive," because he liked to drive. So I'd only been in the band a short amount of time, and I'm just sitting there driving along with John, and it's that thing, he'd comment just gently on little things, like road signs, an observation of something. And we talked, little stories about food or about his family, something came up. . . . But I just remember so distinctly [thinking], "I'm driving to Memphis with John Prine." And he's just commenting about stuff, stop at a Dairy Queen. It was like a little Jim Jarmusch movie or something; even though nothing was really happening, it was just sort of gentle and quirky, something in a gentle way.

JW: Florence, if you want to get a sense of what Fats was just talking about, the best I've ever seen is Tom Piazza's piece, I can't remember where he published it. He wrote about him and John in Florida, going to buy some shoes or something. More than anything I've ever read, he captured John. He captured the way he talks and the way he acts. So I would definitely recommend that if you get a chance. It's not that long of a piece. It's right on the money and that's hard to do, to capture John, I think. But he did it.

FD: What you're saying is so wonderful, starting with Pat's comment about the hang, and what you said, Fats, about he's just living this, that's who he is, so the songs are like just another part of the day, as Pat put it. A little like John was just in touch with aspects of human life that people aren't used to noticing, and that enrich life. We should appreciate the road sign if it's got something interesting about it.

DJ: Of course, you know, John looked through newspapers voraciously. He'd buy all the papers, always. I always felt when he was looking in the newspapers, he was looking for the small stories. The stories on the front page, I don't think he cared about that stuff. But he'd look through the newspapers and it was the small stories that interested him the most.

FD: That's back to the Jim Jarmusch. I had another friend who didn't know Prine's work who I brought, I think y'all might have met her, and she was like, "Oh, it's like the Coen brothers." I was like, okay, not as violent . . . although there's "[Lake] Marie," you know . . .

DJ: A friend of mine who came to a show years ago, who didn't know John's work, was just totally blown away, like, "How did I not know?" And then he said, "It's like an emotional roller coaster, there's everything." But everything can be in one song, too.

Another thing I used to always think was amazing, and really summed up John in a way, was that in the Lost Dogs band, John would end the solo set with "Space Monkey." I don't know if you know the song. And Maple Byrne was the tour manager at the time, and we'd be in the dressing room, and Maple would open the door and say, "Space Monkey." And his face saying "Space Monkey" will always be. . . . But then we'd go up and play "Sam Stone." And I'd think, this is the set: we're going from a song about a monkey that the Russians shot into space, and he comes back and there's no more Soviet Union when the monkey comes back. To go from that to "Sam Stone," which is one of the most heartbreaking songs ever—who else could do that? How do you do that? But it's all John. And that's why it worked seamlessly. That's John: you're [talking about] a space monkey and then you can talk about Sam Stone all in one breath. And it all works.

FD: Last thing I'll say is when you guys are talking about, say, "Lake Marie," that you can interpret them and what do they mean. I teach literature, and that's what I do, I sit around and try to figure out what it means. But when I teach songwriting, I can't do that. I tried to do it the same way, and I've gotten better at [teaching songwriting], but it's hard—because it's not about trying to unearth the metaphors. Somehow there's something wrong with that. So coming from years of doing literary criticism back to songwriting, it's a relief, like I'm just gonna let this be. Rather than trying to understand it.

JW: Yeah, well, it's like if you talk about some really good food, like [Andrea Reusing's] that night, we can talk about what's in it, and why it's good, and how much of this and how much of that, whether you should use this kind of ingredient, or whether you should do this part first or this part first, you can figure it all out. But the part that really matters is eating the food and experiencing that. The rest is certainly interesting, and you can do it, but that's not the essence of the thing.

FD: In some ways it sounds like what you guys are saying is that John was sort of the master of finding the thing that it should be.

PM: Yes, and that people would emotionally connect with. Like "all dressed up in his corduroys": Man, when you had to put those corduroys on, your day was totally screwed up. And John knew that, and it's such a gem that he was able to bring that out.

FD: It's a tiny detail.

PM: Really small.

FK: But that's being an artist. You know you can do that.

JW: That's why he was so great. It's funny, he could do that in his writing, so that someone else could take that and perform it and there'd be magic in that, but he also had the ability to do it as a performer. It was kind of a dual thing there.

PM: I agree, and you know, I'm more impressed with his fingerpicking today than even anytime previously, I've just become more amazed by his guitar playing as time goes on. What he pulled off. He had really good time.

DJ, JW, and FK: Yep.

DJ: Most of the time it was just so easy to play with him. I think of the sessions I did, the easiest things I've done in my life were doing sessions with John. With John and Rooney, it'd be like, okay, we're done. He's capturing a performance of a song, and "all right, that's good." It was nice.

JW: We all got to be a part of something incredibly special, and I think we all appreciated it then and now.

FK and PM: Oh, yeah.

DJ: One thing I want to say before I forget, this is a Jason quote. Jason and I were standing on the side of the stage one time watching John's solo set, and Jason referred to John as "the reluctant genius." That never left my consciousness. I can't remember what you said around it, what the whole quote was, but I just remembered the "reluctant genius."

JW: I don't remember it, but it was probably in reference to something he said.

DJ: I don't remember what the song was or anything. But it kinda sums John up in a way. "Well, I didn't mean to be a genius . . ."

FD: That might just end up being the title of this section. It should be. In a way, it ties everything you guys have been saying together, back to the beginning when you were talking, Fats, about his songs as mundane and huge at the same time, small and large at the same time. "I am an old woman named after my mother": it doesn't sound like much, but it's a lot. The reluctance and the genius at the same time.

FK: Yep. Perfect.

JW: I would say so.

FD: I want to ask, and you can tell me to buzz off if you don't like the question, but can anybody tell me a favorite song? Does it change? A favorite John song?

DJ: Yeah, that one always changed. Pat, do you have one?

PM: I like the corduroy song ["Sabu Visits the Twin Cities Alone"]: "Jungles of East St. Paul . . ." I like his ability to change the time signature, like in "Illegal Smile," I love "Illegal Smile," the way he changed the time signature in those choruses. "Illegal Smile" is awful good, god dang.

FK: I was just about to say that's one of my favorite songs, "Sabu Visits the Twin Cities Alone." It's one of my absolute favorite songs, it's just so quirky.

JW: It paints a picture . . .

DJ: You almost never got to play it, because he'd do it in his solo set. When it was just the three of us, I think we got to play it more.

JW: Yeah, we played it a few times.

PJ: I heard y'all play it. But there wasn't one word that didn't absolutely belong in that song. It was just amazing.

FK: I agree.

DJ: The story, and the whole concept, of course. And the way the story plays out.

JW: And it's similar to "Jesus, the Missing Years." You realize at some point during the song that this is really John describing his own experiences under the cover of this character. You know, he's the one who had the manager send him off to places. And "Jesus, the Missing Years" is similar in that. Obviously Jesus never opened up a three-way package for old George Jones.

PM: And the elephant boy was like the guy that everybody was lookin' at and didn't necessarily enjoy it, and he was uncomfortable. . . . Oh man, it was just too much.

FK: And I should also say that I have a great fondness for "Lake Marie" just because of the strangeness of it. And we'd always end with that. I played a couple of years and did a couple of albums with Jack White, and I always used to think, when we started doing "Lake Marie" and I'd think, "This is the 'Seven Nation Army' of the singer-songwriter." We start "Lake Marie" and everybody goes "Waaaa!"

FD: Punk rock moment, right?

FK: Yeah, it's . . . anthem!

DJ: We were playing in Chicago, actually I think it's when we played John's high school, Jason and I got to play at John's high school. And we're on the road and John goes, "that's the forest preserve." And it was the forest preserve he's talking about [in "Lake Marie"]! And he did the same thing with the stairs that he swept the snow off of [in "Bruised Orange"]. Were you in the car, Jason?

JW: Gosh, I don't remember that. He showed you the church where he swept the stairs?

DJ: Yeah, where he swept the snow off the stairs.

JW: Like in "Bruised Orange."

DJ: Yeah, it's like those moments where you go, "wow."

JW: I had a similar moment when we were working on the book, the *Beyond Words* songbook, and I was at his house, and he had all these pictures spread out over his dining room table and he was looking through trying to pick out ones to put in the book. And I was trying to get him to say stuff about the pictures. And he pulls up one, and I was like, "What's this a picture of?" "Oh, that's me and Billy and my cousin . . ." I can't think of his name, on the stairs on Airdric Hill. The picture of them at that iconic spot in the song "Paradise," where the air smelled like snakes and they went to shoot pop bottles. That was a picture from that day! Of them as kids, doing that. Not the same as being at the place, but similar kind of experience of, "This is really a picture of the thing you've been singing of."

FD: These are snapshots for reality that you can point to. That would in somebody's language mean, "Yeah, well, I went to get the newspaper this morning," but in John's hands it's transcendent.

JW: John liked that movie *Big Fish*.

FD: Daniel Wallace, the novelist who wrote that, has a piece in this volume.

JW: Oh, that's great! Well, the thing I think he liked about it so much was that scene where you saw all the people and you realized all the kernels of truth that led to all those fantastic stories.

DJ: Yeah because that, it's like John.

FD: Jason, you are a songwriter.

JW: I think I am. [*laughter*]

FD: Did playing with John affect your songwriting?

JW: I think it did, but I really think, like I was saying earlier, I realized pretty early on that John had a brilliance to his songwriting that was so individual and personal to him that there really wasn't a lot to take away. At least not a lot that I ever found to take away. You know, it's funny, I've often had people come to me over the years, friends or usually people I didn't know, or even people I did know, and they'd say, "Hey, I wrote a John Prine song." Meaning that they wrote something that they thought was in the style of John. And they were always bad, they were always terrible. Because John wasn't doing a shtick.

So I know there's tons of things I learned from John, not that I could necessarily articulate them. He was not the type of person who would give you advice.

FK: It's like an artist going, "Hey, I painted a Jackson Pollock." [*laughter*]

FD: But what you're saying is cool because it's related to what Pat said, as somebody who actually did a lot of cowriting with him, which is that he tried to learn what John did, and he couldn't because you can't learn someone else's essence.

JW: Yeah, because what John did, it was so innate. It just came from him and who he was. It's just really hard to deconstruct.

DJ: He managed to take the way he saw the world, which he probably had since junior high or something, staring out the window, he managed to take that and be able to put it down and share it with people.

JW: Thank God he did. Or he just would've been a mailman.

DJ: Thinking about what I was saying about the stairs, the "Bruised Orange" thing, I think it was when John Hiatt had interviewed him for *Sessions at West 54th* or whatever, I don't remember where I heard the story exactly. But when he talked about when the kid got hit by the train, so the moms know somebody got hit by the train but they don't know whose kid it is. And then they find out. And he talked about that moment when all these moms are relieved, thank god it's not my kid, but the mom whose kid it was is there too. And I just remember that story—to be that open to what's going on in a moment like that . . .

FD: . . . when you're a male at whatever teenage year, and empathizing and picking up on a very small, specific, emotional, potent moment.

JW: I'm getting way out of my realm of knowledge here, but if you have, you know the idea of emotional intelligence, John was off the charts on that EQ.

22

The Day the Live Concert Returns

By Dave Grohl

Where were you planning to be on the Fourth of July this year? Backyard barbecue with your crankiest relatives, fighting over who gets to light the illegal fireworks that your derelict cousin smuggled in from South Carolina? Or maybe out on the Chesapeake Bay, arguing about the amount of mayonnaise in the crab cakes while drinking warm National Bohemian beer? Better yet, tubing down the Shenandoah with a soggy hot dog while blasting Grand Funk Railroad's "We're an American Band"?

I know exactly where I was supposed to be: FedEx Field, outside Washington, D.C., with my band Foo Fighters and roughly eighty thousand of our closest friends. We were going to be celebrating the twenty-fifth anniversary of our debut album. A red, white, and blue keg party for the ages, it was primed to be an explosive affair shared by throngs of my sunburned hometown brothers and sisters, singing along to more than a quarter century of Foo.

Well, things have changed.

Unfortunately, the coronavirus pandemic has reduced today's live music to unflattering little windows that look like doorbell security footage and sound like Neil Armstrong's distorted transmissions from the moon, so stuttered and compressed. It's enough to make Max Headroom seem lifelike. Don't get me wrong, I can deal with the monotony and limited cuisine of quarantine (my lasagna game is on point!), and I know that those of us who don't have to work in hospitals or deliver packages are the lucky ones, but still, I'm hungry for a big old plate of sweaty, ear-shredding, *live* rock and roll, ASAP. The kind that makes your heart race, your body move, and your soul stir with passion.

There is nothing like the energy and atmosphere of live music. It is the most life-affirming experience, to see your favorite performer onstage, in the flesh, rather than as a one-dimensional image glowing in your lap as you spiral down a midnight YouTube wormhole. Even our most beloved superheroes become human in person. Imagine being at Wembley Stadium in 1985 as Freddie Mercury walked onstage for the Live Aid benefit concert. Forever regarded as one of the most triumphant live performances of all time (clocking in at a mere twenty-two minutes), Freddie and Queen somehow managed to remind us that behind every rock god is someone who puts on their studded arm bracelet, absurdly tight white tank, and stonewashed jeans one pant leg at a time just like the rest of us. But, it wasn't necessarily Queen's musical magic that made history that day. It was Freddie's connection with the audience that transformed that dilapidated soccer stadium into a sonic cathedral. In broad daylight, he majestically made seventy-two thousand people his instrument, joining them in harmonious unison.

As a lifelong concertgoer, I know this feeling well. I myself have been pressed against the cold front rail of an arena rock show. I have air-drummed along to my favorite songs in the rafters, and been crushed in the crowd, dancing to dangerous decibel levels while lost in the rhythm. I've been lifted and carried to the stage by total strangers for a glorious swan dive back into their sweaty embrace. Arm in arm, I have sung at the top of my lungs with people I may never see again. All to celebrate and share the tangible, communal power of music.

When you take away the pyrotechnics and confetti of an arena rock concert, what are you left with? Just . . . people? I will never forget the night I witnessed U2 perform at what used to be called the MCI Center in DC. This was their 2001 Elevation Tour, a massive production. I waited for the lights to go out so that I could lose myself in a magnificent, state-of-the-art rock show. To my surprise, the band walked onstage without any introduction, house lights fully illuminated, and kicked into the first song beneath their harsh, fluorescent glow, without the usual barrage of lasers and LED screens we've all become accustomed to. The brilliant move stunned the audience and began an unforgettable concert on a very raw, personal note. This was no accident, mind you. It was a lesson in intimacy. Without all the strobes and lasers, the room shrank to the size of a dirty nightclub at last call, every blemish in plain view. And with that simple gesture, we were reminded that we are all indeed just people. People that need to connect with one another.

One night, before a Foo Fighters show in Vancouver, my tour manager alerted me that the "Boss" himself, Bruce Springsteen, was in attendance (cue paralyzing nerves). Frozen with fear, I wondered how I could possibly perform in front of this legendary showman, famous for his epic concerts that span four hours. I surely could never live up to his lofty expectations! It turns out he was there to see the opening band (cue devastating humiliation), so I was off the hook. But we chatted briefly before the gig, and I was again reminded of not only the human being behind every superhero, but also the reason millions of people identify with him: he is real. Three hours later, as I sat on a locker-room bench recovering from the show, drenched in my own sweat, there was a knock at the door. Bruce wanted to say hello. Having actually stayed for our set (cue jaw crashing to the floor), he very generously thanked us and commented on our performance, specifically the rapport we seem to have with our audience. Something he obviously understood very well. When asked where he watched the show from, he said that he'd stood in the crowd, just like everyone else. Of course he did. He was searching for that connection too.

A few days later, I received a letter from Bruce, handwritten on hotel stationery, that explained this very clearly. "When you look out at the audience," he wrote, "you should see yourself in them, just as they should see themselves in you."

Not to brag, but I think I've had the best seat in the house for twenty-five years. Because I *do* see you. I see you pressed against the cold front rails. I see you air-drumming along to your favorite songs in the distant rafters. I see you lifted above the crowd and carried to the stage for a glorious swan dive back into its sweaty embrace. I see your homemade signs and your vintage T-shirts. I hear your laughter and your screams and I see your tears. I have seen you yawn (yeah, *you*), and I've watched you pass out drunk in your seat. I've seen you in hurricane-force winds, in 100-degree heat, in subzero temperatures. I have even seen some of you grow older and become parents, now with your children's Day-Glo protective headphones bouncing on your shoulders. And each night when I tell our lighting engineer to "Light 'em up!," I do so because I need that room to shrink, and to join with you as one under the harsh, fluorescent glow.

In today's world of fear and unease and social distancing, it's hard to imagine sharing experiences like these ever again. I don't know when it will be safe to return to singing arm in arm at the top of our lungs, hearts racing, bodies moving, souls bursting with life. But I do know that we will do it again, because we have to. It's not a choice. We're human. We need moments that reassure us that we are not alone. That we are understood. That we are imperfect. And, most important, that we need each other. I have shared my music, my words, my life with the people who come to our shows. And they have shared their voices with me. Without that audience—that screaming, sweating audience—my songs would only be sound. But together, we are instruments in a sonic cathedral, one that we build together night after night. And one that we will surely build again.

23

Unknown Band on a Forgotten Stage

By Greil Marcus

Why do I remember this? It was in a basement bar in Aspen sometime in the late 1960s. I have no idea what we were doing there—maybe I'd thought I'd heard of the band the hand-lettered sign outside had announced, though it turned out I hadn't.

They were a loud, completely typical bar band playing covers. Almost all current hits. Not badly, but in that setting, so what? Nobody cared. It wasn't so loud that you couldn't keep talking, and that's what everyone was doing. In real life, Creedence's "Lodi" played a thousand times more often than the song ever played on the radio, and it was on the radio for years. The band didn't cover "Lodi"—"If only had a dollar / For every song I've sung / And every time I've had to play / While people sat there drunk"—but they didn't have to.

Subtly, the numbers the band was playing got a little older, a little less obvious. And then at one point the leader stepped closer to the lip of the stage and said, "And this next one is *the best song Paul Revere and the Raiders ever did!*"

Paul Revere and the Raiders were a Portland band that dressed up in costume-store Revolutionary War outfits. In 1963 they recorded "Louie Louie" in the same Portland studio where the Kingsmen recorded their version; the Kingsmen had the national hit, but the Raiders' recording, if only for its weirdly distracted opening—"Grab your woman—it's *Louie Louie* time!" someone shouts with untrammeled delight. "Uh, hey, yeah, uh, that's right," someone answers, as if the first person has just told him it's impolite not to remove one's hat when entering a house—was all over the radio on the West Coast. But "Just Like Me" was the best song Paul Revere and the Raiders ever did, I said to myself, sitting in the bar the split second it took to think of all that, even though I was sure the band was going to play "Kicks." "Kicks" was a big hit in 1966, a terrific song, so good it sort of rolled right over its own anti-drug message ("You better get straight—But not with kicks—You just need help, girl")—it delivered what it said it was protesting against. But "Just Like Me," from the year before, was completely meaningless. It was just a shout, with an engine of hysteria. You couldn't believe it ever got recorded—how do you make a 45 out of people running in panic out of a burning studio, or for that matter running with joy into one?—let alone on the radio, and it seemed to appear on the radio and vanish in the same moment. Did that happen? Did I hear what I thought I heard? Who was that masked man?

The band went right into "Just Like Me" and played it with such drive and desperation I was convinced they actually were Paul Revere and the Raiders, moonlighting, maybe hiding out from an old, pre-"Kicks" drug arrest warrant, trying to see if they could get over on a crowd without their Paul Revere costumes and their name (weird name, really: Paul Revere and the Raiders, but wouldn't the Raiders have been the British?).

I've thought about that night, that stage announcement, hundreds of times. Every other time I wonder why I'm remembering it, and I know: it was the heart of the leader as he made his declaration, his complete abandonment of any pretense toward cool, his testament that he and the band were now going to play a song they loved, and they were going to do everything they could to live up to that song. I don't know if, immediately, everyone in the place was on their side, but the song was. I have the Paul Revere and the Raiders 45, but I'd trade it for a tape of the other band's version if I had the chance.

24

Right on Time

An Interview with Amy Helm

By Florence Dore

Florence Dore: Thank you so much for doing this.[1] I really appreciate it. I'll bet you get tired of talking about your dad.

Amy Helm: Not really.

FD: Okay, good. I'm very interested in talking about your own career too. You read the introduction to *The Ink in the Grooves*, so you know I used your song "Record Needle." It's sort of the through-line for the whole piece—and for this book in some ways. I'm not really sure why. And it actually didn't have anything to do with your dad when I first put it in there. It was a matter of, what am I listening to a lot right now and what am I reading a lot right now? So can I just ask you to tell me about the song and what it's about? I just love "Drop the record needle"; it's such a great line.

1. Zoom interview with the author, May 7, 2021.

AH: You know I wrote that song with Byron Isaacs, who was in [the band] Ollabelle. We were in Ollabelle together for many years and he also played in the Midnight Ramble Band with my dad for another ten years after that. Byron and I did a lot of writing together and the song was meant to be about two people maybe falling in love or losing themselves in whatever they were going into. That that line was supposed capture that, which I think it did. I think it does kind of capture that feeling of a free-fall.

FD: Right. I do too. Dropping the record needle is kind of [the other line from the song] "fast we fall into the night," those are the same things.

AH: Yeah, right.

FD: So dropping the needle is like—sorry, I'm a literature analyst—dropping the record needle is the figure for the falling that doesn't feel like regular life. Right? You're falling in love or some other thing. The needle dropping is that.

AH: Yes.

FD: That's really great. I love that, and it relates to one of the questions in the introduction. You're younger than I am, but we are vaguely of the same generation. The question is about that—our generation. The novelists Jonathan Lethem and Dana Spiotta—and a bunch of other middle-aged people—contribute work to this volume describing the influence of rock and roll on their form. I think that people in our generation have a particular relationship to rock. I'm wondering if the dropping the record needle, I don't know how old Byron is, but . . .

AH: Byron's my age, or maybe a year or two younger.

FD: Okay, so the needle as a description of something pretty profoundly human, even though it's a mechanical thing related to records. One of the things I describe in the introduction is not remembering a time without rock records in the house. The Beatles on *The Ed Sullivan Show* didn't happen to us. So do you have something to say about being middle-aged and your relationship to rock?

AH: What's interesting is that radio was so different for our generation. When I was in high school—when I was fifteen or sixteen years old, around 1985—there were hits, and you could hear them on the rock and pop stations. The mass index of music that you were taking in was so much less. And even videos were so different. Before social media you weren't getting small, short memes that had layered references, you were just getting the song and the video, which was like a movie that went with it. I was thinking about this in relation to your question, when I was a teenager every kid I knew, no matter whether hip-hop was your thing and you listened to Run DMC or modern pop music—you still knew all the classic rock and roll songs. Everybody knew the words to "Helplessly Hoping," for example. You'd start hearing that song at a party and everybody knew it. Maybe not everybody was listening at home. But I think that was an interesting piece of our generational experience, and I imagine that's due to the way radio was structured at the time. Even you were listening to R.E.M. and the Cure, you knew "The Weight" and you knew Jimi Hendrix's "Purple Haze" and you knew the Allman Brothers' "Sweet Melissa"—you knew the hits; you knew the playlist.

I don't think it's the same now for teenagers. I don't think that they know those songs in that way, except for the ones that are resurfacing on TikTok. (A catchy chorus is still a catchy chorus.) Whatever you're going to get turned on by musically, it finds you—whether through your parents' record collection, or your friend's mix tape that they made you. It's gonna find you. And so for me, I discovered Aretha Franklin's singing and just . . . that was it for me. I was like, OK everything's gonna be all right, because this world exists, you know, and it can just be in this song, and she's singing just to me, I can feel it. This is everything I'm feeling. And of course the words didn't even necessarily sing a story I related to. I didn't know about "Do Right Woman" or falling in love, I was a dorky teenager with braces, and I was nervous and didn't have a boyfriend. I wasn't a cool chick; I was a nerd.

FD: But moved.

AH: But moved and I found not just an oasis, but a place I wanted to reside in from there on. And then of course that world had Jimi Hendrix, and all the other people that I got influenced by as a singer.

FD: That's really interesting what you're saying about the radio. Jonathan's novel, *The Fortress of Solitude*, kind of kicked me into rock and roll as relevant to my work as a literary analyst. *The Fortress of Solitude* echoes what you're saying because there's a bit of a soundtrack going through that novel, as if it's a radio. There's "Play That Funky Music" in one scene in some New York apartment; "Chimes of Freedom" starts to go through this one character's mind when he is coming of age; Brian Eno is part of his road trip to the Midwest. So there is this canon of music that exists for people maybe in generations after the Beatles were on *The Ed Sullivan Show* that you're suggesting radio created in a certain way. That's a really good point.

AH: I really think that's true, a canon that radio created. I think it's very different now.

FD: How old are your kids?

AH: Thirteen and nine.

FD: Right, so you have a newly minted teenager and you're watching how different it is for him as well.

AH: I mean, our kids are different because we're musicians. They know all the stuff that maybe their friends don't know, and my teenager is actually a musician himself—he's just in love with the drums, and he's kind of a lifer already, you can see. It's interesting; he has such a wide range of stuff that he listens to. A lot of the modern hip-hop and rap that he listens to, the referential piece seems so different from the rock and roll canon. Some of that has made me very hopeful, actually; that's where I hear the most interesting poetry in music. There's a different kind of freedom and a different kind of rebellion in it. I can't speak to it as well as I'd like to because I haven't studied it, but when I hear it in the car I'm like, man that's really brilliant and really different. It's very original and doesn't relate to anything I knew coming up musically.

FD: Thinking about people like your dad, who were much older. They were there creating and watching rock as it emerged—there were actually there, witnesses of this new form being born. For me, I find I have to go back, and I think this marks our generation as well. We have to go looking for it. I didn't know who William Bell was, for example, to take somebody that you've worked with. I had to learn about William Bell from Peter Guralnick's book. And then I went back and listened, immersed myself in it. I feel like there is some sense of belatedness for people our age. Maybe not for you because your dad was Levon Helm. But for me, I mean, my dad was into pop music, but it was Frank Sinatra. So for me when I would get obsessed with Aretha Franklin as you've described—and as a young singer I had that same experience with that same song—I would have to go back and try to understand her place. But we can only do that retrospectively. Maybe it's different for you because of your parentage.

AH: Honestly I think I had to do the same thing, especially with female artists, frankly. Not because anybody was a bad guy—my dad or his friends. It just wasn't as known. They loved it, they loved that singing, but no one went into the deep dive especially about a lot of female singers, I've found, except a lot of women. Who would start to ask, wow, did you know that she was raising . . . three kids and working as a fucking house cleaner when she recorded this? I think it was Mahalia Jackson. As a woman, you start to go into that. I unwound it. There were some people whose history my dad made sure I knew about—like Ray Charles and Sonny Boy Williamson and Muddy Waters and all those guys that were his heroes—oh, and Ralph Stanley. And of course he turned me on to so many musicians. But I think I had to discover the history and the development of each artist like anybody would have to do.

FD: Right, because you were not born yet. So then when you make it your own, it's a process of putting pieces together yourself. And what about that? I saw in your promo for your new record, *What the Flood Leaves Behind*—what a great title—that you returned to where you came from, going back to the studio—the Levon Helm studio. And I guess I would love to hear more about how you made it your own and what that process was like. I mean I remember when I became a professor and somebody said, oh, it's because your dad was a professor, and I thought, no way, that is not why I'm doing this. I mean, of course there's some relationship. Of course I'm influenced; but I was doing it for my own reasons too. I wonder about that with you.

AH: Sure. I tried to turn away from it, and I think that my dad was a big part of pulling me back onto the rails, onto the path at an age and a time where I really had to make that decision. Like, OK, I've been doing music and it keeps kind of finding me and I keep trying to get a waitressing job or a teaching job but it keeps pulling me back in. And then he and I had a very significant [change in] our relationship. We really reconnected and healed a very fractured relationship in my late twenties, and at the point we're going through this profound change in our relationship, and that also solidified my commitment to being a singer and being a working singer.

FD: Is that around the time you produced his record?

AH: No, that was born from the repair, though. In my late twenties my dad was diagnosed with throat cancer, and when we got that diagnosis and he had to start treatment, that was a really just a transformative time for both of us. We kind of came back together, walked through it, didn't really know what we were walking through, or what the result would be. He was also just newly sober, just off of twenty-five years addicted to heroin and all kinds of drugs and weighed less than I did. You know, he was not in strong shape emotionally or physically; we really didn't know what the outcome was going to be. It was an incredible time. He healed himself from that and I walked through it with him, and he pulled me right in. Then he formed his blues band and put me in it as the singer. That was kind of the beginning of a baptism by fire for me in a lot of ways—and for him too.

FD: That's a beautiful story. Why was it a baptism by fire?

AH: There's a couple of pieces. I could probably do a three-hour interview just about this period of time.

FD: I feel like we've arrived. This is really interesting.

AH: It is really interesting, and I want to someday paint it really clearly, especially for musicians. It was such an interesting time in his life. It was a baptism by fire for him because he couldn't speak, couldn't sing. All he could do was drum. Not being able to sing any of those hit songs led him to put this band together and master the shuffle. That was his blinders-on, vision-forward thing, and he packed his drums in the back of his car, his falling-apart car. We had no money. He had no money. We drove up and down the country back and forth for years just playing tiny clubs, sometimes for a hundred people, sometimes more people would show up. But it was like he had completely lost everything about his identity as a rock star and a great musician. It was flattened: back to dust, back to ashes. He was just right there, focused. That was his baptism by fire. Mine was walking out onto a stage very green, very insecure, given a natural singing voice but never having had the experience to use it and work it and develop it. And coming out under the spotlight of Levon Helm's daughter everywhere I went. It didn't matter if we were playing in a shitty club for fifty people. For me, that may as well have been Carnegie Hall. Also, I will say, just because we're in it, I'll share this with you, I realize we're off topic from the book . . .

FD: I don't care.

AH: So the other interesting thing about this is that the guys in the band, these three young guys with these blues musicians from Poughkeepsie were not very happy about me being in the band. They didn't quite have an understanding of what was happening. It's all right. I mention this not to vilify these guys but to say, a lot of female singers can relate to this, I was coming out on stage standing up as that, not being very good or experienced at all, trembling, insecure, and these guys were like goddammit.

FD: What the fuck.

AH: What the fuck. It was a really fucking interesting time. So that was my baptism by fire. And really falling on my ass figuratively speaking, really falling on my ass just about every night until I had to decide what that was going to be.

FD: I don't think this veers from my book at all. I mean, at least the personal part. My father was an alcoholic too. And there's a tiny line in the introduction which I decided not to make a big deal about, where I narrate his careening around the post on his way out the door when my mother threw him out. But yeah he was an alcoholic. And I guess it's sort of like an analog moment in a certain way. Like I remember hearing your dad's voice. And it's ironic what you went through, and I would love to hear if you're open to talking about it, some of that fracturing. Because my house was crazy. It was the seventies in Nashville. It was fucking insane. There was an alcoholic. I have a borderline narcissist mother. Standing there, listening to your dad: there is some kind of poetry in this I think. I was in chaos and of course I recall other musicians and other songs, but I remember so distinctly hearing the "na"s in "The Night They Drove Old Dixie Down" and just being stopped. But in a good way. In a way that felt comforting and maybe singing is like this too. For me the beauty of it and the weirdness of it, the sound was just, it pulls you out. It pulled me out. I didn't care what crazy fucking shit was going on in my household. It's like what you're saying about Aretha singing to you. I just felt anchored by the beauty of the sound.

AH: Absolutely. Isn't it weird how music can do that? Like just the refrains that you and I have quoted from our personal stories, the "nananas" from "The Night They Drove Old Dixie Down" or "take me to heart and I'll always love you" well that doesn't really connect to the fact that my dad is nodding on the table. I could go on and on painting dark imagery—and I do that with a lot of love and forgiveness for them. But it was similar to you. I grew up in a fucking crazy environment. I mean I just remember being ten years old and thinking if I just had my driver's license I could get the fuck out of here. But it's so interesting how those songs can speak to a kid's heart—a kid who is feeling something that has nothing to do with the line and yet be moved. It's really humbling.

FD: It's beautiful. And it's also weird and interesting—and problematic I suppose in many ways—that I was getting that from your dad's voice. I guess there's some beauty in the connection as well. That out of chaos and misery and darkness, there are these spaces of sweetness.

AH: It's why we play. I mean back to what you were saying about being a professor, that's the calling. When you get called to it you're not going to be happy unless you do it. That's kind of it, no matter what that looks like. And no matter what the disappointments could end up being.

FD: Maybe just veering a little more into the personal again. I'm interested in our generational connection to music. I love what you're saying about radio and your own experience with your dad when he's sober at that point when you guys were out?

AH: One year sober and three months complete with radiation treatments for throat cancer. No voice.

FD: Yeah. My dad never got sober. Actually alcoholism was one of the things that was listed as the cause of death.

"Lifelong alcoholism." But I'm interested, how old were you when you made your first solo record?

AH: Jeez Louise. I just turned fifty, and I was in my early forties when I began to try to poke around at it. I took a long time to do it. And then I rerecorded the thing after I started doing gigs on my own. Because after playing for a year, my friend said you can't put this out. You've grown exponentially as a singer. You've held the mic and learned how to hold the song. I think I was forty-four. Six years ago when I put my first record out.

FD: That's amazing. I think I was thirty-five when I put my first record out and I'm now finally going to get back into the studio . . . at fifty-uhm-something. So middle-aged and coming into music. Any thoughts about that?

AH: I mean I think it's just right on time. You can't control how your art is going to grow in you. And so if you have something to say at twenty, you say it. And if you have something to say at seventy, you say it. I don't think you can even compare it. I see how I've gotten stronger as a singer but I also watched a video of myself recently singing at thirty years old doing a gig with Ollabelle, and I was watching all of us and I was like, it's always right there, it's just different colors that you learn to paint with. So I feel really good because I feel like I'm doing what I'm supposed to do and I feel really trusting that things fall into the place they're meant to with it.

FD: Cool. And you said that you have a recording of your dad doing "Record Needle," playing drums on "Record Needle."

AH: I do. I do.

FD: Tell me about that recording. How come that came to pass?

AH: Well, because Byron, who I wrote the song with, helped me and produced my first record and helped me jump into my first run at making a solo record. We were writing a lot for that record and we were also looking over what we had written. So we tried that song to see what it would sound like, a different arrangement of it, and for whatever reason it just didn't match the other stuff we did, so we didn't use it. But I've got it. . . . Yeah, I mean, needless to say it's like the funkiest shit you've ever heard. Everything he played was just like, Jesus. And that's taking nothing away from Tony Leone, who's the drummer from Ollabelle. He's a dear friend. He now holds the Ramble Chair. He plays in place of my dad when we do Ramble Band shows. It all comes full circle.

FD: Speaking of full circle: your son is a drummer.

AH: My son is a drummer. It's really funny. I didn't push anything on him. Nothing. I knew he was really drawn to music at a young age. And then drums. He abandoned the drums for a minute and I never pushed him. I can't even remember how he came back to it. But you see this with your kids. Some kids it's soccer or it's whatever it is. And with Lee it's music. It's pretty cool—he just did his first full-length gig with us the other night. We had a long rehearsal from noon to five and then a full gig, playing double drums with Tony—who I was just talking about. He's really taken him under his wing as his mentor. It's really cool to watch.

FD: That is incredibly cool.

AH: Yeah it is. He sang the first verse of "The Weight" the other night at a gig in the barn; he wanted to try it. It's cool. It's amazing to watch him hold himself in that legacy because he's so centered about it. Lee, whose named for my dad, Levon—we call him Lee—has so many music teachers in this. And some of them are connected to my dad, like Tony. All these musicians who played with my dad are now pulling him into the fold. But he's also got Jason Bowman who runs the rock academy here, he had Harvey Boyer, who does the middle school jazz ensemble that he was a part of. He's got all these different influences and teachers and it is really special.

FD: So some of them are connected to your father and some are not?

AH: Absolutely. Yeah. And he doesn't compare himself to my dad, he doesn't feel self -conscious about it. He's got a very clear head on his shoulders about it. It's pretty cool.

FD: That's really sweet. It's so lovely. We'll see what happens with my girl. She's a singer too. She's a very good singer. She's got an old guitar of mine in her room, and once and awhile I'll think, sounds good in there. We asked her to do some background vocals on a song her dad recorded about Trump, actually, and she said no thanks. She declined. But by the time I finished my record last summer she had changed her mind and agreed to sing on my record. It's funny. We'll see how it all goes. She wants to do it. But I think she wants to do it herself, which is cool.

AH: And you know I'll say to your daughter too, and I say this to a lot of singers, you know, I spent a big part of my youth hiding out in my living room and listening to music. I did not want to get out there. I didn't want to join a band. I didn't want make it happen and network. I sat in my living room and sang along. My playlist was incredible. I found all the secret, incredible gems. Irma Thomas's "Ruler of My Heart." I just hid out and studied music in my house.

FD: My daughter, when Will my husband was playing with Steve [Earle], we would take her on the bus and she just . . . well, one time we took her to Asheville and it was time to go to the show and she stayed for like a half a second and was like, can we go back to the bus? She was bored by all these old men with beards. Did you experience that when you were young?

AH: Definitely. And then when you really start to experience it is when you're singing, and you're on some gig, and it's like "Not Fade Away" is the encore and you're up there like, "note to self, split before 'Not Fade Away.'" Stagehand hands you a tambourine and I'm thinking, this is not for me.

FD: At what age?

AH: Like yesterday. [*Both laugh.*] I'm just being cheeky about the long, endless jams, where it's like your feet are hurting and those heels hurt and shit, I want to be in my car.

FD: It's been really nice talking to you. Thank you so much, Amy.

AH: Thank you. And I look forward to meeting you.

FD: In person out there . . . middle-aged woman road dogs.

AH: Yes!

FD: Some place with a foot basin.

AH: Perfect. I'll put that on my rider.

Afterword

By William Ferris

Having followed Florence Dore's work and used her book *Novel Sounds: The American Novel in the Age of Rock and Roll* (2018) in my Southern Music course, I am thrilled with her latest work, *The Ink in the Grooves*. I share Florence's love for both literature and rock 'n' roll, but I was not prepared for the sheer pleasure of reading her book.

While *The Ink in the Grooves* focuses on the decades of the sixties and seventies, it also reminds us that literature and music have been joined at the hip since humans first appeared. Language and music have been, from the beginning, blended into a single sound, over time, morphing into epics that required days to perform, some of which were eventually written down and attributed to a single writer.

This long history reminds us how language and music have been preserved through oral tradition. The publication of the first modern novel, *Don Quixote*, in 1605 was a recent event on this timeline. Albert Lord's *The Singer of Tales* convincingly argued that Homeric epics originated in oral performances that long predated their written form. The writers and musicians featured in *The*

Ink in the Grooves are also singers of tales and should be viewed as part of this long tradition.

A significant link between American literary and musical traditions was when W. C. Handy first heard blues sung in Tutwiler, Mississippi, in 1903 and described how:

> A lean, loose-jointed [Black man] had commenced plunking a guitar beside me while I slept. His clothes were rags; his feet peeped out of his shoes. His face had on it some of the sadness of the ages. As he played, he pressed a knife on the strings of the guitar in a manner popularized by Hawaiian guitarists who used steel bars. His song, too, struck me instantly.
>
> Goin' where the Southern cross the Dog
>
> The singer repeated the line three times, accompanying himself on the guitar with the weirdest music I had ever heard. The tune stayed in my mind.

Blues poetry sprang onto the literary scene in 1926 with the publication of W. C. Handy's *Blues: An Anthology*. Handy's blues compositions were illustrated by Mexican artist Miguel Covarrubias, and Abbe Niles, a white Wall Street lawyer, wrote the introduction. In this historic volume, Handy claimed the blues as part of his "mother tongue," and his lyrics shocked music scholars like H. E. Krehbiel, who considered blues a music "from the lips of harlots and the frequenters of low dives."

Handy's work inspired Langston Hughes to publish his own blues poetry in *Weary Blues*. Edmund Wilson praised Handy's *Blues: An Anthology* as a model for a long overdue anthology of American folklore and literature. Wilson's call was answered by Robert Penn Warren, Cleanth Brooks, and R.W.B. Lewis, who included Handy's lyrics for "St. Louis Blues" in their 1973 edition of *American Literature*, along with lyrics by blues artists Robert Johnson, Leadbelly, Ma Rainey, and Blind Lemon Jefferson. The relation in these works between white anthologizers and Black artists is of course troubling and fraught, but these early inclusions by architects of the high literary indicate acknowledgment of the importance of vernacular music to the American literary tradition.

Florence Dore and the impressive team of writers and musicians whom she includes in her book view the dialogue between music and literature as the central question of our time. They cite Bob Dylan's 2016 Nobel Prize in Literature—which Patti Smith accepted on his behalf—as a watershed moment that formally recognized music as part of the modern literary canon. Together, they offer a deeply felt confessional, a freeze frame about the power of music and language through the lens of rock. Some of the writers, including their editor Florence Dore, are also accomplished musicians.

Dore opens her book by describing how she enters a trance when she reads a great book while listening to music, and she declares that, "rock is as important culturally as literature." Significant literary voices in her book include Randall Kenan, Rick Moody, Dana Spiotta, Daniel Wallace, Lucinda Williams, and Colson Whitehead, all of whom are equally comfortable in the worlds of books and records. Dore focuses on rock music as a key to the porous membrane between music and literature.

Dore consciously selected contributors who understand the exchange between vernacular music and literature. Author Michael Chabon's life is defined by music, he says, acknowledging that "words . . . by the lyricists of rock soul, and hip-hop constitute the body of writing that I know best, that I have studied most intensively, puzzled over longest . . . entire skeins of the synapses in my cerebral cortex by now are made up entirely of all this unforgettable literature." Jonathan Lethem believes that "Dylan offers us nourishment from the root cellar of American cultural life." Dylan once confessed to Lethem that, "I own the sixties—who's going to argue with me? . . . I'll give 'em to you if you want 'em. You can have 'em." Lucinda Williams reinforces Dylan's claim to own the sixties. In 1965, when Williams was twelve, she first heard Dylan's *Highway 61 Revisited*. She recalls how the record, "basically changed my life. . . . I could see the connections between the traditional folk music like Woody Guthrie and the literary world which were the two worlds I came out of." Those worlds are also intimately familiar to Dana Spiotta, who tells Dore, "most of the people I know, including myself have music and movie and book references running through their minds all the time. These artifacts are part of how we make sense of the world, and it is part of how we build our identities."

Steve Earle cast a wide net to find musical inspirations. In the interview included here, Earle explains that he was inspired by Shakespeare's use of iambic pentameter, eventually incorporating it into his songwriting. His long list of writers and musicians who shaped his music includes David Bowie, James Brown, Bob Dylan, Mick Jagger, John Lennon, John and Alan Lomax, Carl Sandberg, Harry Smith, Bruce Springsteen, and Izzy Young. Shifting from Steve Earle's global perspective to the intensely local scene of

Sag Harbor, New York, Colson Whitehead explores the town's lone radio station, WLNG, that featured, "the oddball tune, the one-hit wonders and fluke achievers. . . . They came to WLNG to die, these misfit ditties. . . . Picking up a ditty from WLNG was hard to explain, like claiming you got VD off a toilet seat in a bus station. You walked around with it to your shame." Roddy Doyle has similarly mixed memories of RTE, the Irish state radio station and its host who finished his weekly program with, "'If you feel like singing, do sing an Irish song.' 'Fuck off,' I answered, silently, every Saturday." Rejecting "music as an arm of the state," Doyle declares "I spat on any boy who ever popped out of any Irish song." Doyle's rebellion from Irish music inspired *The Commitments*, his novel about a Dublin band who play soul music because "superimposing the Black American form on Dublin would be fun." Years after the novel was published and Alan Parker's film adaptation was released, Doyle was at a wedding, "and the band started to play 'Mustang Sally.' There was uproar, delight. Arguments stopped, flirting was put on hold. Pints were put back on tables, trousers were hitched. Everyone stood up. Everyone sang along. Everyone. 'Mustang Sally' had become a traditional Irish song." Doyle then confesses, "I hate 'Mustang Sally' but that's a different story."

Richard Thompson reflects on "Dragging ancient ballads into the twentieth century, and what that can do to fragile young minds" as he recalls the British Folk Revival and his band Fairport Convention. Both he and his British audience felt connected to their history through the ballad. "Once you sing a traditional song . . . you feel the resonance of history . . . and you are altered." Tension between tradition and contemporary music is also on the mind of Dom Flemons whose music is influenced by both Black cowboys and Jimi Hendrix. Flemons proudly identifies with his Black and Mexican American ancestors, and music allows him "to navigate between multiple worlds. When he read *The Autobiography of Nat Love*, Flemons was moved by "his story of being born into slavery and then becoming a cowboy and then a Pullman porter . . . my dad use to be an apprentice porter. . . . To be able to connect cowboys and porters . . . was a beautiful juxtaposition of modernity as well as telling the history of the past . . . there's the literal West . . . but then there's the imagined West. . . . And to bring Black cowboys into any of that starts to create this very fascinating tapestry.

Peter Guralnick shows how a single song—"I Got A Woman"—launched the career of Ray Charles, when he broke away from the gospel tradition associated with groups like the Five Blind Boys of Mississippi and announced to his producers Jerry Wexler and Ahmet Ertegun, "This is what I'm going to do." Charles later recalled, "The minute I . . . said, 'Okay, be yourself,' that was all I knew. I couldn't be nothing else but that." Another single recording—"Dueling Banjos"—saved Daniel Wallace's life and is forever burned into his memory. "That call and response, what amounts to a conversation between a banjo and a guitar, tentative at first, checking each other out, finding common ground, gathering speed, the way all really good songs do. . . . Without 'Dueling Banjos,' I don't think I'd ever have become a writer . . . that song . . . led me toward a new world, and gave me a pinhole view of everything we think of as art." In "Two Blue Suedes," Laura Cantrell recalls that she has heard the term "poet" applied to musicians. "Hank Williams was called 'The Hillbilly Shakespeare,' Merle Haggard earned the variant 'The Poet of the Common People,' while Tom T. Hall was called simply 'The Storyteller.'"

Over the course of my career, I have witnessed live blues concerts that end with musical performers who play as they march out of the theatre. I am reminded of those players as I follow the beautiful pieces in *The Ink in The Grooves* with my afterword. Like New Orleans marching bands who sing after the deceased is buried, this book assures us that as long as the human voice is heard, music and literature will both celebrate and console the human spirit.

Didn't he ramble . . . he rambled,
Rambled all around . . . in and out of town.
Didn't he ramble . . . didn't he ramble,
He rambled till the butcher cut him down.

Notes on Contributors

Laura Cantrell is a country music artist based in New York City. Born in Nashville, she came to New York to attend Columbia College and found her way to campus radio station WKCR, where she cultivated interests in the history of country music, broadcasting, and performing. Cantrell's program *The Radio Thrift Shop* ran for thirteen years on noted freeform station WFMU, and as a summer-replacement on BBC Radio Scotland in 2005–2006. In her twenty-year recording career, Cantrell has released six acclaimed albums, *Not the Tremblin' Kind*, *When the Roses Bloom Again*, *Humming by the Flowered Vine*, *Kitty Wells Dresses*, *No Way There from Here*, and *Laura Cantrell at the BBC*. She has toured extensively in the United Kingdom, Europe, and Ireland, and was a favorite of pioneering British disc jockey, John Peel, who called her 2000 album *Not the Tremblin' Kind* "my favorite record of the last ten years, possibly my life." Cantrell has performed on "Prairie Home Companion," "Mountain Stage," and the "Grand Ole Opry" and has appeared on the television programs, *Late Night with Conan O'Brien* and the Sundance Channel's *Spectacle: Elvis Costello.*

She has also been a contributor to the *New York Times* and *VanityFair.com*. Cantrell is currently the host of *Dark Horse Radio*, a program about George Harrison on SiriusXM's The Beatles Channel and *States of Country* on the streaming service GimmeCountry.

Michael Chabon is a Pulitzer Prize–winning novelist whose books include *The Amazing Adventures of Kavalier & Clay* and *The Yiddish Policemen's Union* (which won the Hugo and Nebula Awards for best novel). Born in Washington, D.C., and brought up in Columbia, Maryland, he graduated with an MFA in creative writing from the University of California, Irvine and now lives in Berkeley. Most recently he is the author of *Moonglow*.

Florence Dore is a Nashville-born, North Carolina-based, musical artist and professor of English at the University of North Carolina–Chapel Hill, where she teaches both literature and songwriting. She has made two albums, *Perfect City* (Slewfoot Records, 2001) and *Highways and Rocketships,* which were produced by Don Dixon and Mitch Easter. The Posies covered her song "Christmas" for a 1996 Geffen release called *Just Say Noel*, and she has published scholarship on the rock novel, the blues, and censorship. She is the author of two books, most recently *Novel Sounds: Southern Fiction in the Age of Rock and Roll* (Columbia University Press); she is a founding member of the board at the Bob Dylan Institute at the University of Tulsa; and she created and was co-executive producer for the *Billboard*-charting compilation album, *Cover Charge: NC Musicians Go Under Cover to Benefit Cat's Cradle*. She has held conferences on rock and literature at the Rock and Roll Hall of Fame and the National Humanities Center.

Roddy Doyle has written twelve novels, the first of which was *The Commitments*, which was self-published in Dublin, Ireland, in 1987. The other novels include *Paddy Clarke Ha Ha Ha*, for which he won the Booker Prize in 1993; *The Woman Who Walked into Doors* (1996), *A Star Called Henry* (1999), *Smile* (2017), and *Love* (2020). He has also written three collections of short stories and eight books for children. He cowrote the screenplay for the film adaptation of *The Commitments* (1991), with Dick Clement and Ian La Frenais. *Family*, a four-part TV series he scripted, was broadcast by the BBC in 1994. His latest book, *Life Without Children*, is a collection of stories set in

Dublin during the COVID-19 pandemic. He is a cofounder of Fighting Words, an organization that encourages and mentors Irish children and young people who want to write creatively. He lives and works in Dublin.

Bob Dylan is an American singer-songwriter, author, and visual artist. Regarded by many as one of the greatest songwriters of all time, Dylan has been a major figure in popular music culture during his sixty-year career.

Steve Earle is one of the most acclaimed singer-songwriters of his generation. A protégé of legendary songwriters Townes Van Zandt and Guy Clark, he quickly became a master storyteller in his own right, with his songs being recorded by Johnny Cash, Waylon Jennings, Joan Baez, Emmylou Harris, the Pretenders, and countless others. 1986 saw the release of his album *Guitar Town*, which shot to number one on the country charts and is now regarded as a classic of the Americana genre. Subsequent releases *The Revolution Starts . . . Now* (2004), *Washington Square Serenade* (2007), and *TOWNES* (2009) received consecutive Grammy Awards. Restlessly creative across artistic disciplines, Earle has published both a novel and collection of short stories; produced albums for other artists such as Joan Baez and Lucinda Williams; and acted in films, television (including David Simon's acclaimed *The Wire* and *Tremé*), and on the stage. He currently hosts a radio show for Sirius XM. In 2009, Earle appeared in the off-Broadway play *Samara*, for which he also wrote a score that the New York Times described as "exquisitely subliminal." Earle wrote music for and appeared in *Coal Country*, a riveting Public Theater play that dives into the most deadly mining disaster in US history, for which he was nominated for a Drama Desk Award. His 2020 album *Ghosts of West Virginia* was named one of the "50 Best Albums of 2020 So Far" by *Rolling Stone*. Earle was recently (November 2020) inducted into the Nashville Songwriters Hall of Fame, and released his twenty-first studio album, *J.T.*, on January 6, 2021, as a tribute to his late son Justin Townes Earle.

William Ferris is the Joel R. Williamson Eminent Professor of History Emeritus at the University of North Carolina at Chapel Hill. The former chairman of the National Endowment for the Humanities (1997–2001), Ferris has written or edited sixteen books and created fifteen documentary films. He coedited with Charles Wilson the *Encyclopedia of Southern Culture*, which was nominated for a Pulitzer Prize. His books include *Give My Poor Heart Ease: Voices of the Mississippi Blues*, *The Storied South: Voices of Writers and Artists*, and *The South in Color: A Visual Journal*. A box set of his documentary recordings and films *Voices of Mississippi* received two Grammy Awards for Best Liner Notes and for Best Historical Album. Ferris curated "I Am a Man: Civil Rights Photographs in the American South—1960–1970," an exhibition that is accompanied by his latest book *I Am a Man: Civil Rights Photographs in the American South—1960–1970*. His honors include the Charles Frankel Prize in the Humanities, the American Library Association's Dartmouth Medal, the Mississippi Institute of Arts and Letters Award, and the W.C. Handy Blues Award. In 1991, *Rolling Stone* magazine named him among the Top Ten Professors in the United States.

Dom Flemons, a Grammy Award–winner and two-time Emmy nominee, is known as the American Songster. His repertoire covers more than one hundred years of American popular music. He's a music scholar, historian, record collector, and multi-instrumentalist. In 2018, Flemons released his critically acclaimed solo album *Dom Flemons Presents Black Cowboys* on Smithsonian Folkways and the National Museum of African American History and Culture. The album was nominated for a Grammy Award for Best Folk Album, a Blues Music Award for Best Acoustic Blues Album, and peaked at number 4 on the Billboard Bluegrass Charts. Flemons had his solo debut on the Grand Ole Opry and was selected by the Country Music Hall of Fame to be featured in the American Currents Best of 2018 exhibit. In 2020 he released a two-CD reissue with new material titled *Prospect Hill: The American Songster Omnibus* and the first wax cylinder recording release of the new millennium. His recent collaborations include recordings with Steve Cropper, Old Crow Medicine Show, and Tyler Childers. In 2005, Flemons cofounded the Carolina Chocolate Drops, winning a Grammy for Best Traditional Folk Album. He left the group to pursue his solo career in 2014. In 2016 they were inducted into the North Carolina Music Hall of Fame.

Rhiannon Giddens is an acclaimed musician who uses her art to excavate the past and reveal bold truths about our present. A MacArthur "Genius Grant" recipient, Giddens cofounded the Grammy Award–winning Carolina Chocolate Drops, and she has been nominated for six additional Grammys for her work as a soloist and collaborator. She was most recently nominated for her collaboration with multi-instrumentalist Francesco Turrisi, *There Is No Other* (2019). Among her many diverse career highlights, Giddens has performed for the Obamas at the White House, served as a Carnegie Hall Perspectives curator, and received an inaugural Legacy of Americana Award from Nashville's National Museum of African American History in partnership with the Americana Music Association. Her critical acclaim includes in-depth profiles by *CBS Sunday Morning*, the *New York Times*, the *New Yorker*, and NPR's *Fresh Air*, among many others. Giddens is featured in Ken Burns's Country Music series, which aired on PBS in 2019, where she speaks about the African American origins of country music. She is also a member of the band Our Native Daughters with three other Black female banjo players—Leyla McCalla, Allison Russell, and Amythyst Kiah—and coproduced their debut album *Songs of Our Native Daughters* (2019), which tells stories of historic Black womanhood and survival.

Dave Grohl has been one of the most beloved and respected figures on the international music scene since his drumming propelled Nirvana's generation-defining *Nevermind* in 1991. Grohl took center stage with Foo Fighters' 1995 self-titled debut, the first album in a massive twelve-Grammy-winning catalog that now includes several albums, most recently, *Medicine at Midnight* (2021). In addition to his day job, Grohl has collaborated with Paul McCartney, David Bowie, members of Queen and Led Zeppelin, Mick Jagger and too many more to name. Grohl's work as director/producer in the worlds of film and TV include the acclaimed documentary *Sound City* and the double-Emmy-winning eight-part HBO docuseries *Foo Fighters: Sonic Highways*. Dave Grohl made his debut as an author in 2021 with *The Storyteller: Tales of Life and Music*.

Peter Guralnick has been called "a national resource" by critic Nat Hentoff for work that has argued passionately and persuasively for the vitality of this country's intertwined black and white musical traditions. His books include the prize-winning, two-volume biography of Elvis Presley, *Last Train to Memphis* and *Careless Love*. Of the first Bob Dylan wrote, "Elvis steps from the pages. You can feel him breathe. This book cancels out all others." Ta-Nehisi Coates named *Sweet Soul Music* as "one of the ten books he couldn't live without." Guralnick's *Dream Boogie: The Triumph of Sam Cooke* was hailed as "monumental, panoramic, an epic tale told against a backdrop of brilliant, shimmering music, intense personal melodrama, and vast social changes." Of his latest book, *Looking to Get Lost*, Michael Eric Dyson wrote: "Peter Guralnick is one of the three or four greatest writers in the country today. His searching intelligence, his unquenchable curiosity, and his stunning scope of knowledge are all on display in this breathtaking volume"; Rosanne Cash described it as the work of "a dedicated explorer, a writer of great sensitivity and intuition, who lyrically untangles the network that exists between artist and art and, seamlessly, his own relationship to everyone and everything he contemplates."

Amy Helm is an acclaimed American singer-songwriter and multi-instrumentalist. A member of the New York–based alt-country ensemble Ollabelle, Helm and her father, Levon Helm, of The Band, built the Midnight Ramble concerts at his home in Woodstock, New York starting in 2004. The Midnight Rambles started as rent parties and rapidly grew into an institution of their own, featuring such artists as Emmylou Harris, Alain Toussaint, and Elvis Costello, among many others. Amy is a producer as well, involved with three of her father's records, all of which won Grammy Awards. Amy has appeared on records by dozens of artists, including Levon Helm, Linda Thompson, Rosanne Cash, and William Bell, just to name a few. In addition to the four albums she recorded with Ollabelle—including *Neon Blue Bird*, which includes the song "Record Needle"—Helm has made three solo albums, including *What the Flood Leaves Behind* (2021).

Dave Jacques toured with John Prine for twenty-five years. His distinctive bass playing can be heard on John's *The Tree of Forgiveness* and Grammy Award–winning *Fair and Square*, as well as on *For Better, or Worse*, *In Person & On Stage*, *Standard Songs for Average People*, *Souvenirs*, *In Spite of Ourselves*, and *Live on Tour*. In addition to his work with John, Dave has toured and/or recorded with Emmylou Harris, Buddy Miller, Daddy, Iris Dement, Steve Forbert, Patty Griffin, Lucinda Williams, Greg Brown, Rodney Crowell, Kevin Gordon, Jason Wilber, Jimmy Rankin, Jeff Black, Greg Trooper, Todd Snider, and many more. *What Was I Thinking!* is Dave's first solo album.

Fats Kaplin has been described as a "wizardly" multi-instrumentalist. Violin, guitar, mandolin, banjo, steel guitar, dobro, button accordion, oud, are all in his wheelhouse. He has recorded and toured with hundreds of artists including Jack White, John Prine, the Manhattan Transfer, the Tractors, Beck, and his own group, the Fats Kaplin Gang, which includes his wife, the songstress, Kristi Rose. Raised in New York City, he now resides in Nashville.

Randall Kenan was an American author who was born in Brooklyn, New York, but moved, at six weeks of age, to Chinquapin, North Carolina, where he lived with his great aunt. Kenan was the author of several works of fiction, including *If I Had Two Wings: Stories*, as well as *Let the Dead Bury Their Dead*, which was named a *New York Times* Notable Book in 1992. Kenan was the recipient of a Guggenheim Fellowship, a Whiting Award, and the John Dos Passos Prize. He died in 2020.

Jonathan Lethem is the author of twelve novels, including *The Fortress of Solitude* and *You Don't Love Me Yet*. He teaches at Pomona College and lives in Los Angeles and Maine.

Greil Marcus was born in San Francisco in 1945 and attended the University of California at Berkeley when the Beatles first appeared on *The Ed Sullivan Show* and the Free Speech Movement turned the school upside down, events that—with studies in American history and literature with John Schaar, Michael Rogin, and Norman Jacobson—have been the underpinning of any work he has done since. His books include *Mystery Train* and *Under the Red White and Blue*. He is the author of one rock 'n' roll song, "I Can't Get No Nookie," which was recorded in 1969 by the Masked Marauders and reached the "Bubbling Under" Billboard chart for one week as a result of statistical manipulation. His column "Real Life Rock Top 10," which began at the *Village Voice* in 1986, continues today; he is still waiting to get tired of the Mekons and Sleater-Kinney. With Werner Sollors, he is the editor of *A New Literary History of America*. He lives in Oakland, California.

Pat McLaughlin is a Grammy Award–winning singer-songwriter living in Nashville. McLaughlin has two Capital Records releases under his belt, and his songs have been covered by George Strait, Dan Auerbach, Marcus King, Yola, John Anderson, Rag 'n Bone Man, Bahamas, Steve Wariner, Bonnie Raitt, Alan Jackson, Taj Mahal, Trisha Yearwood, Al Kooper, Nanci Griffith, Josh Turner, and Gary Allan. As a studio musician he has contributed guitar to projects by Jamie Hartford, Rosanne Cash, Julie Roberts, Don Williams, Al Kooper, Shawn Camp, Cowboy Jack Clement, Neil Diamond, Johnny Cash, and many more. McLaughlin also cowrote songs with John Prine and toured in his band up until Prine's death.

Rick Moody is the author of six novels, three collections of stories, two volumes of memoir, and a collection of essays, *On Celestial Music.* His music writing has appeared at *Salon*, *Talkhouse*, *New Music Box*, the *New York Times*, the *A.V. Club*, *Salmagundi*, and, from 2009 to 2020, at *The Rumpus*, where he was a founding editor. His most recent musical release is *The Unspeakable Practices* (Joyful Noise, 2015), in collaboration with drummer, Kid Millions. He teaches at Tufts University.

Lorrie Moore is an acclaimed American author and the Gertrude Conaway Vanderbilt Professor of English at Vanderbilt University. She has published several novels and short story collections, including *Birds of America* and *A Gate at the Stairs.* Her fiction and nonfiction have appeared in the *New Yorker*, the *New York Review of Books*, the *New York Times*, the *Paris Review*, and elsewhere. She lives in Nashville.

Dana Spiotta is the author of five novels, including *Wayward*, which was published in 2021. She has been a finalist for the National Book Award and the National Book Critics Circle Award. She was a recipient of a Guggenheim Fellowship, the Rome Prize, the St. Francis College Literary Prize, and the John Updike Prize from the American Academy of Arts and Letters. She has worked as a waitress, a political canvasser, and a record store clerk (at Cellophane Square, Seattle, Washington). She now teaches in the Syracuse University Creative Writing Program.

John Jeremiah Sullivan lives in Wilmington, North Carolina, where he works with a non-profit research initiative called Third Person Project. TPP's mission is to recover the region's lost Black history, much of which was obscured after the massacre of 1898. He's a writer for the *New York Times Magazine* and the Southern Editor of the *Paris Review*. He has been a Guggenheim fellow, and in 2019 he wrote about Rhiannon Giddens for the *New Yorker*. His forthcoming book is *The Prime Minister of Paradise*.

Richard Thompson is widely regarded as one of the greatest rock guitarists of all time. A British singer-songwriter and founding member of the group Fairport Convention, Thompson helped create British folk rock during the 1960s and has had lasting influence in popular music.

Scott Timberg was an American journalist, culture writer, and editor. He was best known as an authority on Southern California culture and for his book *Culture Crash: The Killing of the Creative Class*. After writing *Culture Crash*, Timberg wrote for *Salon* and kept a busy schedule as a freelancer, writing for the *Los Angeles Times*, *Vox*, and other outlets. For the *Los Angeles Review of Books*, he interviewed many musicians, including Rhiannon Giddens, Aimee Mann, Patti Smith, and Jeff Tweedy, about their literary influences. He also collaborated with musician Richard Thompson on *Beeswing: Losing My Way and Finding My Voice 1967–1975*.

Daniel Wallace is author of six novels, including *Big Fish*, *Ray in Reverse*, *The Watermelon King*, and most recently, *Extraordinary Adventures*. His memoir, *This Isn't Going to End Well*, will be published by Algonquin Books in 2023. He teaches in the creative writing program at the University of North Carolina at Chapel Hill.

Colson Whitehead is an acclaimed American novelist who has written several novels, including his 1999 debut work *The Intuitionist*, *The Underground Railroad* (2016), and *Harlem Shuffle* (2021). A recipient of the Pulitzer Prize, Whitehead has also won a Guggenheim Fellowship and the MacArthur "Genius Grant." He lives in New York.

Jason Wilber is an American singer-songwriter. He was lead guitar player and musical director for John Prine for twenty-four years. His work with John Prine includes the Grammy Award–winning album *Fair & Square* and the Grammy-nominated albums *Live on Tour*, *In Spite of Ourselves*, and *For Better, or Worse*, on which he also served as executive producer. From 2006 to 2016, Jason hosted the syndicated radio series *In Search of a Song*, which featured interviews with singer-songwriters and producers. Highlights from his years with John Prine include performing with the Colorado Symphony Orchestra at Red Rocks; duet recordings with Iris Dement, Emmylou Harris, Lucinda Williams, Josh Ritter, Sara Watkins, and many others; and appearances on *The Tonight Show*, *Late Night with Seth Meyers*, *The Late Show with Stephen Colbert*, the *Grand Ole Opry*, *Austin City Limits*, and *The Late Show with David Letterman*.

Lucinda Williams is a Grammy Award–winning American singer and songwriter who has received critical acclaim for her label-defying music, which ranges from folk to country to rock. She recorded her first albums, *Ramblin' on My Mind* (1979) and *Happy Woman Blues* (1980), in a traditional country and blues style and received very little public or radio attention. In 1988, she released her third album, *Lucinda Williams*, to critical raves. This release featured "Passionate Kisses," a song later recorded by Mary Chapin Carpenter, and this garnered Williams her first Grammy Award for Best Country Song. Williams's commercial breakthrough came in 1998 with *Car Wheels on a Grave Road*. Williams has been dubbed both the "grand dame of Americana" and the "queen of alt-country."

Warren Zanes was seventeen when he joined the Del Fuegos, a Boston-based rock and roll band that went on to make three albums for Warner Bros. A more traditional education followed, with Zanes eventually picking up a PhD from the University of Rochester's program in visual and cultural studies. While teaching at Rochester Institute of Technology and finishing his dissertation, Zanes signed a solo recording deal with the Dust Brothers, producers of Beck, the Beastie Boys, and more. From that point forward he made an effort to make music while remaining active as a professor. Accepting a position as vice president of education and public programs at the Rock and Roll Hall of Fame and Museum allowed him to teach as a visiting professor at Case Western Reserve University while rebuilding the museum's programs. In that same period he wrote *Dusty in Memphis*, the first volume in the celebrated 33 1/3 series. Since that time, Zanes has spent a decade as executive director of Steven Van Zandt's Rock and Roll Forever Foundation, served as the consulting producer for Morgan Neville's Oscar-winning *Twenty Feet from Stardom*, earned a Grammy nomination as producer of the PBS/Soundbreaking series, conducted interviews for Martin Scorsese's George Harrison documentary, wrote Thom Zimny's Johnny Cash documentary, and published several books, including his bestselling *Petty: The Biography*. Having released four solo recordings in addition to a *Collected Warren Zanes*, he's currently back in a band as a member of Paul Muldoon's Rogue Oliphant, cowriting several songs with Muldoon, while teaching at New York University. A series of books he's worked on with Garth Brooks is currently in its fourth volume, while another, about Bruce Springsteen's *Nebraska*, is forthcoming.

continued from page iv